Gallo Be Thy Name

THE INSIDE STORY OF HOW
ONE FAMILY ROSE TO DOMINATE
THE U.S. WINE MARKET

Jerome Tuccille

JEROME TUCCILLE

PHOENIX
BOOKS

ISBN-13: 978-1-59777-590-8
ISBN-10: 1-59777-590-8
Library of Congress Cataloging-In-Publication Data Available

Book Design by: Marti Lou Critchfield

Printed in the United States of America

Phoenix Books, Inc.
9465 Wilshire Boulevard, Suite 840
Beverly Hills, CA 90212

10 9 8 7 6 5 4 3 2 1

To my *famiglia*: my wife, Marie; children, Jerry and Christine; son-in-law, Jim Merry; daughter-in-law, Wendy Katzenstein Tuccille; and grandsons, Jasper, Hugo, and Tony.

Table of Contents

Prologue

Fresno, California, was a small and dusty town in 1933, populated by down-at-the-heels farmers and idle men and women with too much time on their hands and not enough work to fill their days. It, like the rest of the country, was dry. But after thirteen long, violent, and turbulent years, Prohibition would soon be coming to an end. It had been a puritanical and ignoble experiment in social engineering that was widely ignored and almost universally considered to be a failure.

With the repeal of the Eighteenth Amendment about to become a reality, the fortunes of the Gallo family supposedly took a turn for the worse. Having lived like royalty for a decade, Joseph and Susie Gallo found themselves deeply in debt, reduced to living in a modest house on a scrubby, dust-covered ranch in this agricultural working-class town in the Central Valley of California, midway between Sacramento and Bakersfield. The house they moved to had neither a telephone nor electricity.

For those thirteen years—1920 to 1933—Joseph Gallo and his brother Mike had prospered in the illegal California wine industry. Competition was sparse during Prohibition. Grape-growers and winemakers with connections to the lucrative mob-controlled markets in Chicago and New York made a pretty good living, while those without ties fell by the wayside or ended up in jail.

The morning of June 20, 1933, broke hot and sunny. The heat could be brutal from late May through late September in the parched valley, and this particular day was no exception. According to Julio, the Gallos' second son, he and his wife, Aileen, had driven his truck to his parents' home to pick up the youngest brother, Joe Jr., and bring him back with them to Modesto. Julio first unloaded some irrigation equipment that his father had asked for. Then he strolled behind the house to the barn, where he found his father pacing back and forth, distraught, muttering to himself.

"Where's Mother?" Julio asked.

Joe pointed toward the field alongside the barn, where Julio saw his mother standing on top of a haystack, pitching hay into a truck. Julio cursed and ran over to her.

"Here, Mother. I'll do that," he said, taking the pitchfork from her. "You and Aileen go make lunch and get Joe ready to leave."

When he returned to the barn, Julio spoke harshly to his father, the Gallo patriarch, berating him for treating his mother so badly. Joe had raised his family with an iron fist, abusing his wife both verbally and physically and brutalizing his older sons, Ernest and Julio. But now Julio stood up to him. Why was his mother pitching hay, he wanted to know.

Instead of joining the others inside the house for lunch, Joe Sr. stayed out on the front porch, where he slumped in a chair with his head buried in his hands. Julio, who had gone into the house, now went outside and tried talking to his father, but Joseph continued to babble incoherently. Julio, then twenty-two, knew that his father had been borrowing heavily from banks—and from his mobster brother, Mike—just to keep his vineyards operating. But Julio claimed that he did not know the full extent of his father's debt, nor could he pry details out of him in his current state of mind. Later, as Julio and Aileen prepared to leave with Joe Jr., Susie walked over to Julio, grabbed his shoulders, and whispered in his ear, "I don't care what happens to me. All I want is for you boys to work together and get along."

Julio had a sense of foreboding but said nothing. This was not the first time Susie had tried to be a buffer between her husband and her sons. And how many times had she attempted to intervene when her oldest son, Ernest, took out his resentment of his father on Joe Jr.? Julio figured it wouldn't be the last time his mother intervened. It was just the family dynamic, he decided, and no amount of pleading with his father or Ernest would change anything. Julio revved up his truck and headed north to Modesto.

The youngest Gallo son, Joseph Jr., remembered that day differently when he recalled it later in life. According to him, his mother had not been pitching hay on the ranch. When Julio and Aileen drove up in their truck, Joe Jr. was in the house with both his parents. The three walked outside together to greet them. Julio tossed thirteen-year-old Joe the keys to the truck and told him to drive the two women around the ranch for a while. It was clear to young Joe that his older brother wanted to speak to their father alone.

When Joe Jr. returned with his mother and sister-in-law more than a half hour later, he saw Julio and his father arguing under a tree in front of the house. Then Julio told his younger brother to go inside and get his bag because they were leaving immediately. Julio and Aileen did not stay for lunch, as Julio had claimed, and according to Joe his father did not seem upset before Julio arrived. When little Joe left the house with his suitcase, however, his father was sitting on the porch in silence, looking troubled. Like his older brother, Joe Jr. also recalled his mother walking over to Julio, clutching him by the shoulders, and whispering, "I don't care what happens to me. All I want is for you boys to work together and get along."

But Joe Jr. added that his father suddenly got up, walked over to where he was standing next to Julio's truck, and said to him in Italian, "Be good and mind your brothers." Then his father turned away and walked back inside his house by himself.

Around noon the following day, June 21, Joe Sr.'s right-hand man, Max Kane, and a field hand named Frank Madrigal arrived at his house for lunch after finishing their morning chores. Surprisingly, neither Joe nor Susie was inside the house. Normally, the smell of Susie's cooking would have wafted through the air as she prepared the midday meal. Max and Frank looked forward to lunch every day, ravenous after a long morning spent working hard around the ranch or running errands in town.

They pulled their horse and wagon around the house toward the barn in back. Max felt a sinking sensation in the pit of his stomach even before he had a chance to see what had happened. The first thing that caught his eye was a bright blue cloth on the ground, which at first he thought was a windblown rag. Max jumped off the wagon, handing Frank the reins. The rag was lumped up on the ground beside the pigpen, but as Max drew closer he could see that the blue cloth was actually the edge of Susie's dress. Susie lay facedown in the mud with a bloody wound on the back of her head. Max saw Susie's straw hat a few feet away, a bullet hole visible in its broad, blood-soaked brim. Max howled, yelling for Joe. Joe was nowhere to be seen, so in a panic, Max jumped into Joe's truck and sped to the gas station down the road, where he called the local sheriff from the pay phone.

Fifteen minutes later, two deputies pulled up at the ranch. First they checked out Susie's body and then walked down to the house to see if they could find Joe. There he was, sprawled out on the floor beneath a small mirror in the dining alcove of the house. Beside his outstretched right arm, they could see a .32 caliber Smith & Wesson revolver. Near Joe's feet lay his black fedora, soaked with blood. The blood had come from the bullet hole that Joe had drilled above his ear into the right side of his head.

Ernest claimed that he was the first to get the news of his parents' deaths when a reporter from the local newspaper called to tell him. Another newspaper, the *Fresno Bee*, ran a front-page story that evening with the headline:

FRESNO FARMER AND WIFE VICTIMS OF MURDER AND SUICIDE

The subhead beneath it stated:

Joseph Gallo Believed To Have Taken Own Life After Slaying Wife As She Fed Pigs; No Motive Found For Act Found By Officers

When Ernest called Julio to tell him what had happened, Julio felt a wave of otherworldliness wash over his body. He had seen this coming. He had *sensed* it there in his parents' house the day before. Why hadn't he taken a moment to get out of his truck and try once again to get through to his father? He *knew* it had been inevitable. Receiving the news from his brother Ernest was akin to déjà vu.

But the news of their parents' grisly deaths, as Ernest and Julio described them, did not hold up to scrutiny. Too many contradictions surfaced during the ensuing investigation, fueling speculation that the murders were related to Joe's mob connections and that perhaps his sons were involved. Ernest in particular had sufficient motive to want his father dead. Were Joe and Susie victims of contract killings by the mob? Did Ernest and Julio have a hand in their parents' deaths? Was the pistol found at the crime scene the same one Ernest had bought in Chicago four years earlier?

To understand the business Ernest and Julio inherited from their parents and the tensions in the Gallo household, we have to go back in time, when Prohibition was the law of the land, when beer, wine, and bootleg liquor nonetheless flowed like rivers through the mob-controlled speakeasies of great American cities, when many of the grapes and wines that made their way east from California originated in the vineyards owned and operated by Joe and Mike Gallo.

And if one name was synonymous with Prohibition, it was that of a tough thug from Brooklyn named Al Capone.

Book One

OUR FATHER

Chapter One

Al Capone, whose real name was Alphonso Caponi, was born to Italian immigrants Gabriele and Teresina Caponi on January 17, 1899, in Brooklyn, New York. Like many other first-generation Americans from minority backgrounds, Capone's primary goal was to climb out of poverty the quickest way he could. But he discovered that his family background made it virtually impossible for him to get hired in many industries. The business world and society at large discriminated against Italians and the working class, and Capone was both. Embittered by the reality of the American dream, he gravitated to crime as a means of achieving success in what he perceived to be an unjust society.

He showed early on that he was a natural leader—ruthless, amoral, and as tough as nails. A shrewd businessman, he gained the loyalty of those who worked for him by rewarding them handsomely for a job well done. He inspired confidence through sound judgment, intimidation-style diplomacy, and the steely nerves of a gambler. He left school at age fourteen and married an Irish girl named Mae Coughlin at fifteen. He spent the next ten years making his mark with neighborhood street gangs, particularly the Brooklyn Rippers, the Forty Thieves Juniors, and the notorious Five Points Gang headed by a psychopathic stone killer named Frankie Yale. Yale put Capone to work as a bouncer and bartender in one of his bars, a seedy Brooklyn joint called the Harvard Inn. It was there that Capone was slashed in the face by another hood, Frank Galuccio, after Capone told Galuccio's sister that she had a nice ass. The three knife wounds left deep scars that gained Capone the nickname "Scar Face."

In 1919, the same year the U.S. government ratified the Eighteenth Amendment prohibiting the manufacture, sale, and transportation of alcoholic beverages, Capone fled Brooklyn to Chicago to avoid the wrath of another mobster. Bill Lovett, boss of the White Hand Gang, had accused Capone of murdering two of his associates. In Chicago Capone joined forces with James "Big Jim" Colosimo and another former Brooklyn hood named Johnny Torrio. Before long, Capone was running Torrio's infamous Four Deuces bar, the headquarters of the bootleg operation that had been spawned by Prohibition. Capone was only too happy to assuage the thirst of normally law-abiding citizens. As he told the popular reporter of the time, Damon Runyon, "I make money by supplying a public demand. If I break the law, my customers…some of the best people in Chicago, are as guilty as me."

When Torrio fled the country following an attempt on his life by the capo of the rival North Side Gang, he turned his entire enterprise over to Capone. The thug from Brooklyn proceeded to build his operation into a fabulously profitable bootleg monopoly catering to a large segment of the community, including police and city officials. By the time the Gallo family of California established its ties with Capone in the early 1920s, he was viewed as the real ruler of Chicago— a man who had slapped the face of the mayor on the steps of city hall for not clearing a piece of legislation with Capone first.

* * *

The railroad tracks snaking eastward from northern California toward Chicago, Illinois, traversed the broad western expanses of the country. Every time Ernest Gallo made the trip at the behest of his father, he cursed the inevitable inconveniences along the way. He was accompanying the railroad cars full of Gallo grapes and giant vats of vine-glo, the jellied "wine juice" that fermented into bona fide wine in about two months when mixed with water. Capone's lieutenants, and sometimes the rough but jocular scar-faced man himself, would be waiting for him in the grape markets at the Santa Fe yards in the dark streets on the South Side of Chicago.

The Gallo family was not without serious competition as a supplier of the fruit of the vine. During Prohibition, wine was treated a little differently than other types of alcohol. In some cases, it was enough to slip a government inspector a twenty-dollar bill with a wink that told him to look the other way. Wine had to be purchased through warehouses owned and monitored by the government unless it was for sacramental purposes, an exemption that allowed rivers of contraband wine to slip through to market. A 1925 study revealed that the demand for sacramental wine increased by 800,000 gallons in a two-year period; apparently Prohibition did more to usher in a religious revival in America than all the bible-thumping fundamentalists in the country. There was enough demand to satisfy well-connected winemakers like Joe Gallo and his sons, considering that the consumption of wine doubled during the 1920s.

Many wineries closed since it was hard to get their product to market without the proper connections. The wineries that survived did so by establishing ties with distributors like Capone while pretending that their primary business was growing grapes. The Gallos and other prospering winemakers actually doubled the size of their vineyards during Prohibition to more than 640,000 acres in California alone. They planted mostly a hardy variety of grape known as Alicante Bouschet, which was dark and dense and resisted spoilage. A gallon of the thick, syrupy wine was usually adulterated with a gallon or more of water and sugar, producing a concoction that came to be known as "Dago Red."

Dago Red and hard cash were much on Ernest Gallo's mind as he made his annual journeys eastward from the vineyards of California to the warehouses of Chicago. He had learned from his father, who had made the initial runs to the Windy City in 1925, that the most treacherous part of the trip could well be *after* he had gotten paid for his delivery.

"If they give you a check, deposit it immediately before it bounces," Jacob "Jake" Matkovich had told Joe Gallo. "And if they pay you in cash, drive as fast as you can to the bank or back to your hotel. The hoods hanging out down there will rob you blind before you know what hit you."

Jake was a Yugoslav who owned a grocery store on Wentworth Avenue, which also doubled as a bank of sorts for winemakers like Joe Gallo and some fellow distributors. Jake was scrupulous with their money, but he did skim a commission off the top for keeping it safe. Some of the hoods who mugged the winemakers belonged to the Genna Gang headed by Sam Genna, the "Wine King of Little Italy," before Capone folded Genna's operation into his own.

After being stiffed with a bad check once, Joe Gallo insisted on cash for his shipments and began carrying a pistol under his suit jacket. He had learned to drive back to his hotel with his headlights off, following a circuitous route to make sure no one found out where he was staying. The safest deliveries were those made directly to Capone's Chicago headquarters in the Lexington Hotel on South Michigan Avenue, or to his other base in Cicero, outside of Chicago. No one dared mess with any of Capone's suppliers on his own playing field. The streets around both compounds were well patrolled by Capone's men, who dealt harshly with freelance thugs looking for an easy score.

Joe liked being paid by Capone himself. He felt that cash that had been touched by the de facto ruler of Chicago was safe money. No one in his right mind would attempt to take it from him. Joe enjoyed the handsome profits he was raking in for both his grapes and his Dago Red—and in some cases, 100-gallon tankers full of superior wine that he had cultivated himself. But he hated staying in a lonely hotel room, hated being on the road for weeks, and hated the cooking he had to endure away from home, which was a poor substitute for the meals Susie prepared for him. So, after putting up with the ordeal for a year or more, Joe reluctantly took Ernest under his wing and trained him to make the runs on his own.

Later on in life, Ernest acknowledged his father's "bootlegging activities" during Prohibition, and early in 1926 he bragged to friends and associates that he had "all but taken over" his father's grape-growing and wine business—a brash claim for a boy of seventeen with a tyrant for a father. Paul Alleruzzo, a California wine distributor, laughed at the idea of Joe's son puffing himself up like that.

"The Joe Gallo label was highly regarded and very competitive," said Alleruzzo. "Joe Gallo had a good reputation. People would see his name, and his grapes and wine were in big demand. I remember the first year I met Ernie. He was like a smaller version of his father. They both wore black fedora hats, and they walked almost exactly alike, their hands behind their backs, their shoulders hunched forward. His father was training him, but Ernie was already a shrewder businessman and a hard bargainer. We knew Joe was managing the growing and shipping in California. We just had to work harder to get the price we wanted. Ernie never forgot the time I forced him to take a dollar instead of a dollar-ten per box for a car of overripe grapes. I proved that I could be as stubborn as he was. But he just hated to lose, I could see that."

In 1926, Ernest replaced his father on the shipments to Chicago. Alleruzzo was impressed with the boy, whom he regarded as a more stable version of his father. He once overheard two of Capone's men saying to Ernest, "We can put you on a regular contract with us. That way you'll have a guaranteed sale and a guaranteed price."

Ernest made the cross-country trip to Capone's lair several times a year and dealt with Scar Face himself on several occasions. He liked to tell stories at the time about how he would take the cash Capone handed him, wrap it in a newspaper, and carry it back to his hotel. Ernest was only a senior in high school, and his classmates began to tease him about his "city slicker ways," with his black suits and dark fedoras that made him look like one of Capone's henchmen. Schoolwork to Ernie was little more than a necessary step he had to take before running his father's business full-time. Even so, he proved to be a good student, receiving all A's and B's in his senior year despite his long absences from the classroom.

A year or so later, Joe sent his second-oldest son, Julio, farther east to the grape markets of New Jersey to see if he could expand the family operation all the way across the country. The markets there were centered in Kearny and controlled by the New York mob. Most of them were connected to one of the five families headquartered in Manhattan's Little Italy and in Brooklyn. In Kearny, auctions were held regularly for the finest grapes from California growers, as well as for the illegal Dago Red, for which federal inspectors were always on the lookout. Julio accompanied Ernest to Chicago, then continued eastward on his own. As new shipments of Gallo grapes and wines reached Ernest, he sent the excess produce to Julio in Kearny to be auctioned there. Unfortunately, Ernest turned out to be a better salesman than Julio, and he was more in tune with the rough-and-tumble mobsters and their lifestyle than his kid brother was. Julio felt ill at ease with the gangsters, whom he was dealing with reluctantly; he was out of his element, as though he had plunged into the deep end of a pool not knowing how to swim and without a life jacket to keep him afloat.

A life jacket came along in the person of Jack Riorda, a former winemaker for Italian Swiss Colony who knew the right people in the east coast auction yards. Riorda took Julio under his wing and introduced him to his New Jersey contacts. He also taught Julio a few tricks of the trade that the Gallos had yet to master. To keep wine from spoiling on the long journey across the country, Riorda added a chemical called metabisulfite, which helped stabilize the fermentation process. Riorda also taught Julio how to blend different varietals to enhance their flavor and durability. Julio was an apt, eager, and grateful student. He learned a lot about winemaking from his older mentor that would serve him well in the years ahead, lessons he would put to good use when Ernest and Julio expanded the family bootleg operation into a thriving wine empire. Still, Julio hated being on the road and feared being busted, just as his father had loathed traveling far from home to sell his wine a few years earlier. Ernest reveled in his role, however, and enjoyed the rough banter and camaraderie of his contacts in Chicago.

The biggest complaint both Ernest and Julio had was the way their father treated them when they returned home following their long weeks on the road. They were doing the jobs of grown men, taking great personal risk in their father's illegal enterprise, and they felt they deserved to be made equal partners in the Gallo family business. Joe, on the other hand, continued to treat them like indentured servants, entitled only to whatever he cared to dispense under the law of *patria potestas*, with him playing the iron-fisted ruler of an Old World Italian family; he had the right of life and death over his wife and offspring. Joe's tyrannical style was particularly hard on Ernest, who was expected to work hard in the vineyards after putting in a full day studying agriculture at Modesto Junior College.

Young Joe Jr., the youngest son and his father's namesake, was the only one who got off lightly. He had chores to do as well, but when he was kept after school for acting up in class and failed to get home on time, his father feigned gruffness, then broke into a smile, tousled the boy's hair, and told him to mind his teachers and stay out of trouble. Ernest fumed. Joe Sr. had assigned him and Julio arduous work, a lot of it involving heavy lifting, from the time they were eight or nine years old. If they messed up for any reason whatsoever, their father beat them with a strap, directing the worst of his wrath at Ernest, who was smaller and weaker than Julio. Ernest grew up hating his youngest brother because his father openly favored Joe Jr. and treated him as his natural heir, usurping Ernest as next in line to the father's throne. Ernest felt that he should have been the one to carry his father's name. Ernest's hatred of Joe Jr. would survive long after their parents died that tragic day in 1933, when Ernest was only twenty-four. It would fester inside for decades, finally erupting in a bitter, costly, and mutually destructive lawsuit over the rights to the family name more than half a century later.

Although they downplayed it later, Ernest, Julio, and Joe Jr. knew their Uncle Mike was a high-powered racketeer with influential contacts in law enforcement agencies. Joe Gallo's younger brother had achieved celebrity status in the East Bay wiseguy circles and even across the bay in North Beach, in the heart of San Francisco. Mike had a flair for making a quick buck by the time he was seventeen, long before Prohibition got under way. While still in his teens, he enticed a woman he met in a gin mill to start a so-called "badger game" with him. She would serve as bait to lure married men to her hotel room, and at just the right moment Mike would burst in and shake them down at the point of a gun. Either they paid up or Mike would let their wives know about their husbands' extracurricular activities. The scheme worked well for a while, until a well-to-do local businessman had second thoughts about the thousand bucks he had just handed over and threatened to turn Mike in to the cops for running a blackmail operation. Mike pocketed the money and ran from the room with his girlfriend, then wisely decided to leave town and find a new place to work his schemes.

He relocated to Oakland, where he joined up with his older brother Joe. The two brothers began to socialize in the neighborhood bars in Oakland and across the bay in North Beach, where their fellow countrymen hung out after work, imbibing vast quantities of homemade wine served in five-gallon kegs that sat right up on the bar. They soon learned that this homemade wine was being supplied to the bars by local family winemakers through distributors.

Mike and Joe knew something about winemaking, having watched their parents pressing their own grapes back in the old country, in the Piedmont region of Italy. Mike was a natural salesman, with a quick boyish smile and easy charm, while Joe was more cut out to be an executive. With the thousand-dollar stake Mike had pried out of the businessman in the hotel room, they bought a secondhand truck, a load of wooden barrels on which they stenciled *GALLO* in red capital letters, rented an office in Oakland, and hung out their shingle. They were now in the wine distribution business under the name of The Gallo Wine Company. Joe drove around to the small wineries, which were always looking for distributors, and Mike visited the saloons in the Italian neighborhoods of San Francisco and Oakland, lining up customers for their new line of wines.

In 1906, Mike and Joe were legitimate businessmen with a thriving wine distributorship, and they weren't about to stop when Prohibition became the law of the land fourteen years later. Mike, the flashier of the two, soon discovered the benefits of Prohibition for those who had no qualms about bending the law in their own favor. He corrupted the local authorities, paid off federal investigators, and prospered even more after the law had reduced his competition. As early as 1921, he was branded a "notorious East Bay bootlegger" by federal agents, who busted him regularly—only to see him get off with a light fine and a slap on the wrist. Invariably, whenever the feds shut Mike down, he and Joe just rented an office in the next town and continued as before. Through the middle and late 1920s, Mike and Joe stayed one step ahead of the authorities thanks to Mike's well-placed contacts within their ranks.

On May 6, 1922, Joe was returning home with Ernest after making a wine distribution run in nearby towns. As Joe pulled his flatbed truck onto the dusty road leading to the Livermore ranch he managed for Mike, he came upon the incongruous sight of a group of men, dressed in dark suits and fedoras, swinging axes against his padlocked barn, which housed the stills.

"It's a raid!" Joe yelled, then accelerated through a U-turn and beat it back down the road. Father and son hung out in town, waiting for the sun to sink well into the horizon, hoping the marshals would be gone when darkness fell. The coast looked clear when they returned later that night. But they were wrong. The marshals had not left as Joe had hoped. They were waiting there in ambush and pounced out of the brush, surrounding Joe's truck as soon as he cut off the engine.

"Is that your barn with the stills?" one of the agents asked Joe.

"No, we're just renting it," he answered.

Joe had no choice but to submit to the indignity of being handcuffed on his own property, in front of his oldest son. The agents left Ernest, who had recently turned thirteen, standing in the dust as they carted his father off to jail.

Joe's first and only phone call was to his brother Mike.

"Don't worry about a thing," Mike said, putting Joe's mind at ease. "I'll be right down and fix it."

Indeed, the next morning Mike accompanied Joe as he was released from jail. Five months later, all charges against Joe Gallo were officially dismissed.

Chapter Two

These two brothers, Joe and Mike—or Giuseppe and Michelo—were as tight as any two brothers ever were from the time they were kids. They were working-class sons of the Italian soil, offspring of a Piedmontese butcher and winemaker and a woman who ran a *pensione* in the village of Fossano along the northwest edge of Italy, due west of Genoa. Giuseppe entered the world first on July 15, 1882, and Michelo followed two and a half years later on February 25, 1885. There were seven siblings in all, including four other brothers and a sister. Giuseppe and Michelo decided together and early in life that they were not cut out for the harsh manual labor imposed upon them by their strict, grim, and sometimes brutal father. Like most European men of his generation, the family patriarch regarded his children as little more than sources of cheap labor, mere chattels on his land. They left home at a young age, first Michelo in his early teens, who headed for the fabled sun-soaked coast of California, which resembled his native country with its abundant natural beauty. There, on the western rim of the New World, he had been told, a young man with ambition and imagination could find his true calling and make a fortune while pursuing it. What he found, though, was the hard labor he had tried to avoid in Italy; he was soon digging ditches to build up a stake before getting a job as a bartender in Oakland, across the bay from San Francisco.

Giuseppe wandered in a different direction a couple of years later. His itinerary took him first to Argentina, where he found little opportunity for a young Italian immigrant with grand designs for his future. He returned to Italy before moving to Philadelphia, where he stayed with some cousins who operated a saloon and boarding house. Giuseppe, too, had to resort to manual labor to make some money, working long, grueling days in the coal mines in western Pennsylvania before abandoning those mines and moving to Oakland.

Michelo, now known as Mike, had already embarked on a series of schemes that were to put him on the road to riches that he had been looking for since leaving Italy. More conventional adventurers lit out for the foothills of the Sierra Nevada in search of gold. Mike, however, went there in search of a different kind of fortune—one that could be found in the brothels, gin mills, and gambling halls in the heart of Amador County. A veritable new Barbary Coast had sprung up in Jackson, a pivotal point in the gold-mining region, to satisfy the demands of miners for strong drink and willing women. In 1902, with the thousand dollars that Mike conned out of the businessman his girlfriend had lured to her hotel room, Mike returned to Oakland and set himself and his brother up in the wine distribution business—their first foray into the lucrative world of wine.

* * *

The Biancos were another Italian family who knew something about wine. Battista Bianco and his wife, the former Virginia Campadelli, relocated from the agricultural region north of Genoa to the vineyards and wheat fields of Hanford, California, south of Fresno, where they established the Bianco Winery at the turn of the twentieth century. By 1901 they were producing enough wine to supply the saloons and restaurants in the Italian quarters of San Francisco and New York City. The Biancos were a hardworking family, respected in the community. They were God-fearing Catholics who attended mass and hosted local farmers and vineyard workers in their home on Sunday afternoons. Battista was solidly built; he sported a thick, bushy mustache, and he usually walked around with a long-stemmed pipe hanging from his mouth. Virginia was thick, running to stout, with pretty features beneath her fleshy cheeks.

Battista and Virginia had several distributors for their wine in the area, among them Mike and his older brother Giuseppe, who now called himself Joe. The Gallo brothers took particular interest in two of the Biancos' daughters, Assunta and her younger sister Celestina, who Americanized their own names to Susie and Celia. Joe started to show up at the Bianco vineyard more than Battista liked, slickly groomed in a three-piece black suit, starched white shirt and tie, and a wide-brim fedora. He lingered longer than he needed to, engaging the shy and self-effacing Susie, who was an inch or so taller than he, in conversation. Joe was twenty-five, slim and wiry, and wore his thick dark hair parted down the middle.

Battista was even more alarmed shortly afterward when Joe's brother Mike, who was two and a half years younger, accompanied him on his visits, similarly attired and directing his attention to Susie's younger, vivacious, assertive sister Celia. Susie was born in 1889, which made her seven years younger than Joe, and Celia was two years younger than her sister. Mike was quite a bit fuller than his older brother, and his hair had already begun to thin out. He glared at the world through unblinking brown eyes—unsettling eyes, some might say the eyes of a stone-cold sociopath. His face was almost perfectly round, expressionless when he needed to intimidate someone, but also capable of breaking into a broad smile when it suited him. Mike was the more polished of the two, more attractive to women with his bull-like physique and engaging manner, while Joe had some rough edges, a short fuse, and was unable to control his temper, especially when he thought Battista overcharged him for his wine.

Battista knew his daughters were attractive and desirable. There was no shortage of young men eager to make their acquaintance. His house was filled on Sunday afternoons with countless young would-be suitors from the area. Battista didn't like the look of these slick *paesani* from the city. He neither approved of their flashy clothes and glib conversation, nor did he trust their motives when it came to his daughters. But Joe would not be deterred. He was nothing if not determined, even ruthless, in pursuit of his goals. And he resented this country bumpkin Battista, just a *cafone* really despite his high standing among the yokels, who openly disapproved of him and his brother. Joe was determined to get his way, to remove this roadblock from his path to riches, and the key to doing that was through Susie—who, he knew, was infatuated with him.

Joe sold his interest in the wine distribution business to Mike and used the proceeds to buy a hotel in Jackson—the town where Mike had pulled off his badger-game scheme a few years earlier.

Jackson was situated up the line from Fresno, southeast of Sacramento, in the foothills of the Sierra Nevada. The town sat in the most stunning hill country outside of Tuscany. Rolling olive-green hills stretched to the soaring mountains, visible in the distance, their caps glinting white with snow reflecting the bright midday sun. Today, Jackson is a sleepy town of less than 4,000 year-round residents. But in the early 1900s, Jackson was the center of gold-mining activity, which was still in full swing half a century after gold was discovered there in 1848. The gold camps around Jackson had grown quickly, fueling an explosion of bars, hotels, poker parlors, and whorehouses that served the needs of rough-hewn men traveling between Sacramento and other gold- mining camps in the area. One of the most prominent hotels in town, if not the most profitable, was the Central Hotel, which Joe planned to run as a combination hotel and saloon. Susie was anxious to leave the sleepy village of Hanford and the family winery, so when Joe proposed and asked her to join him in his new venture, she accepted at once without asking for her father's approval.

Battista was enraged by both Susie's defiance and Joe's gall in proposing to her without asking him for her hand in the Old World tradition. He refused to sanction the match and boycotted the civil ceremony at the Hanford Town Hall on March 18, 1908. Celia, who was even more defiant than her older sister, was the only Bianco family member present. Joe, for his part, fumed silently that Battista had not provided Susie with a dowry as he had expected. Instead, Battista loaned Joe $1,000 at ten percent interest, payable in full in two years, to help him get the hotel business off the ground. The terms of the loan rankled Joe. Battista might as well have stuck him with a knife. As ruthless as Joe fancied himself, his father-in-law was equally determined to go to the mat with him, if that's what it took to win the war he felt Joe had started.

So there they were in Jackson, proprietors of a shabby hotel, a boarding house really, with more than two dozen rooms that Susie had to clean by herself every day while also cooking for the foul-mouthed, ill-tempered, frequently drunk gold miners who lodged there. Joe tended bar downstairs, drinking with the miners, and soon discovered that the overhead on the property far exceeded the income from his establishment. He had made a poor business decision. He had married Susie to gain a foothold in her father's prosperous winery, and instead he found himself drowning in debt, overwhelmed by bills he couldn't pay, operating a godforsaken business catering to drunks, gamblers, and whoremasters. The more Joe drank, the more violent he became, and Susie bore the brunt of his rage.

"*Fica! Puttana!*" Cunt! Whore! He swore at her in Italian, smacking her back and forth, punching her with closed fists, blackening her eyes, bruising her face and body. Small and wiry, vicious to the core, Joe lost his temper quickly and lashed out repeatedly with his hands and fists, particularly when he had too much to drink. He was at his worst when he felt the financial pressures building. His marriage to Susie was supposed to have ended all that, yet here he was, saddled with a failing business made worse by the terms of his father-in-law's loan.

Joe cursed Susie time after time and pummeled her without mercy, holding nothing back even after Susie got pregnant. If anything, her pregnancy infuriated him more because it limited the amount of work she could do around the hotel. Joe had to hire help, adding to his considerable overhead and plunging him deeper into a financial hole. Susie gave birth to a frail runt of a child on March 18, 1909, a boy they called Ernest.

While Joe grappled with financial misery in the hellhole of Jackson, Mike prospered in the thriving markets of Oakland and San Francisco. He continued to operate the wine distributorship on his own under the name Gallo and Company, and he bought a saloon in Oakland that did a bang-up business in inverse proportion to Joe's floundering enterprise. Mike had always had a dramatic flair. He was outgoing, a back-slapper, a storyteller who knew how to make people laugh, but underneath it all he was as ruthless as Joe and infinitely more cunning. He had a taste for dark suits and bright ties, and now he could afford to have his clothes tailor-made. He added the trappings of wealth to his wardrobe: a gold watch and chain to adorn his vests; diamond pinky rings; shoes polished to a mirror shine. And he traded in his old truck for late-model cars with gleaming chrome trim—suitable vehicles for a junior league Al Capone.

Celia was more attracted than ever to Mike and grew increasingly infatuated with his big-city lifestyle, which was totally alien to the rural environment in which she had been raised. She continued to see Mike despite her father's objections, often visiting him in the city and accompanying him to Jackson to visit Joe and Susie. Mike responded with true affection, clearly taken with the vivacious Celia and her gregarious personality. He showered her with expensive presents, which maddened Battista Bianco all the more. He had not raised his girls to take on fancy, flashy, highfalutin ways. They were country girls; respectable, God-fearing Catholics. When Mike proposed, also without asking for her father's permission, Battista refused to attend their wedding as well, which took place on August 17, 1909. The one saving grace for Battista and Virginia was that Mike had married Celia in church, unlike Joe, who was impertinent enough to take his own vows with Susie before a justice of the peace. As far as Battista was concerned, Joe and Susie were not married in the eyes of God.

With the hotel failing, Joe put an ad in the local newspaper announcing the sale of his business. All he needed was one rube foolish enough to pay good money for the hotel and bar. He found his mark in Pietro Genolio, a recent arrival from the old country who was staying at the hotel with his wife. Pietro had his doubts, but his wife bought Joe's sales pitch that the place was "doing good business and making money." She convinced Pietro that it would be a good investment for them in the New World, so on August 31, 1909, Joe registered the sale of his hotel and bar with the county for the substantial sum of $2,000, which Genolio paid in cash. It was all Genolio had in the world, his entire life savings.

Little more than a week later, the *Amador Dispatch* carried this story on the front page: "Peter Genolio, about noon Wednesday, attempted to end it all by slashing his throat with a razor." The article continued, "Just prior to committing the rash act, Genolio had quarreled with his wife, blaming her with inducing him to buy the business. He had been drinking heavily and, telling her he would settle the matter, went to his room. His absence was noted soon, however, and he was found on the floor in a pool of blood, a three-inch gash in his throat and a bloody razor at his side."

Genolio had failed to sever his carotid artery and jugular, however, and he survived. He went on staggering beneath the burden of a money-losing, labor-intensive business with poor prospects. Whether his marriage survived as well is a fact lost to the dust-strewn annals of history.

With Genolio's money safely tucked away in their bank account, Joe and Susie Gallo hightailed it all the way back to Hanford, where the couple moved into one of the houses Battista Bianco owned, this one on West Fourth Street. Joe's father-in-law had been suffering from bouts of pneumonia and exhaustion, and he needed help running his winery while he and Virginia took a long-needed vacation in Italy. Joe now found himself in the uncomfortable position of depending on Battista's good graces to support his wife and their son. Battista had Joe exactly where he wanted him: under his thumb where he could control him and keep an eye on him, making Joe dependent on him for the very roof over his head. When Battista returned from Italy, Joe refused to pay back the $1,000 Battista had lent him, and Battista was forced to sue him for it. Joe took his fury out on Susie. Once again, the curses flew in Italian.

"*Puttana!*" Joe slapped and punched her, knocked her down on the floor, and kicked her black and blue, shouting that he was going to kill her.

Finally, Susie had had enough. She was physically unable to withstand another beating, and she worried about the effects of Joe's tantrums on their baby. Susie bundled up Ernest and escaped to the sanctuary of her parents' home. "Good riddance to him," Battista told his daughter. "You're better off without him." Battista would have run a pitchfork through Joe for the abuse he had heaped on his daughter, but Joe was smart enough to get out of town before his father-in-law could exact his revenge. He gathered together his own belongings and escaped to Oakland to stay with Mike.

Celia was unhappy with her sister's tormentor living under her roof, even if temporarily. Mike had always treated Celia well, although he was known as something of a ladies' man. Rumors about his romantic escapades had swirled about him ever since she met him. But Mike was not a violent man, at least not toward her, and she despised his surly, abusive older brother, who was so quick to use his fists at the slightest provocation. Her husband, on the other hand, did not need to use his fists. One look at those riveting eyes of his was enough to send a chill through anyone who crossed him.

Susie filed for divorce on January 27, 1910, alleging that her husband treated her "in a cruel and inhuman manner," subjected her to "mental and physical cruelty," and beat her "with his fists or club or anything his hand could get hold of," putting her "in fear of her life." Within a month, however, Joe had managed to convince her that he was a changed man. He had stopped drinking, he loved her dearly, and he would never abuse her again. He was now the proud proprietor of a new saloon, this one a moneymaking establishment in the Italian section of Oakland.

Perhaps Susie found life back in her father's house more stifling than ever. Perhaps Battista was just as cruel in his own way as her husband was in his. Perhaps Joe had a sexual hold on her, an expression of physical passion that was the polar opposite of his outbursts. Perhaps it was because she was pregnant with their second child and wanted her children to have a father, as troubled as he was. Whatever the case, Susie withdrew her divorce petition, left the town of her birth, the home in which she was raised, and joined Joe in Oakland, once again to be his partner in marriage and in his new business venture. There she gave birth to their second son on March 21, 1910, a boy they named Julio Robert. (In their unsophisticated attempt to Americanize the Italian name *Giulio*, Joe and Susie inadvertently spelled it with a Hispanic twist, prompting others to pronounce it *Hoo-lio* until they were corrected.)

Chapter Three

Joe Gallo's Saloon on Broadway in Oakland was, indeed, a moneymaker. Joe began to prosper to the point where he could afford to buy the adjoining hotel and re-create the type of establishment that he had in Jackson, only this time with the kind of success that had eluded him. He also resumed his partnership with Mike in the wine distribution business, and it seemed to Susie that Joe really had changed for the better. It wasn't terribly long, though, before his mood darkened again.

His insults and his beatings commenced with a vengeance. Joe pummeled and kicked her until her face and body were bruised black and blue. She began to look forward to his long absences from home, when he was on the road distributing wines from the local vintners. Susie took the abuse for as long as she could possibly stand it, then packed up one day and returned with both boys to her parents' home in Hanford. This time their separation was a long one. Ernest and Julio's early years were spent with their grandparents in the Bianco family homestead on their winery south of Fresno. Ernest was a small, frail boy, often sick, while Julio was bigger and more robust. Aside from their difference in size, they looked as though they had been cloned from the same seed, with dark brown eyes and hair and a medium-fair complexion. Ernest, in particular, looked just like his father—a resemblance that alarmed Battista, who had to wonder what kind of man the child would become.

Joe seemed to do best financially when he linked his fortunes to those of his brother. The formula worked, but Mike finally overreached and ended up in jail—inevitably, it would seem, considering the notoriety he attracted. Mike had teamed up with some other charlatans to sell land they didn't own. His undoing occurred on December 20, 1912, when he and his partners in crime induced a gentleman named Charles Folda to sink $900 into one of their land investment schemes. Mike decked himself out in priest's attire, complete with black tunic and starched white collar, and diverted Mr. Folda's attention while Mike's partners absconded with the gentleman's satchel full of cash.

"Father Mike" didn't know that Mr. Folda was part of a sting operation orchestrated by several detectives who had been out to nail Mike and his partners for some time. Mike had been bribing another group of bunko squad cops who turned a blind eye to his racketeering. The arresting detectives, however, had been left out of the action and were looking for revenge. Mike was charged with grand larceny, and the prosecutor convinced the judge that he was the head of a bunko ring consisting of about forty people who had bilked their victims out of more than $300,000. The judge sentenced Mike to five years in San Quentin and then went after Frank Esola, the lead detective who had protected Mike and his cohorts over the years.

At Esola's trial in June 1913, Mike appeared as the main witness for the prosecution in a plea bargain agreement that allowed him to avoid prosecution for other bunko schemes—a catchall term for various swindles—that he had perpetrated. Mike showed up as nattily dressed as ever, wearing a dark sharply pressed hand-tailored suit. He took the witness stand and listened bemusedly while Esola's attorney presented a laundry list of his con games over the years, including his land swindles, extortion, and blackmail schemes. Hadn't Mike extorted $1,000 from a businessman at the point of a gun? the lawyer asked.

"That was just an accident," Mike replied, staring back at his interrogator with a smile. "I caught him in a room with a woman everybody called my wife."

"You got a thousand dollars, didn't you, because you had worked what is commonly known as the badger game on him?"

"No. He offered me one thousand dollars."

"But you took it?"

"Yes, of course I took it."

Celia was as brazen as her husband as she took the stand in his defense. Dressed to the nines in a white lace blouse, a wide-brimmed hat adorned with a plume, and a well-cut suit, she listened carefully to Esola's attorney when he asked her how long she had known about her husband's illegal activities.

"For quite a while," she answered.

"But you testified before that you'd been aware that he was involved in bunko games only two and a half months before his arrest," the lawyer persisted.

"At the time I made that statement, I believed it to be correct. I have learned differently since then."

Mike couldn't have asked for a better partner in marriage. She was the perfect mobster's wife—attractive, well dressed, and totally unflappable. Mike beamed approvingly at her before they trundled him away to serve his five years at San Quentin. When Esola's lawyer asked him what he was laughing at, Mike replied, "I'm laughing at you because the bunko man gets his money from his victims the same as a lawyer does from his." Both Esola and his lawyer fumed as the judge sentenced the corrupt detective to five years in Folsom Prison. Fifteen other San Francisco cops were indicted along with him for accepting Mike's bribes, a scandal that was covered on the front page of the *San Francisco Call-Bulletin* for a solid week.

With his brother now behind bars, Joe was forced to scramble on his own to keep his hotel, saloon, and wine distribution business afloat. He continued to do well without his younger brother's help, adding a retail liquor store to his expanding operations in Oakland. Susie gave in to Joe's requests to resume their marriage after a separation of about three years. He put the saloon and hotel in Susie's name as a gesture of good faith, and Susie returned with their sons to live with him in Oakland in 1915, when her father's health took a serious turn for the worse. Battista failed to recover from his latest bout of pneumonia, and he died on January 17, 1916. The estate he left behind included about 9,000 gallons of red wine, his vineyard and houses in Hanford, and a couple of apartments in San Francisco. Property and wine! This was what had attracted Joe Gallo to the Biancos in the first place, and he welcomed Susie and the boys back under his roof with open arms. He was furious shortly afterward when Virginia had to sell the vineyard and houses to raise cash for herself.

Joe's enterprises generated a comfortable living for him and his family. Talk of prohibition was already in the air, however, and in 1917 Congress passed the necessary legislation to outlaw the manufacture, sale, and transportation of alcoholic beverages. Thirty-six states needed to ratify the measure to change the Constitution and put the ban into law—a hurdle that seemed impossible to surmount in the beginning. But the forces favoring the ban were vocal and well organized, and the wine growers of California grew increasingly nervous that their livelihood was threatened and their worst fears might become reality.

* * *

When Mike had finished serving his time in San Quentin, he returned to Oakland and picked up precisely where he had left off five years earlier. The two brothers put their heads together and decided to prepare themselves for the worst. They sold their operations and raised cash. In 1917, Joe plowed his share of the proceeds into a vineyard in Antioch, at the edge of the Sacramento River delta. He didn't know at the time that the property became a wetland during the annual rainy season. It was land more suitable for growing vegetables than the grapes Joe planned to crush and turn into wine.

Joe turned ugly the moment he realized that he had made another monumentally bad business decision. And when Joe was in a foul mood, he tended to drink too much and direct his wrath toward the usual punching bag, Susie, as well as his two boys, who were now old enough, in Joe's estimation, to put in long, hard hours working the vineyard. Ernest was eight and Julio a year younger. Their childhood quickly became a nightmare. They were treated no better than serfs, forced into backbreaking labor on their father's vineyard, which refused to yield the grapes Joe dreamed of when he bought the property. When Joe thought they were slacking off, when their small bodies collapsed from exhaustion, Joe cursed them, screamed at them, and beat them black and blue just as he beat up his wife.

When Ernest was ten, Susie gave birth to her third child, another boy, whom they named Joe Jr. The arrival of a younger brother on September 11, 1919, became another point of contention between the first two sons and their father. Ernest, in particular, felt that he should have been christened as his father's namesake, a privilege normally bestowed on the first-born son. And from the start, Susie cooed in awe over little Joe. The father—as Ernest and Julio referred to him, not "our father"—favored his youngest son. Ernest and Julio would grow up to resent this little contender for the father's affection and throne, such as it was at the time. Later in life, Ernest told at least one of his employees that little Joe was actually the product of an illicit affair that his mother had with a local farmer. But this seems more vindictive than anything else. If that were the case, it seems incredible that Joe Sr. would have honored the boy with his own name. It is more likely that he would have killed both wife and son on the spot.

* * *

It was Mike, once again, who came to Joe's rescue and saved him from insolvency. Mike opened a bottling plant in preparation for the bootlegging operation he planned if Prohibition were ratified. He also built his own stills on land he owned in Livermore, southeast of Oakland, and he brought in Joe as a partner shortly after Prohibition became law. Susie was happy to leave the wetlands of Antioch and relocate to a region with better prospects for her family. The two older boys helped their father load the family's possessions into a pickup truck, then climbed atop of the pile for the ride south to Livermore. Little Joe sat up front between his parents.

Ernest and Julio worked harder than ever, tending the stills on Mike's property after putting in a full day at school. By 1921, Mike had already established a reputation as one of the biggest bootleggers in the region, a man who had the local authorities in his hip pocket thanks to the bribes he generously bestowed upon them. On the Livermore property, the Gallos produced not only wine but also enough brandy to keep the speakeasies in Oakland and San Francisco stocked with Gallo products. While Mike had competition from other winemakers, the Gallo brand was visible enough to earn him the sobriquet "West Coast Al Capone." The illegal production and sale of alcoholic beverages became so widespread that it attracted the attention of federal agents. In 1922, they descended in force on Livermore and snagged many of the local bootleggers in their web. Mike escaped most of these roundups, but he did get stopped by a local cop who caught him with a load of contraband in his truck. If the cop had known who he really was, a "notorious East Bay bootlegger" who had already served time for other crimes, he would have thrown the book at him. But the cop took him at his word when Mike said his name was Mike Bianco.

"Mike Bianco, Livermore rancher, was arrested on Steiner Street early today…while transporting 10 kegs of liquor," read the story in the *San Francisco Bulletin*. The newspaper reported that he also had several vats of wine in his possession.

As a "first-time" offender, Mike got off with a light fine. The locals chuckled when they read the story, knowing that Bianco was the name of Mike's in-laws, a name he had adopted on the spur of the moment as a matter of convenience. Mike emerged from the mishap virtually unscathed, and he and Joe continued to expand their operations throughout California and into the markets controlled by Capone and other mobsters farther east. With the money rolling in, Joe was in a better frame of mind—at least as far as Susie was concerned, although he continued to drive Ernest and Julio as hard as ever.

The boys followed different paths in school. Despite his small stature, Ernest was contentious and argumentative with his classmates, quick to pick a fight at the slightest provocation, a true chip off the old block.

"Although I was smaller in stature than most of my classmates," Ernest said, "I usually won fights using the element of surprise by striking first to the nose."

Julio, on the other hand, was more popular, more laid-back with his classmates, a natural athlete who was bigger than his older brother; a slugger who could hit the long ball for the school baseball team. But neither Ernest nor Julio had much time to enjoy childhood. Joe was all over them the moment they came home, loading them down with chores, which consisted mainly of tending to the family stills, stoking them and finessing them just right to keep them from blowing up. There they were, out behind the house, day after day, sweating profusely at their labor, cowering as the father paraded up and down, cursing them, whipping them, making sure they were not slacking off after putting in a full day in the classroom.

"Take it easy on the boys," Mike repeatedly said to Joe. "They're just kids."

But Joe refused to let up. Mike, with all his notoriety and illegal schemes, was far more self-assured and well adjusted than Joe. Mike knew exactly who he was—a con man, "a professional liar," as he described himself on at least one occasion. And he was happy in his own skin, fun to be around and generous to those who were loyal to him, including Celia. Joe was his opposite, as dark and brooding as Mike was cheerful and fun-loving.

"In those days whippings from Father were frequent," Julio admitted in the autobiography he coauthored with Ernest. "His temper was like a volcano; he was very volatile and excitable.... We learned to do as we were told in the hope of not setting him off."

"Give them a break once in a while," Mike would say to Joe. But in this area of his life, Joe refused to take Mike's advice.

Joe's world crashed down on him that memorable day in 1922, when the feds descended on the ranch and busted up the stills. Though Mike was able to get all charges against Joe and his sons dismissed later that year, thanks to his valuable connections in various law enforcement agencies, Joe decided that it was time to move on. The Livermore ranch had become a target for federal investigators.

Susie hoped the incident would persuade her husband to get out of the bootlegging business for good and set himself up in a safer—and legal—type of business. Joe did move on, but not to the enterprise Susie would have preferred. In June 1922, he and Mike bought a twenty-acre ranch and farmhouse in Escalon, east of Livermore and due north of Modesto. The ranch was actually a vineyard in disguise, located in the heart of the Central Valley grape-growing region.

Joe tended the vineyard, growing mostly Alicante Bouschet grapes, which were hardy enough to withstand the long journey to eastern markets. The grape produced more wine as well, thanks to its thick skin and ability to keep yielding juice after several pressings. A ton of less durable grapes normally produced about 150 gallons of wine in a pressing, but bootleggers managed to squeeze more than 600 gallons from a ton of Alicante Bouschet after several pressings, to which they added sugar and water. Joe and Mike reserved part of the vineyard for Petit Bouschet, which was sweeter and darker, and also for Carignane, which produced a heavy, coarse wine but had the advantage of being another high-yield grape. Joe's success with the Escalon vineyard during Prohibition encouraged him to buy another twenty-acre vineyard in the small town of Keyes, about ten miles farther south, just outside of Modesto.

It was ironic that Ernest and Julio would later deny that their father made and distributed wine—with their help—during the long years of Prohibition. It became a matter of shame for the family; the general populace, however, largely viewed bootlegging as a public service, considering that the consumption of all sorts of alcohol skyrocketed during the era. And Joe Jr. would openly recall accompanying his father on various wine and brandy deliveries in the region, including one memorable occasion when his father ran over a sheep and brought his "near" roadkill back home to be slaughtered for dinner.

While Uncle Mike flaunted his wealth at the time, building lavish homes and driving expensive cars, Joe preferred to keep a low profile, investing his money in more grape-growing land in surrounding towns. Despite their father's growing success, Ernest and Julio continued to have it rough at home. "Julio was my friend then," said Joe Sciaroni, a classmate of the older Gallo boys, "and he had to work harder for his father than any of the other farm kids who helped out at home." He added that he never visited them at home, though. "Julio said they weren't allowed to have friends over, and everyone talked about what a terrible temper his father had, how he was always yelling at his wife and sons."

Besides acquiring new vineyards, Joe bought some commercial and residential parcels in Modesto. He planned to build a shipping facility on the commercial plot after analyzing the success of another local grower and shipper,

Giuseppe Franzia. Franzia accompanied his shipments of produce to the Chicago markets as did Joe, and the two men got to know each other and develop a friendship on those trips.

Joe's residential land included a forty-acre tract on the west side of Modesto and another thirty contiguous acres he bought later. Joe built the most lavish home he had ever occupied, a stately white Mediterranean-style villa with tall pillars in the front and a red-tile roof, set on the edge of his land on the north side of Maze Road. This was a major extravagance for a man who had suffered his ups and downs in life; a man who preferred to keep a low profile, unlike his flashy brother, who wanted the world to know just how far he had risen. These two sons of the Italian soil, Joe and Mike, had succeeded on their own terms in the New World, to which they had come more than two decades earlier. Joe's new house would not be complete, of course, without his beloved brandy stills, wine presses, and barrels in the basement. Ernest and Julio denied their existence later in life, but Joe Jr. was not ashamed to discuss them.

"Of course the stills were there," he said. "Ernest and Julio tended them, just as they had to do in Livermore."

Chapter Four

Shortly after Joe moved his family into the Maze Road house, Ernest began to challenge his authority. Ernest's trips east to the Chicago markets had matured and toughened him. He dealt regularly with some of the roughest people in the country. He did business with them and earned their respect.

"Being unarmed, I decided, was not advisable," Ernest admitted in the autobiography he coauthored with Julio. So in the fall of 1929, according to the book, "I bought the .32 Smith & Wesson for ten dollars."

His "holster" was a large pocket that he had sewn inside his suit jacket, and he often bent over deliberately to show his weapon so that anyone who thought about relieving him of his cash might have second thoughts about it.

Back in California, he joined the agricultural club and enrolled in Modesto Junior College to continue his education. There he learned more sophisticated methods of planting grapes with the use of better, up-to-date equipment. But the more he approached his father with his ideas on improving the family business, the more Joe dug in his heels and tried to slap him down. How dare one of his offspring, who was still just a boy really, try to tell *him* how to run things? Who the hell did he think he was, anyway? Ernest got nowhere with his old man, *the* father, who continued to treat him like his personal property even as the boy was growing quickly into a man.

As Joe's fortunes were on the ascendant, his brother Mike ran into stiff headwinds of his own making. Normally it was Mike who paved the way for Joe, but suddenly their roles were reversed when Mike overreached once again. His undoing this time coincided with his purchase of the Woodbridge Winery with another winemaker in the area, Samuele Sebastiani. The sale took place on February 28, 1928, and the deed to the property indicated that Mike was the senior partner, with two-thirds equity in the corporation, and Sebastiani owned the other third. The vineyard was situated in Lodi, where the conditions were perfect for the growth of Zinfandel grapes.

Mike went to work immediately, turning the Woodbridge operation into a major facility for the production and distribution of wine and brandy. In the past, he had always taken some precautions to camouflage his activities, but this time he threw caution to the wind. Perhaps he believed that he could buy his way out of any run-in with the law. Perhaps he had begun to believe the myth surrounding him that he was untouchable, a man who could do anything he wanted to with impunity. But the illegal entrepreneurial zeal at Woodbridge was so flagrant, so out in the open, that everyone for miles around knew that Mike was producing rivers of alcohol for distribution throughout California and other markets. The local cops and federal Prohibition agents had become the butt of jokes; they were toothless, ineffective. Mike ran the area like a warlord and the authorities were his flunkies. His brazenness backed them into a corner. They had to do something about him, and the local cops pounced on May 22, 1928. Three of his men were seized transporting about 400 gallons of wine to a depot in Richmond, in the East Bay.

Mike stormed into the sheriff's office the next day, demanding to know, "Where are my men?"

When the sheriff refused to release them, Mike informed him, "You may not realize who I am, but I intend to run liquor through Contra Costa County. I suggest you get together with me. I'll make it worth your while. I have all the other counties fixed, so you'd better play ball here."

This time the authorities refused to play ball. They indicted him and went after some of his other partners as well. On June 21, 1928, the cops raided the Oakland home of John Severino, one of the Woodbridge operatives, and confiscated a still and nineteen fifty-gallon barrels of wine, sherry, and muscatel, plus hundreds of cases of champagne. Mike's lawyers were able to get him and his cohorts off on a technicality relating to the legality of the raids, which infuriated the police even more. They responded by redoubling their efforts to shut him down, and they made no secret of it when they sent a press release to the *San Francisco Chronicle*.

"Federal investigation of the activities of Mike Gallo, alleged Oakland rum runner, has been launched here," the newspaper reported. "Ramifications of what is asserted to be a conspiracy to divert 'blending' wine from a winery near Lodi to illegal channels, flooding not only Oakland but San Francisco with the product, has been brought to the attention of the Federal Grand Jury."

Further indictments were launched against Mike and several of his partners, including Samuele Sebastiani. Sebastiani decided to do what was expedient and agreed to testify against his partner at Mike's trial on August 29, 1929, in return for dismissal of the charges against him. Mike, after all, was the one the authorities really wanted to take down. Uncharacteristically, Mike panicked and sold his shares of the winery to Sebastiani, a move that essentially left him without his formidable winemaking and storage facility. The sale, however, turned out to be premature. Had Mike held on a bit longer, he would have emerged on the other end of his legal ordeal better than he had anticipated. His lawyers convinced the prosecution that the judge had withheld evidence during the trial, weakening the state's case against him, and a year later all charges against Mike and the other defendants were dropped. But Mike was now without a headquarters for his various enterprises.

A new disaster occurred on October 29, 1929, when
the stock market imploded, further damaging the financial
interests of the Gallo brothers and their families. Black
Tuesday, as the day has come to be known, sent not only stock
prices plummeting off a cliff, but grape prices as well. Mike
and Joe were both caught up in the tumult. Joe had grapes
ripening on the vine ready to be shipped or pressed, but his
buyers were suddenly in a position to lowball him. The
demand had dried up. Nobody but the incredibly rich had any
money, since whatever wealth they possessed had evaporated
into the ether after the roaring good times of the decade.

Ernest and Julio had advised their father not to ship
any more grapes to the eastern markets. "We'd have to give
them away," they said. Mike, more imaginative and
entrepreneurial than Joe, came up with a plan to build
underground storage tanks in order to salvage their
investments.

"What's Father doing out there?" young Joe Jr. asked
his mother. "Why is he digging such a big trench?"

"It's for underground tanks," said Susie. "Your father
and Uncle Mike need it for the business."

It took Joe about a week to dig the huge rectangular
trench and fit it out with cement walls. When his labor was
complete, he feverishly began to press his grapes directly into
the underground storage pit, which held more than 30,000
gallons of wine. Joe was not the only winemaker in the area
who had resorted to this crude method of storing wine in
response to Black Tuesday—and also in anticipation of the
end of Prohibition, when they would be able to distribute the
juice of the grape legally.

"Underground tanks became essential during
Prohibition," said Robert Mondavi, son of wine magnate
Cesare Mondavi. "My father told me that hundreds of
wineries went into business during those years, largely because
of the use of those tanks. After all, over three hundred
thousand acres of vineyards were planted during Prohibition,

and not all of those millions and millions of tons of wine grapes were shipped to the grape markets." After Black Tuesday, he added, "Growers had to crush them into juice and store it just to save their harvest."

While Joe bent to the task at hand, Mike was growing increasingly erratic and self-destructive. Celia knew of his reputation for philandering, and by and large she had turned a blind eye to his extramarital affairs, even though she was concerned about them. Mike was who he was, after all. She had never taken him for a saint and was willing to put up with a certain amount of infidelity as long as he continued to treat her well. He was the type of man who was even more generous to his wife, and more content with himself, when he had the leeway to indulge his sexual appetites on the side once in a while. For the past year or so, however, he had become reckless and less discreet about both his professional and personal activities. Without warning, his womanizing took an alarming turn the same year the market crashed.

"There's another woman taking your place," he announced one day without fanfare. "What are you going to do about it?"

Celia filed for divorce and warned him up front that it was going to get ugly, that she intended to go public with his crimes and reveal where he hid his money. Stung by her threats, Mike attempted reconciliation. Celia relented at first, but his ugly side resurfaced when she refused to sign a note for some money he wanted to borrow. Mike slapped her, pounded the table, and smashed dishes against the walls.

"You bitch!" he screamed, reaching for a knife. "I'll murder you as sure as you walk the streets."

During the divorce hearing in January 1930, Mike claimed that Celia had pulled a gun on him, saying, "I'll kill you first, you son of a bitch!"

Celia's divorce was granted the same month. She ended up with $25,000 in cash, plus some property Mike owned that her lawyers had uncovered—sizable assets at the time, considering that he had successfully hidden much of his fortune. Mike retained his bottling plant and a few other holdings. The *San Francisco Chronicle* covered the breakup on January 22, 1930, referring to Mike as "a wealthy Oakland merchant."

* * *

By 1930 Ernest, then twenty-one, had grown to a point where he was as big as his father. Their relationship deteriorated as he grew in size, stature, and his knowledge of the family business. The frequent confrontations between them got uglier and threatened to erupt in physical violence. Their antagonism reached the boiling point when Joe, in an effort to save money, ignored Ernest and Julio's advice and ruined the soil he was replanting for a new grape harvest. Ernest exploded into rage, essentially calling his father incompetent. Even Julio protested his father's stubbornness.

"That vineyard was always poor because the father killed the soil," Julio said later. "It took years to subsoil and try to recover the land."

When Ernest heard that Giuseppe Franzia was planning to make his sons, whom Ernest had met in Chicago, full partners in his Ripon winery, Ernest demanded that Joe promote him and Julio to equal status in their operation. Joe vacillated between screaming at his oldest son one day and saying he would think about it the next day. Finally, he just dragged his feet and refused to discuss the matter any longer, hoping that Ernest would forget about it.

Ernest dealt with the situation in basically the same manner that Joe had when he'd attempted to feather his nest some twenty years before. Ernest suddenly took an interest in nineteen-year-old Amelia Franzia, just as his father had courted Susie Bianco in an effort to gain a foothold into *her* father's winery. Understandably, Giuseppe Franzia was suspicious of Ernest's interest in his older daughter, the "ugly duckling" among his brood at that. Ernest was smart enough to avoid making the same mistake his father had made, however, and asked Giuseppe's permission to take his daughter to the movies. Giuseppe said it would be all right, if they took Amelia's younger sister Ann along with them.

Ernest told his father that he intended to marry Amelia and needed to know when he would be on more solid financial ground. This time, Julio backed him up when he confronted Joe about a partnership in the family enterprise.

"A partnership or not?" Ernest demanded. "Otherwise I quit."

"That's right," said Julio. "We need an answer."

Joe went berserk. "You'll work for me if I say so!" he screamed. When Susie tried to intervene, Joe told her to shut up. "Not another word or I'll kill you!"

Joe grabbed the shotgun he used to kill the rabbits that were always eating his grapes and leveled it at Susie.

"Run, Mama, run!" Ernest and Julio yelled in unison.

Susie turned and ran into the vineyard, with Joe following her. When the boys chased after their father to get him under control, Joe wheeled around and aimed the shotgun at them, yelling that he would kill both of them as well.

According to an eyewitness who worked at the ranch, Ernest and Julio turned tail and fled from the property. Another family associate claimed that Joe ran after them with an axe, threatening to chop them to pieces. It was clear that Joe, who had been drinking heavily, intended to follow through with his threat. It's hard to believe that two grown boys, especially the feisty and aggressive Ernest, who was more like his father than he cared to admit, would abandon their mother so cravenly in such a perilous situation. Evidently, they were disgusted with their mother for tolerating her husband's abuse over the years, and they reasoned that she deserved her fate. Whatever the case, Ernest and Julio drove to the bus station in Modesto and boarded a bus headed for El Centro, California, a vegetable-growing area north of Calexico, across the border from Mexicali, Mexico. There they holed up for a couple of months, living on the few dollars they had in their pockets when they fled. They stayed with a sympathetic farmer who fed them and rented them a room for next to nothing. They returned to the family homestead only after Joe promised to stop brutalizing their mother and make them equal partners in the vineyard.

With wine grapes going for rock-bottom prices after the stock market crash, Joe and Ernest stepped up their shipments of highly overripe grapes—the gelatinous, near-liquid concentrate known as juice or vine-glo—to the Chicago market. But this time they attempted to find buyers without making a deal with Capone. The Gallos were not the only winemakers who had tired of Capone and his henchmen siphoning off a hefty percentage of their profits. When they tried to bypass the Chicago syndicate, Capone drew up a list of California shippers whom he threatened to target for execution if they tried to cut him out of the action. Joe Gallo was among the names on the list, which drew the attention of the FBI.

Capone's threats unsettled Ernest, but he was not concerned enough about his own safety to avoid making the trip. By then he had hardened into a tough young man who, at twenty-one, knew how to take care of himself. Assured by Joe that he would soon become a full partner in the business, Ernest married Amelia Franzia with her father's blessing on August 23, 1931, and then brazenly took his bride on a combined honeymoon–business trip to—where else—Chicago. Either he was supremely reckless or confident that Capone, for some reason only he was privy to, would leave him alone. And Ernest, as the world would discover later, was more shrewd and calculating than he was reckless.

"Who's the lucky girl?" grape shipper Paul Alleruzzo asked him when he heard about the marriage.

"Amelia Franzia," Ernest replied.

"Giuseppe Franzia's daughter. Well, you son of a gun," said Alleruzzo. "You'll be fixed for life, Ernie."

But Ernest was sadly mistaken if he truly believed that his father would keep his promise to make him and Julio equal partners. When he and Amelia returned home from Chicago, he found Joe in a black funk, ready to explode into one of his trademark temper tantrums. Mike had just been arrested, and Joe too had become a target of federal investigators cracking down on grape growers who were distributing and selling juice with an alcoholic content. On August 14, 1931, federal agents had stopped Mike, who was driving a truck outside of Oakland transporting a cargo of 600 gallons of wine.

"He has the general reputation of being very wealthy," the feds said in their report, "having made all his money from the illicit liquor business." He was "reputed to own several wineries," the report added.

Mike told the authorities that his name was George Bruno, and he offered them $1,000 to let him go. This time his ruse didn't work. They fingerprinted him and discovered his true identity. The feds raided his home in December and seized hundreds of printed wine labels. A few days later, they closed in on one of his storage depots and confiscated bottling and capping equipment, labels, and a large assortment of wines. The authorities were on a roll, determined to shut him down. None other than Earl Warren, future governor of California and future chief justice of the United States, who was then the district attorney of Alameda County, had trained his sights on Mike and crowed about "halting the extensive activities of the wine baron Mike Gallo."

Federal investigators and California law enforcement agencies continued to tighten their dragnet around Mike. They shut down his headquarters on 23rd Street in Oakland, which served as a warehouse for his wine and brandy and assorted distilling equipment. They confiscated his car and his pistol, and they seized several of his trucks elsewhere in the state, trucks carrying hundreds of gallons of contraband beverages. Mike's luck had run out. The magic was gone. And Mike's demise sent his brother Joe into a panic. Joe was frantic and reverted to form, telling his sons that he had second thoughts about what he had promised.

"What do you mean you're not going to make us partners in the business?" Ernest screamed.

Joe's word was final, he said. Ernest was concerned— his father seemed to be more scared than angry. Joe was apparently worried that Mike would tell everything he knew to get a lighter sentence. Mike's plea bargaining, if that was the route he intended to follow, would not only implicate his brother but some high-level racketeers as well, with whom Mike and Joe had conducted extensive business over the years. Ernest pleaded with his father to reconsider. Prohibition wouldn't last forever, he argued. There already was talk of repeal in the air. They would continue as before, only the next time their operations would be legal. But his father refused to budge.

Then one morning, early in 1932, Ernest drove over to his parents' home in Modesto, only to discover that they were nowhere around.

"Where are they?" he asked Julio and Joe Jr.

"They're gone," Julio said.

"Where?"

They went on a trip, the brothers answered. But they didn't know where.

They were all astonished. Joe and Susie never went anywhere. Their habits, their entire lifestyle, were as regular as clockwork. All anybody knew was that Joe and Susie had vanished just like that, without telling anyone where they were going.

Chapter Five

Joe and Susie disappeared during the early months of 1932, leaving twelve-year-old Joe Jr. in the care of Julio, Ernest, and Amelia. On March 4, Joe and Susie returned to Modesto as abruptly and mysteriously as they had departed. Joe told the boys that he had bought a ranch in Fresno, nearly a hundred miles south of Modesto. The boys were shocked. Why had he done such a rash thing when he still owned his place in Modesto? The Great Depression was taking hold, grapes were withering on the vine, and the entire economy was sinking into a quagmire. Buying more land to expand his operations didn't make any economic sense. Could it be that he had disappeared and bought a nondescript parcel of land with no telephone or electricity because he was afraid of something? Had he gone there just to hide out?

Joe Jr. was told that his father had moved to Fresno to appease Susie, who was concerned because Ernest and Julio were not getting along with their father. "Those were tough times during the Great Depression," Joe Jr.'s son Mike said years later. "There was no question that Ernest and Julio were worked very hard. My father, who was ten years younger, got the better end of the deal. My grandmother was concerned that the boys should get along. The story was that my grandfather moved to the ranch in Fresno to appease my grandmother. The house didn't have electricity. (It had a vineyard with it, and my grandfather borrowed some money to buy the property.) According to my father's recollection, everything was fine. It was a happy home there for him."

But it appears unlikely that a man who had brutalized his wife and older sons would have inconvenienced himself like that to keep peace in his family. Julio was mystified by the move. He described his father's Fresno property as "a run-down raisin-grape ranch.... Most of the 225 acres were hardpan clay overrun with weeds and Bermuda grass. It was some of the most godforsaken land I had ever seen. The Thompson and Muscat vineyards on the ranch were old, and they were infested with weeds that quickly grew higher than the vines."

Ernest, Amelia, and Julio continued to live in the house on Maze Road in Modesto, and Joe and Susie brought Joe Jr. to live with them in their Fresno hellhole. Joe was as bewildered as his brothers by his parents' reduced circumstances. He later described the Fresno home as old and dilapidated, with a sagging front porch. The walls inside were dark and stained, and the house was sparsely furnished. Why would his parents choose to live there, away from his older brothers, he wondered, when they had their comfortable spread in Modesto?

Ernest, he remembered, never came to visit; the bad blood between young Joe's father and Ernest had apparently boiled over and created an unbridgeable gulf between them. If anything, their feuding had grown more heated. Ernest applied for a license to open a bonded wine storeroom, anticipating the repeal of Prohibition, but his application was denied because he had no vineyards in his own name. His father owned the vineyards, and he still refused to make Ernest and Julio partners. Both of little Joe's brothers were furious with their father. Julio drove down to Fresno only sporadically, mostly to check that Joe Jr. was okay.

Julio had begun to court a girl he had met in high school named Aileen Lowe, a pretty blonde from a German-Austrian background. Ernest made his annual trip to Chicago in the fall, while Julio stayed behind to tend the vineyards. On May 5, 1933, Julio and Aileen eloped to Reno, where they were married by a Catholic priest. Aileen was the first non-Italian to marry into the Gallo family.

A month later, on that foreboding morning of June 20, Julio and Aileen drove down to Fresno. Though Julio and Joe Jr. recalled the specific events of that day differently, both agreed that the father and his second son had an altercation at the Fresno ranch. The following day the ranch hands, Max Kane and Frank Madrigal, found Joe and Susie dead—victims of an apparent murder-suicide. But was that truly the case?

The investigation that followed raised more questions than answers. Ernest had only this to say: Joe and Susie "had been found by the hired hands shortly before lunch. Mama was dead on the ground out by the barn, where she had been feeding the livestock when she was shot in the back of the head. My father was in the house, dead from a self-inflicted gunshot wound to the temple. A handgun was on the floor next to him. No notes were found."

Asked whether he was satisfied that it was a case of murder and suicide, Ernest said "yes." He did not comment in his own book about the murder weapon found at the crime scene, which was the same caliber and make as the one he had bought in Chicago four years earlier. When questioned about the pistol by Deputy Coroner William Creager, Ernest replied that his father's handgun was only "about a year old."

Julio said that Aileen heard about the deaths first, when a local reporter called the house in Modesto and told her that "Mr. and Mrs. Gallo were just found shot to death at their place in Fresno." Aileen told Julio, who then informed Ernest about the phone call.

"I made the drive to Fresno in a daze," said Ernest.

But in another account, a reporter from the newspaper in town called the Modesto house and told Ernest directly about the tragedy, and Ernest then told Aileen and Julio. During the inquest that followed, Creager asked Ernest a question about Susie's murder:

"Do you know of any motive for it, or your father's suicide?"

"Possibly, financial reverses," answered Ernest.

More likely, Joe "owed money to the wrong people," according to one family associate.

The sheriff's report indicated that Joe and Susie had combined bank balances of more than $3,000, and a later hearing unearthed other bank accounts owned by the couple in addition to their various properties. At the beginning of the most impoverishing and soul-searing depression in the nation's history, their financial profile was hardly one of a family on the verge of bankruptcy. Some estimates put their net worth at over one million dollars, adjusted for inflation today. If they had been in such dire financial straits, why had Joe and Susie purchased another 225 acres of land—hardscrabble as the land was—adding to the property they already owned? Why wouldn't they have sold their considerable acreage, vineyards, and wine storage facilities to raise cash if they were faced with insolvency? Surely Joe's wine alone, which he had stored in his underground tanks, would have found an eager buyer, with repeal of Prohibition just months away.

One of the investigators was intrigued that Joe's palm print was found on the barrel of the gun, not on the pistol grip. The pistol was supposedly found across the room wiped clean, except for the prints on the barrel. The inconsistencies in the case troubled him; the evidence found at the crime scene, along with the personal circumstances of the victims, required further investigation, not a rush to judgment that Joe had shot his wife and then himself.

Why had Susie written a check for their property taxes just hours before their deaths and put it in their mailbox for the carrier to pick up? She wouldn't have done so unless Joe told her to, and it makes no sense that a man about to murder his wife and take his own life would make sure his taxes were paid first.

Why wasn't Julio, who had been at the Fresno ranch just the day before, called to testify at the inquest?

And why did Joe Jr. say that he had learned of his parents' deaths from Julio and Aileen at nine in the morning, some three hours before the farmworkers found the bodies?

Joe's neighbor in Fresno, Peter Brengetto, and his older son had discovered the bodies around 9 or 10 a.m. when they went over to see Joe Gallo, according to Brengetto's younger son, Gene. Brengetto and his wife had invited Joe and Susie to dinner the night before, and they never showed up, which was totally out of character for them. He found Susie first, out by the hog pen where she had been shot to death, and then Joe, who lay inside the house with a bullet hole in his temple. Brengetto also found the bodies of their two dogs, which had been shot and killed—a detail not mentioned in the official report. Brengetto called the sheriff immediately to report the deaths. Later in the day, one of the ranch hands must have discovered the bodies and called the sheriff as well, Brengetto assumed, since an article in the local paper stated that sheriff's deputies arrived shortly afterward, at 12:25 p.m., in response to the latter's phone call. Yet Peter Brengetto had never been called to testify at the inquest, while the ranch hand had been.

Gene was eighty-five years old in 2007, still spry and active, living in Fresno ten miles up the road from Joe Gallo's old ranch. "I used to play with Joe Gallo [Jr.] when I was a kid," he said. "I was born in 1922, and he was three years older. I never saw him again after his parents were killed, and he moved away to live with his brothers. We lived two and a half or three miles away from the Gallos' ranch in Fresno at the time, on Kearney and Monroe. Everyone made wine in their cellars in those days. The Gallos used to come over or we'd go over there. The men would go down into the cellar and eat bread, cheese, salami, sausage, and drink the homemade wine. It was a terrible thing that happened. My father always wondered why he was never called to give his own testimony, and he also wondered why Joe Gallo would have shot his own dogs before he murdered his wife and committed suicide."

Why were the dogs not mentioned in the report? Was this oversight a deliberate attempt by the authorities to cover up the true facts of the case?

The only explanation that made any sense was that Joe and Susie were hiding out in Fresno because they were afraid. Perhaps it had something to do with Mike's mob connections, about money Joe owed to the wrong people. Was Joe targeted by his brother's confederates because he knew as much as Mike about their joint bootlegging operations? Were mobsters worried that Joe would also be called in for questioning and cop a plea by implicating them to save his own skin? If so, Susie would have to be killed along with Joe, as well as the dogs, since they were likely to raise a ruckus at the sight of strangers.

Did Ernest and Julio know what was about to take place? Was that the reason for Julio's visit the day before—to warn his father? Did Ernest have a hand in it, as some speculated? Did he and Julio know about their deaths as early as nine in the morning, three hours *before* their bodies were discovered by the ranch hands? Ernest and Julio certainly had motive to kill their father, but it's hard to believe that they would have targeted their mother along with him.

Too many unanswered questions, too many conflicting details!

"I never understood what might have caused their deaths," Joe Jr. said later, "although I don't remember my father being ill or financially ruined, as Ernest and Julio say he was. But after my parents' deaths, we weren't supposed to talk about it, so I was left in the dark."

"My father always said that his father was not depressed," said Mike Gallo, Joe Jr.'s son. "His father didn't seem capable of these acts, and my father always suspected that the so-called murder-suicide was not what really happened."

And so the dark family secret, and the truth surrounding the demise of Joe and Susie Gallo, was buried in the California soil along with their tormented remains.

Book Two

THY WILL
BE DONE

Chapter Six

The fresh, cool wind of repeal blew across the length and breadth of the land. And it roared high over the western rim of the country on the edge of the Pacific. Prohibition had been, perhaps, the most brazen attempt by government to restrain citizens from doing the things they wanted to do—and continued to do anyway, despite the law. No amendment to the U.S. Constitution had ever been repealed, but this one would be discarded like rubbish in the junkyard of history. A popular verse of the day captured the spirit of the times:

> *Prohibition is an awful flop.*
> *We like it.*
> *It can't stop what it's meant to stop.*
> *We like it.*
> *It's left a trail of graft and slime,*
> *It don't prohibit worth a dime,*
> *It's filled our land with vice and crime.*
> *Nevertheless, we're for it.*

The prevailing sentiment emerged that the law did not deserve to be obeyed. More and more Americans came to believe that, if the politicians refused to change the law, then it should just be ignored. The government finally took action because of dollars and cents. Before the income tax in 1913, the federal government raised about one-third of its revenue from liquor taxes and most of the rest from customs duties. All that changed after 1913, when the income tax raked in revenue on an unprecedented scale for the government—so much so that by 1920, income taxes supplied almost ten times more money than liquor taxes for the bottomless maw of federal coffers. The government decided it could afford to cave in to the demands of the Safety Nazis of the day and outlaw so-called "demon rum."

Then the Great Depression hammered the country with a knockout punch following the stock market collapse in 1929. The spreading wave of economic hardship triggered a downturn in the incomes of average Americans. In one year alone, from 1930 to 1931, income tax revenues nosedived fifteen percent. By 1933, the government's take from income taxes fell a whopping sixty percent from the amount it sucked in three years earlier. The government was going broke, particularly as President Franklin Delano Roosevelt ramped up spending on public works programs to relieve the suffering of his fellow citizens. The bottom line was crystal clear for federal number crunchers: the government needed cash to fund its expanding operations in the face of the nastiest economic reversal in the nation's history.

Where to find it? The answer was alcohol: re-legalize it and tax the hell out of it. Al Capone and his confederates understood the marketplace better than anyone else; if the government really wanted to break up their monopoly, all it had to do was make the sale and consumption of alcoholic beverages legal again. The same holds true for any enterprise. Just legalize it and invite competition. No one dreaded the repeal of Prohibition more than the mobsters did. There were just too many knees they'd have to break to restrict competitors from entering their sacrosanct turf. The government had been losing money, and now the mob was about to see its own profit margins contract.

Ernest and Julio Gallo had positioned themselves well for the repeal of Prohibition when it officially arrived at the end of 1933. Although Joe had left behind neither a will nor a suicide note, Susie had scrawled out a handwritten will a few years earlier, leaving each of her three sons a third of her property as soon as they reached twenty-one. This left the two older brothers, who were now twenty-four and twenty-three years old, in charge of family affairs, including raising young Joe.

Ernest wasted no time swinging into high gear following his parents' deaths. He and Julio were now proud owners of Joe's vineyards and, unknown to the authorities, a veritable underground lake full of wine in the storage tanks their father had dug out a few years earlier. Ernest reapplied for the license that had been denied just before Joe and Susie were killed. But another hurdle had to be cleared this time around. On August 21, 1933, an inspector from the Bureau of Alcohol named Leonard Rhodes paid Ernest a visit at his spread in Modesto and informed him that there was a problem with his application. The name Gallo had raised a red flag in his office.

"Are you and your brothers the only parties who have an interest in this winery?" Rhodes asked Ernest.

"Of course," Ernest replied. "Just me and my brother."

"What about this fellow named Mike Gallo?" Rhodes inquired.

"I don't know him," said Ernest.

"So he wouldn't have any part in the management of your winery?"

"No, none at all," said Ernest.

When Rhodes presented Ernest with evidence that Mike Gallo was, indeed, his uncle, Ernest admitted that that was true. Then why did you deny knowing him? Rhodes wanted to know.

"Mike Gallo *was* an uncle," Ernest explained, "but in the last two years he has become an unknown stranger. Our father disinherited him, disowned him, and because of that we felt he had been removed from us as a relative or someone known to us."

At twenty-four, Ernest had already demonstrated a talent for artful obfuscation. If the wine business didn't work out for him, it was clear that he would have been able to pursue a successful career in politics, or perhaps as chairman of the Federal Reserve. But wine was his future, almost inevitably it appeared, which would give him the opportunity later in life to *buy* politicians instead of merely becoming one. Thanks to the intervention of a well-connected Washington lawyer named John Walsh, Ernest and Julio received permission to continue their father's business—legally, this time—on August 28, 1933. They were now in the wine business under the name E. & J. Gallo Winery, a name that became the calling card of the wine empire that they would build over the ensuing decades.

Many competing grape growers and winery owners had gone out of business during Prohibition, and others had been forced to close up shop when their profit margins evaporated like wine fumes during the depression. But a handful of formidable players with deep pockets and good connections had survived the crash of '29. Among them were Cesare Mondavi, Angelo Petri, Lorenzo Cella of the Roma Wine Company, Samuele Sebastiani, the Rossi brothers of Italian Swiss Colony, and the Franzia clan. Ernest, whose friendship with Giuseppe Franzia had begun during his trips to Chicago, now had an additional link to the Franzia family thanks to his marriage to Amelia. Ernest and Julio needed seed money to get their winery up and running, and Amelia's mother, Teresa, came through with a loan of $5,000.

"Julio and I began looking for suitable space to rent for a winery in Modesto," Ernest wrote. "We were shown an empty warehouse for rent downtown on the corner of Eleventh and D Streets…. A rail spur ran directly to an outside loading dock, which would eliminate having to truck barrels of wine to the railhead."

The challenge they faced was almost insurmountable. As the depression bit deeper, the brothers were launching a major wine business in a country that preferred beer and whiskey and could hardly afford either, let alone rivers of wine emanating from California. When Americans did drink wine, their unsophisticated tastes ran to sweet dessert wines instead of dry table wines. Ernest and Julio joined the Wine Institute in San Francisco, in an effort to start an educational campaign to make their fellow Americans more "wine-conscious." They faced stiff competition from better-quality wines imported from France, Italy, and Spain. Meanwhile, the prices of table wines continued to plummet, sinking to less than half of what they were a few years earlier.

Facing a wall of worry stretching as far as the eye could see, the Gallo brothers charged ahead optimistically. They hired none other than Max Kane, the hand who had discovered their parents' bodies on the Fresno ranch. (The second man to discover them, as it turned out. Their tie to Max was another curious variable in the mystery of what really happened that day.) Ernest then flew to Chicago to meet with Charlie Barbera and Tony Paterno, two dealers with whom Ernest had done business during Prohibition.

"In those days, planes stopped every few hundred miles for gas," Ernest wrote in his joint autobiography with Julio. "We flew no higher than 5,000 feet, flying through canyons and skimming around mountains much higher than us. It turned out to be a turbulent, white-knuckle journey. Though flying was expensive and not very safe in those days, it gave me the advantage over rivals who traveled, much more slowly, by rail."

After repeal, Barbera and Paterno founded the Pacific Wine Company and established a wine-bottling business. "I wanted to know if you knew where I could buy some wine," Barbera said to Ernest when they sat down to talk.

"As it happens, I have samples," said Ernest.

Barbera was pleased by what he tasted and ordered 6,000 gallons of wine at fifty cents per gallon. Encouraged by his success in Chicago, Ernest headed east, where he located distributors for his wine in New York and New Jersey. He then traveled south to Florida and Texas, and then swung back west to Southern California, setting up distributors for his wine in every location he visited. Back in Modesto, Ernest and Julio shipped their wine to their new distributors in fifty-gallon barrels, on which the Gallo name was prominently burnt in with a branding iron. The distributors bottled and rebranded it with names created by the bottlers. Growing grapes and selling wine was a cash-intensive business under the best of circumstances, so the brothers liquidated their parents' estate, selling the Fresno ranch for $34,000, cashing in some stock they owned for another $33,000, and refinancing their Modesto property for $30,000. They also filed "letters of guardianship" with the probate court, making their custodianship of Joe official.

Joe lived at the Modesto home with his brothers and sisters-in-law, attended the local high school, and returned home after school to perform his chores on the family ranch and vineyard, just as Ernest and Julio had done ten years earlier. The five of them lived there together, Julio and Aileen sleeping in the back bedroom that Julio and Ernest had shared as boys, Ernest and Amelia ensconced in their parents' corner bedroom, and Joe occupying the bedroom at the front of the house.

Ernest was the family disciplinarian. He established a routine for his kid brother that was almost as grueling as the one Joe Sr. had laid out for Ernest and Julio. Young Joe worked in the vineyards, fed the pigs and chickens, picked up milk from a nearby dairy, and hunted rabbits for dinner. When his grades were not up to Ernest's standards, Ernest kept him from playing basketball—the sport he loved and excelled in. Joe wanted to study agriculture, but Ernest insisted he enroll in math, chemistry, and physics so he could get into the University of California at Davis and major in subjects that he could put to good use at the winery.

Joe's world at that time "was turned upside down," said his wife, Patricia, many years later. "He was distressed that Ernest forced him into those courses. He missed his parents, he was separated from his old friends and playmates, and I think he must have been a sad, lonely boy."

If Joe's brothers drove him to the point of exhaustion, they were no less hard on themselves. They were trying to launch a major wine operation in the midst of a depression, putting in sixteen-hour days of hard labor, returning home dirty and weary. Amelia did most of the cooking and kept the family books, while Aileen cleaned house, did the laundry, and canned fruits and vegetables from their farm. Late in the evening they would sit around the kitchen table, Ernest and Julio weary but satisfied after a tough day running their business, their wives tending to them, and little Joe looking miserable as Ernest peppered him with questions about his day's activities. Joe had escaped the wrath of the family patriarch, the brutal dictator he was named after, when he was a kid. But Ernest made sure that Joe would get his own taste of what it was like to have every aspect of his life controlled by the heavy hand of a patriarch now that he, the proper heir, had assumed that role. Ernest was a man very much in the mold of the father whom he had detested, except that he had no need to resort to violence against his family. During the rough-and-tumble years of Prohibition, he had learned how to intimidate others with the look in his eye and the tone of his voice.

It was inevitable that the Gallo household would begin to expand now that Ernest and Julio were both married. Julio's wife, Aileen, was the first to deliver a child into the world. Their first was born on August 18, 1934, a boy whom they christened Robert Julio.

Ernest and Julio had established a division of labor many years earlier. Ernest was the front man, the marketing guru, the super-salesman who was the face of the family enterprise. He stood five feet six inches tall and was still slim at 140 pounds. His thick dark-brown hair had not yet begun to recede. Julio was the quiet brother, the one who tended the vines and made the products for the markets that Ernest was opening up. Julio was three inches taller than Ernest, more athletic-looking, and fifteen to twenty pounds heavier. Both brothers had poor eyesight but squinted rather than wear corrective lenses. This, combined with their similar facial features, gave them a strong twin-like resemblance. Later in life, they wore the thick horn-rimmed eyeglasses that became one of their distinguishing characteristics. Ernest and Julio looked more like twins as they grew older, despite their difference in size. Ernest, however, was the more driven.

Even in 1934, with repeal of Prohibition just a few months past, Ernest was determined to position E. & J. Gallo Winery as the number one winery in the country.

Chapter Seven

By 1935, Ernest and Julio were producing and storing 350,000 gallons of wine per year. The brothers had initiated a friendly competition between them that drove business: Julio's goal was to make as much wine as Ernest could sell, while Ernest's was to sell as much as Julio could produce.

The formula worked well. Ernest hoped to expand his enterprise by combining it with his father-in-law's, but Giuseppe Franzia turned him down flat. "Hell no! What do we need with their junk?" he said to Amelia, thereby signing his own death warrant—commercially speaking. When thwarted, Ernest became all the more determined to get his way.

"We don't need them," he said to Julio. "We'll do it on our own."

"Ernest married me for my family's winery," Amelia admitted. "When he couldn't get that, he put them out of business." But at least Amelia was on the winning side when Ernest out-competed his father-in-law and drove him into the arms of the Coca-Cola Bottling Company many years later.

Against the backdrop of a depression that refused to go away, Ernest and Julio forged ahead and bought an additional forty acres of land in Modesto, bounded by the Santa Fe railroad line on one side and Fairbanks Avenue on the other. Together they decided to build a $500,000 plant there, fitted out with concrete storage tanks and the most up-to-date winemaking equipment.

Their 350,000-gallon storage facility "wasn't nearly enough," said Julio. "In 1935, we sold 941,000 gallons. We needed more room."

By the middle of 1936, the new Gallo facility was completed with a capacity for storing a million and a half gallons of wine, more than four times the amount the brothers could store only a year earlier. Making and selling wine involved going deeply into debt and then paying it off as quickly as possible, in an ongoing annual cycle. At harvest time, growers required cash to buy grapes in addition to those they grew themselves, and they sometimes had to buy more wine to blend with their own and pay for extra storage space. So they borrowed from the banks from August through November, then paid back the loans when they sold the wine to distributors in the winter and spring. This treadmill cycle hardly allowed time for aging, but American palates were not yet sophisticated enough to tell the difference between freshly pressed wine and wine that should be drunk in its time. Financially healthy vintners promptly paid off their debts, enabling them to borrow the following summer and fall when they needed cash again. Winemakers who had trouble marketing their inventory fell behind on their loans, sinking deeper into a quagmire of debt and edging closer to bankruptcy.

Julio felt the pressure first, growing fearful that they were taking on too much debt, too much risk, to fund their operation. When he complained that they were moving ahead too quickly, Ernest berated him for slacking off, for falling down on the job, for not holding up his end of the partnership.

"Go make your own goddamn wine!" Julio yelled back, storming out of Ernest's office after one of their periodic battles.

Ernest got his way, as he usually did, but the pressure that he put on himself and Julio finally got the best of him. A persistent, phlegmy cough gripped him early in 1936 and forced him to see his doctor.

"You've got TB," the doctor told him. "You're not going home."

With no miracle drugs yet on the horizon, Ernest's only recourse was a regimen of bed rest and a high-risk procedure that involved collapsing the infected lung, supposedly to inhibit its use and promote healing—if the patient was lucky. Ernest spent the first six months of 1936 in a sanitarium north of San Francisco, leaving Julio alone to deal with their sundry business and legal problems. While Ernest was away mending in isolation, Aileen gave birth to a second child on May 28, 1936, a daughter they named Susann Aileen. Julio began to buckle under the pressure, aggravated by Ernest's extended absence. His responsibilities at the winery, along with the demands imposed by his growing family, weighed heavily on his shoulders. He was exasperated when an agent from the Alcohol Tax Unit visited the winery demanding to see Ernest.

"He's ill," Julio responded. "He's away, unavailable."

The agent was investigating several vineyards for coloring their wines with local tar dyes, an illegal practice. E. & J. Gallo Winery was one of the customers of the company that supplied the dyes.

"Are you aware that your brother ordered coal tar dyes last year for the winery?" the investigator asked Julio, who admitted that Ernest was experimenting with their use.

"Experimenting?"

"My brother travels a lot in the east. Some winemakers back there told him that adding dye to wine was a common practice."

"Who were these winemakers?"

"My brother didn't mention any names."

"Did your brother then start using the dye in the wine?"

"No, he didn't. He found that the dye settled to the bottom of the bottles and left a purple stain on the glass. So he decided not to use it at all."

Without any proof that the dye had, indeed, been used in the brothers' winemaking process, the investigator left in a huff, delivering little more than a warning that the practice was punishable by a fine and a possible loss of their winery license. Ernest returned from the sanitarium shortly afterward, attributing his recovery to his mental toughness as much as to his health regimen.

Joe was now old enough to be brought into the winery. He graduated from Modesto High School in 1937 but failed to get accepted into the University of California at Davis, as Ernest had hoped. Instead, he enrolled at Modesto Junior College, to Ernest's displeasure. Within a year, Ernest insisted that he drop out of school and work full-time for him and Julio. Ernest assigned him an entry-level job in the crushing and fermenting rooms, and also in the distillery, to learn the business from the ground up. Ernest monitored his progress daily and scolded him in front of other employees when he didn't measure up to the older brothers' standards.

"He'd just hang his head and scuff his feet," said Rudy Wagner, an employee who worked with Joe at the time. "Ernest was hard on all of us," said Wagner, but he "was even meaner to Joe, and he just stood there and took it. So we all wondered why Joe wasn't a partner and our boss like his brothers, and why he was always catching hell from Ernest."

"He's a silent partner," Max Kane explained to Wagner. "It's because he's under twenty-one that he isn't called a partner and doesn't give orders."

Suddenly the Bureau of Alcohol, Tobacco, Firearms and Explosives decided to take another look at the claim that local wineries were coloring their wines and other beverages. Having run into a dead end with the initial investigation, the authorities trained their sights on the manufacture of brandy instead. Putting additives in brandy required approval beforehand. Once the brandy had been put into barrels and inspected by the BATF, it was illegal to tamper with it in any way. This time around, a fed investigator named Charles Herd caught Max Kane with a five-gallon jug of caramel in the brandy distillery after he had inspected it. (Distillers used caramel to give the brandy more flavor and a richer, darker texture.) According to Rudy Wagner, Ernest burst in just as Herd was about to seize the caramel as evidence of tampering.

"Can't you forget it?" Ernest asked Herd.

"Better not talk to me," Herd answered. "I may have to use anything you say as evidence against you. These premises are now under detention."

Ernest would not be put off. When another investigator named John Scott returned with Herd to inspect the premises in more detail, Ernest said to him, "You would not lose anything by taking a lenient view of the matter." Scott refused to be swayed.

"But can't you omit telling them about the can of caramel found in the warehouse?" Ernest pressed Scott. When Scott and Herd departed to file their report, Ernest stalked back to his office. He slumped over his desk with his head in his hands, his shoulders heaving. Joe had been in the distillery with Max when Herd arrived unexpectedly. Both of them had been following Ernest's instructions, and now Joe was alarmed to see his oldest brother so upset. Ernest had tears running down his cheeks.

"What are we going to do?" Ernest lamented. "We'll be ruined if they charge us."

"I'll tell them it was my idea," Joe blurted out. "You didn't have a thing to do with it."

Joe remembered Ernest brightening at the idea, then changing his mind.

"No, you're underage. They wouldn't like that either."

"What about Max?" Joe was determined to help Ernest overcome his dilemma.

"That's it," Ernest exclaimed. When he called Max Kane into his office, the loyal family acolyte agreed to take the fall for Ernest. Together, they concocted a story about how Ernest had instructed Max to go through proper channels and obtain permission to color the brandy. Max had taken it upon himself to add the caramel after it had already been inspected.

"I did it all on my own," Kane told the investigators during the hearing that followed, but the authorities didn't buy his story.

All the evidence indicated that Ernest was the boss and dictated policy at the distillery. They charged Ernest in federal court with violating state liquor laws, and the court fined him $5,000 and ordered him to fire Max Kane. The judge let Joe off the hook, with the understanding that he was just a kid following his brother's directives and had no assets of his own.

Max Kane saved the day for Ernest, and Ernest responded by setting him up for life. Ernest was a shrewd leader who understood the value of loyalty. He rewarded Kane with a small ranch of his own and put him back to work off the books for a while, when the inspectors weren't around.

The experience was an eye-opening one for Ernest, one that gave him an opportunity to reassess the marketplace and figure out which direction E. & J. Gallo Winery should take. The United States at the time was still a beer and whiskey–swilling country with little taste for dry, quality table wines. Americans preferred their wines on the sweet side— port, sherry, muscatel, and other dessert wines fortified with brandy to give them an alcohol content around twenty percent—and it took commercial winemakers some thirty years after Prohibition ended to help their fellow citizens acquire a taste for table wines. In 1938, U.S. consumers bought forty-two million gallons of highly fortified sweet wines, compared with half as many gallons of table wines. These percentages had been reversed since the days before Prohibition, when table wines outsold dessert wines by a three-to-two margin. It was only in 1967 that table wines overcame the sales of dessert wines in the American marketplace.

Bad legislation has unforeseen consequences, and Prohibition had the effect of lowering American wine-drinking standards. It started a craving for sweet-tasting plonk with high alcohol content. Before Prohibition, consumers with a taste for fine wine viewed it as a beverage to be drunk in moderation as an accompaniment to food—as food itself. Prohibition also had the effect of turning many drinkers into home-winemakers. It was legal to make wine at home for private consumption as long as it wasn't sold to others, but much of it found its way into the marketplace anyway.

Another aftereffect of Prohibition was that its repeal didn't actually put a complete end to Prohibition itself. The federal government had included loopholes in the new legislation, giving individual states the right to ban the manufacture, sale, and even the consumption of alcoholic beverages within their own borders. As a result, liquor laws across the land became a hodgepodge of conflicting rules, regulations, and tax policies that rendered it virtually impossible to understand them all and establish rational marketing procedures. The U.S. became a crazy quilt of wet and dry states, making it both a state and a federal crime, in some instances, to so much as transport a bottle of wine from one state to another. In this hostile legislative environment Ernest, Julio, and their winemaking confederates had to launch highly complex enterprises in the midst of the nastiest economic conditions the nation had ever experienced.

Ernest observed that his biggest competitors were selling wine under their own labels, while he and Julio had been selling theirs in bulk to bottlers who stamped it with different brand names. About eighty percent of all California wine was sold in bulk at the time. If he and Julio were to break out of the pack and dominate the industry, they needed to put the Gallo name on the map—on the shelves alongside jugs of Italian Swiss Colony, Roma, Petri, Cresta Blanca, and other wines of the day. Ernest was determined that the Gallo name, along with their trademark rooster on the label, would overtake the others in the feverish and sometimes nasty competition for display space. Toward that end, Ernest tried to persuade his distributors to bottle his wine and brandy under the Gallo trademark.

"We had labels printed," said Ernest, "and sent them to a few of our bottlers as an experiment. One brand was Gallo Wine, with a rooster on the label. Our New Jersey and New York bottlers would not even consider putting our labels on our products. A Florida distributor told me Gallo was a terrible name for wine."

Most of the distributors were afraid that a new brand on the shelves would cut into the sales of existing brands. So Ernest decided that he and Julio needed to establish a distributorship and bottling facility of their own. He focused on New Orleans first, after he learned that his distributor there was facing bankruptcy. Franek & Company owed E. & J. Gallo Winery $30,000 for wine, which it could not pay. Franek himself was being indicted for "white slavery" after he transported an underage girl from Mississippi to Louisiana for questionable purposes. When Franek ended up in jail, Ernest bought the company's assets in June 1939 and reorganized it as a separate corporation under the name of Gallo Wine Company of Louisiana. He installed a gentleman named E. R. Anderson as president, with himself and Julio the most prominent members of the board of directors, owning controlling shares of stock.

Thus, adversity—the refusal of his existing distributors to market his beverages under the Gallo brand—created the opportunity for Ernest to reap the rewards of the vertical integration of his expanding enterprise. He did the same thing in Los Angeles with another financially strapped distributor and bottler, Distillers Outlet, buying a controlling majority share of the company and establishing a new Gallo Wine Company outlet, with trusted cronies serving in key positions.

* * *

Aileen delivered a third child, another son, whom they named Phillip, on February 5, 1939. A few months later, on June 12, 1939, Amelia delivered her and Ernest's first child, David Ernest. The Gallo household now had four children at home, the two older brothers, their wives, and young Joe. To accommodate the expanding Gallo *famiglia*, Ernest built a new house on land they owned across the road from the existing homestead. He moved into it with Amelia and David later that year, while Joe remained in the original house with Julio, Aileen, and their three children.

Things seemed to be looking up.

Chapter Eight

"One night at home, Aileen and I were having dinner around ten o'clock," Julio said. "We were just about finished when I felt a stab in my abdomen and started to black out from the pain. I almost fell out of the chair."

In 1939, three years after Ernest's health scare, Julio suffered one of his own. He had a ruptured appendix, which was all the more perilous since the family physician was losing his eyesight and could no longer operate.

"Don't worry, though," Ernest tried to reassure Julio. "We'll call in Dr. Husband, the best surgeon in town."

Dr. Husband may have been the best surgeon in town, but he was also the drunkest. When he arrived at Julio's hospital room, it was apparent that he would require copious amounts of strong black coffee to sober him up. Julio took one look at him and said, "I'm not going to let you operate."

Dr. Husband left to get his coffee while the nurses strapped Julio down and began to sedate him, telling him that Dr. Husband would be sober enough to do a good job when he returned. The last thing Julio thought before he went under was that Ernest would be left alone to shoulder all the responsibilities at the winery, and he was about to be "operated on by one doctor who had been drinking and another who couldn't see."

Julio survived and returned to sixteen-hour workdays in short order, with Ernest barking commands to everyone in sight at their daily luncheon meetings whenever he returned from a road trip. Ernest's overbearing nature began to wear his younger brother down. According to Julio, Ernest tried to convince Joe to take on more responsibilities at the winery, to relieve some of the burden. But Joe had other ideas.

"Joe made it clear that he was not interested in making a career of the winery," Julio said. "He told me he wanted to be on his own and maybe go into cattle ranching. I was very disappointed. Ernest and I were spread awfully thin. Being able to count on Joe joining us as a partner at some point would have been a real weight off us."

Julio was also troubled about having to perpetuate Ernest's lie that the brothers learned winemaking from a couple of pamphlets written by Professor Frederic T. Bioletti, which Ernest had supposedly discovered at the Modesto public library. "These pamphlets were probably the difference between going out of business the first year because of an unsalable product, and what was to become the Gallo winery," Ernest had claimed. When Julio was interviewed late in 1939 by a reporter from the *Modesto Bee*, he sucked it up and explained, "We had to study the pamphlets Ernest had found at the library because we had started with no commercial winemaking experience."

"You mean you started from scratch?" the reporter asked, astonished.

"That's right."

"How many gallons of wine do you make a year now?"

"Three million," Julio admitted, nearly gagging on the absurdity. The reporter, recalled Julio, seemed shocked that one of the state's ten largest wineries—just six years after Repeal—had been launched by two brothers with no commercial experience, who had gleaned everything they knew from pamphlets in a library. Ernest was brazen enough to perpetuate the myth, but Julio lacked the conviction and toughness to carry it off credibly.

Julio knew as much about winemaking as anyone in California—anyone in the country, for that matter. He oversaw the annual cycle of unloading the grapes onto a conveyor belt, which dumped them into huge centrifugal crushers. The stems were then separated from the pulp and juice, which emptied into 20,000-gallon fermenting tanks.

Throughout the fermentation period, the grape sugar turned into alcohol. The dessert wine was only partially fermented over two or three days, then pumped into holding tanks to be fortified by brandy, which increased the alcohol level. Table wine, on the other hand, was allowed to continue fermenting until the process ceased on its own.

Julio then stored the wine in tanks and waited for it to clarify and settle, which took a couple of weeks. Afterward, the wine was cooled to seventeen degrees, stabilized for another two or three weeks, filtered several times through presses, and finally stored in tanks where it could be pumped into railroad cars and transported to their various distributors and bottlers—including the outlets they now owned themselves. It was an exhausting and painstaking process that required meticulous supervision. And if anything went wrong along the way, Julio was the first one to hear about it from Ernest, who returned from his frequent road trips full of spit and vinegar. Ernest was the type of man who was quick to criticize and slow to praise, and Julio had an increasingly difficult time standing up to him.

Ernest continued to focus on the marketing side of the business. He visited retail outlets throughout the country and discovered that "retailers are, as a rule, either too busy or too indifferent to vocally recommend a product for very long." He noticed, however, that they recommended wines silently by prominently placing one brand or another in their stores.

"Having determined that for the time being we would be limited to promoting our brand only by this silent recommendation of the retailer," Ernest explained, "I set about to determine how we could obtain it."

The most prominently displayed beverages were liquor and beer, since they were in the greatest demand. Wines were usually relegated to odd locations around a store, with various brands jumbled together. Ernest designed a steel rack that could hold 120 bottles of Gallo wines, lit up from behind by light bulbs. He went from store to store, selling merchants on the idea that they could make more money pushing his wines if they positioned his racks near the cash register. Ernest also realized that he needed a dedicated sales force of his own since salesmen for wholesale distributors represented as many as 500 products and paid most attention to their biggest sellers, which generated the biggest commissions. Salesmen who walked into a store with only one brand to sell, namely Gallo, would be motivated to push Gallo wines exclusively.

"If he didn't make a sale, he didn't eat," said Ernest, who understood the art of motivation.

Ernest hired eight unemployed soft drink and tobacco salesmen, young hotshots eager to earn a living pushing product in an environment of ball-shriveling economic deprivation. He trained them well: sell my wines and you and your families will go to sleep at night with full bellies; fail and you will starve.

* * *

Ernest and Julio wanted Joe to get more involved in the family business—but not necessarily as a full partner in the enterprise they had created after Prohibition. Joe turned twenty-one on September 11, 1940, which meant that he was no longer under the guardianship of his brothers. According to the terms of their mother's will, Joe was to inherit his one-third share of the estate when he reached his majority. But this was a matter now open to legal interpretation. Upon their deaths, Joe and Susie's assets included their Maze Road home with its illegal winery, their ranch in Fresno, other acreage they owned in the area, some shares of stock, and a few thousand dollars in cash deposited in several bank accounts. The value of E. & J. Gallo Winery in 1940 was something the two older brothers had created through their own efforts after Prohibition. The question—the abiding question, as it turned out, that would resurface more than four decades later—was precisely how much Joe's one-third interest entitled him to: one-third of the estate as it existed in 1933, or one-third of the ongoing Gallo family enterprise.

When the dust settled after the lawyers and accountants had sliced and diced the numbers at the time, Joe's share was valued at $20,000—a sum he claimed later in life that he had never received. He complained that Ernest had shoved some papers under his nose and told him to sign them, which he did because he was brought up to obey his older brothers. So, Joe had been either naïve, obedient, and docile to a fault, or else the revelation of the contents of his mother's will—in fact, the mere existence of the will—came as a total shock when the internecine hostilities erupted more than forty years later.

No sooner had the issue of Joe's inheritance been resolved, for the time being at least, than Julio's health once again deteriorated. "I suppose you've noticed that I sometimes go away," Julio said to Rudy Wagner one day early in 1941. Wagner, who was unaccustomed to such forthrightness from either of the older Gallos, nodded. Not only he, but other employees as well, had been remarking among themselves about Julio's frequent absences from the winery. Julio, in his own way, was as much of a workaholic as Ernest, but he suddenly started to disappear for days and weeks at a time. Always a robust man, Julio began to lose weight and appeared to be ill, with bags under his eyes, his ruddy face taking on a sickly pallor.

"Sometimes the strain just gets too much for me," Julio went on, "and I have to get out of here."

"I'm sure it's good for you to unwind," Wagner said, "especially after all the hours you have to put in here."

"Not just the long hours, but the way Ernest is," said Julio. "It gets so I just can't listen to him anymore. All his talk about what has to be done and has to be done his way."

This was the first time Wagner had ever heard Julio criticize his older brother, and he was alarmed and a bit put off to hear him speak that way. It was clear to everyone who worked there that Ernest was the real boss, the dominant brother, but everyone assumed that they were in sync with each other, that they had formed their partnership in a manner that was mutually agreeable, with a suitable division of responsibilities between them. Wagner was startled to be taken into Julio's confidence like this.

Julio confided in his younger brother as well. No one in the family was allowed to discuss the horrific circumstances surrounding their parents' deaths, so Joe had never brought it up in front of his brothers. Now, here was Julio complaining to him about Ernest's demands and mentioning their parents' deaths with tears welling in his eyes. Understandably, Joe was upset to see his brother in such a state. What no one knew until a few months later was that Julio was undergoing a complete nervous breakdown.

As Julio put it, "The only cure was rest, Dr. Maxwell said. In April 1941, he referred me to a sanitarium south of Livermore for evaluation. Ernest drove me, as he wanted to talk to the doctors himself."

Ernest apparently felt a need to micromanage even his brother's illness.

"After examining me," Julio recalled, "the doctors told us that they would admit me. To get over this, they said, I needed to be away from the business and even the family." Away from *Ernest* was left unsaid. Julio remained there for four months.

It is tempting to speculate on the precise cause of Julio's breakdown. Several Gallo employees believed that Julio was faking his illness as an excuse to be away when investigators came around to check up on charges of illegal activities at the winery. It is also possible that Julio was truly buckling under the stress of living as close to the edge as Ernest enjoyed doing. It was simply not in his nature to constantly be testing the limits of what they could get away with.

It is also understandable that there might have been something deeper gnawing away at him. If there were any truth to the recurring rumors that Ernest and Julio had known what was about to happen to their parents in June 1933—and perhaps had played a role in their sordid demise—the guilt that had been festering inside Julio during the past eight years might finally have gotten the best of him. It's hard to believe that any person could accept the violent deaths of both parents without being affected in some significant way. Simply not discussing the matter was no way to bury the pain for anybody whose emotions were not encased in steel. Even after Julio returned, it would take many months before he was restored to anything approaching normalcy.

"My recovery was not complete the day I walked out of the hospital in August 1941," Julio admitted. "I remained under a doctor's care. In fact, I suffered a relapse in early 1942 and was hospitalized a second time." It wasn't until 1943 that Julio had recovered to a point where he could put in as much as a few hours a day for an extended period at the winery.

If any of the brothers were made of steel it was Ernest, who was not about to let the bullet-pierced corpses of his parents hobble him in any way. Amelia presented him with a second son, Joseph Ernest, on March 12, 1941, a month before Julio's confinement to the sanitarium. In Julio's absence, Ernest ran the show on his own, with his loyal lieutenants Max Kane and Rudy Wagner temporarily taking over Julio's duties. He trademarked the family name and launched a vigorous advertising campaign to promote the brand. Even as cataclysmic an event as the bombing of Pearl Harbor later that year presented him with an opportunity: with the railroads put at the disposal of the federal government's war effort, Ernest bought twelve railroad tank cars and folded them into a new entity, which he called the Gallo Tank Lines Company.

Thus, E. & J. Gallo Winery was ensured that a full complement of Gallo wines would find its way to the markets that Ernest had established throughout the country. With Julio not yet fully recovered from his breakdown, Ernest decided to hire a full-time winery manager named Charlie Crawford, who had completed the courses at University of California at

Davis that Ernest had wanted Joe to take. If his family was
falling apart around him—Julio a psychological invalid and
Joe unable or unwilling, for whatever reason, to live up to
Ernest's expectations for him—Ernest compensated by hiring
the talent he needed to help him run the outfit. And he
continued to be on the lookout for opportunities. One of
the by-products of the winery was something the workers
called "slop." It was an unrefined form of tartar left as residue
on the sides of the tanks, and the government could use it
for gunpowder and medicines. Consequently, it was in demand
by munitions and pharmaceuticals manufacturers. Ernest
decided to spin off a subsidiary called Tartar Incorporated to
sell the slop to government suppliers, and he offered Joe the
chance to get in on the ground floor of the new operation—
for a price.

"You put in five thousand dollars and you'll get two
thousand shares of the five thousand we'll issue," Ernest said
to Joe. "We'll make you a director and president of the
company. It will be a real opportunity for you."

It certainly turned out to be another real opportunity
for the ever-imaginative and dynamic Ernest, who treated Joe
as an employee, paying him a salary. Since Ernest owned a
controlling share of the stock in the privately held
corporation, Joe had little say in how the business was
actually run. Ernest appointed himself treasurer of the tartar
subsidiary, Max Kane secretary, and Charlie Crawford de
facto chief operating officer reporting directly to Ernest. The
vertical integration of the expanding Gallo wine enterprise
continued apace, with Ernest manipulating the levers of power
throughout. He installed Rudy Wagner as overseer of another
operation converting molasses into industrial-strength
alcohol, which was in demand by the military to make
synthetic rubber for tires and other products. The Japanese
had cut off natural rubber supplies when they had advanced
through Indonesia.

"[Ernest] had a government contract for ten percent plus costs," said Wagner. "The more you said it cost to produce the alcohol—torpedo juice we called it—the more the government paid. You can't imagine the costs we put in for! That's when Ernest really started to rake in the dough."

Joe maintained for most of his life that he was devoted to his older brothers, but there is no question that he felt the heavy presence of Ernest weighing upon him, dictating every move he made. His easiest escape was the one open to all young American men of the period—the army. The figurehead president of Ernest's tartar company joined the United States Army in August 1942. At five feet seven, he was an inch taller than Ernest, slim and wiry with a hangdog look. Joe got his basic training in Biloxi, Mississippi, and afterward was dispatched to Denver, Colorado. He spent the next three years there as an instructor in a technical squadron, far from Ernest's relentless and domineering personality.

Ernest, then, had earned the distinction of driving two brothers away—Julio into a nervous breakdown, and Joe into wartime service.

Chapter Nine

World War II had a beneficial side effect for the nation's winemakers, the overwhelming majority of whom were in California. Combat overseas had driven up the prices of wine grapes considerably—they soared from fifteen dollars per ton in 1941 on a trajectory that would put them at $135 per ton three years later, even though the government imposed wartime controls that attempted to cap wine prices at March 1942 levels. Ernest was among the vintners who were temporarily squeezed by the law.

"The government assumed, incorrectly," Ernest reasoned, "that the price of grapes would be limited by the controlled wine prices, and never set a ceiling on the price of juice or table grapes. The high prices of grapes resulted in some very expensive crushes. The average vintner, making price-controlled wine from such expensive grapes, found it difficult to make a profit." No matter. Ernest found ample opportunity to generate profits from his slop and torpedo juice operations.

As good as life had become for those connected to the E. & J. Gallo Winery, the brothers still faced formidable competition. The Gallos' primary opponents in the wine wars were Italian Swiss Colony, Roma, Beaulieu, Wente, Christian Brothers, Paul Masson, Louis Martini, Cresta Blanca, and a few others. The large liquor distillers also attempted to enter the wine market, but with limited success. Schenley acquired Cresta Blanca shortly before the war ended, then bought Roma. National Distillers gobbled up Italian Swiss Colony, propelling it to become California's third-largest wine company. Seagram bought Paul Masson, and shortly afterward Hiram Walker bought three wineries in Sonoma and San Benito counties. Most of the big distilleries would end up gagging on their acquisitions because they failed to understand that making booze is far different from making wine, which is a painstaking agricultural endeavor subject to the vagaries of the weather and the soil.

* * *

Labeling the different products of a vineyard was a haphazard procedure. Essentially, there were two types of American wine—red and white—and there was no discernible logic in naming exactly what subcategories they fell into. Red wine could be labeled Claret, Chianti, Burgundy, or anything else that struck the vintner's fancy. Some winemakers had the gall to bottle some of their plonk with upscale French designations, such as St. Julien, Margaux, and Chateau Yquem. Whites were willy-nilly described as Moselle, White Chianti, White Burgundy, Chablis, and even Sauterne when they added enough sugar to it. Wine drinkers who knew anything about wine understood that they were drinking generic red and generic white tricked out with fancy names that made no sense.

French wine critic and writer Andre Simon said this about American drinking habits of the era: "The men and women in their early thirties today have grown up in the foul air of deceit, gangsters, and bathtub gin. The hipflask was the god of their youth. How can they be expected to turn to the shrine where Bacchus holds his court? They like hard liquor better.... Wine to them, in their state, is nauseating: they want a highball or something with a kick in it. They are beyond reform as beyond civilization altogether."

No one could get himself into a snit like a Frenchman discussing wine. But his disdain was shared by many of his American counterparts, who paraded him around the United States as though he were an oracle from on high descended upon the earth to teach table manners to the barbarians who existed between the Atlantic and the Pacific oceans. And no American cities welcomed him more warmly than Boston, New York, San Francisco, Chicago, Los Angeles, and New Orleans, which established chapters of Simon's Food and Wine Society.

In 1943, around the time that Julio felt well enough to resume his duties at the winery, he and Ernest bought a 1,000-acre tract in Livingston, south of Modesto, from the Valley Agricultural Company. That company had used the land to grow Thompson seedless raisin grapes, but Ernest and Julio set about replacing the raisin crop with a broader array of varietals. Julio wanted to blend the varietals to see if they would produce better-quality wines. The Livingston ranch gave the brothers the capacity to grow over 30,000 tons of grapes a year, more than 400 different varietals, many of which had never before been planted in the area.

According to Ernest, he visited Joe at his base in Denver on one of his sales swings around the country and offered him an opportunity to join his older brothers at the Livingston winery after the war.

"Julio and I are spread very thin," Ernest said. "The time is right for you to come into the winery as a partner. We need you."

"I'll have no part of it," Ernest recalled Joe saying to him. "I know what it is like working with you guys. Anytime I do anything right I never hear from you. Anytime I do something wrong, you holler."

Joe denied that the conversation ever took place. He said he would never have spoken to Ernest like that, since it would have been a sign of disrespect to the de facto family patriarch—a statement that seems to be a bit of a stretch, particularly since he worked for Ernest and Julio there as an employee after the war. Then again, why would he have agreed to work as an employee if he had been offered a partnership? It is possible that Ernest was revising history later in life to justify his and Julio's lawsuit against their kid brother. It is also possible that Joe was speaking on the advice of his lawyer to establish his own legal ground in the dispute.

If the conversation did take place, it appears as though Joe didn't move far enough away from home when he joined the army. He should have been stationed in Guam instead of Denver to escape from Ernest's gravity field. In any event, each brother's recollection appears to have been constructed after the fact; the clear loud ring of truth seems to be missing. Since there were no independent witnesses to the purported conversation, it has to go down as a case of one brother's word against another's.

The Gallo brothers did manage to agree that they were better off buying their bacon, ham, and sausage from a commercial butcher rather than slaughtering pigs by themselves, as they had seen their father do when they were kids: there had been a pig on the Livingston property when they acquired the land, and the brothers figured it would be an easy matter to slaughter and butcher the animal.

"Ernest tied the pig's hind legs with a rope," Julio recalled. "I swung the rope over a rafter and pulled the oinking pig upside down. As we'd seen Father do, Ernest stuck it hard in the chest with a butcher knife, expecting to hit the heart, as Father always did. Sure enough, the pig stopped squealing."

They dropped the pig into a laundry tub filled with hot water and started to pull the hair off when the pig suddenly jumped out of the tub and started racing for its life across the ranch. It was the last time they attempted to do their own butchering. Perhaps Ernest should have used his .32 caliber Smith & Wesson instead of the butcher knife on the frantic porker.

Joe returned to California on leave in 1944, visited his brothers at the winery, and promptly fell into the embrace of a pretty young blonde whom he had met through his sister-in-law Aileen.

Her name was Mary Ann Arata. She was the daughter of a successful grape grower in the region who had been a colleague of Joe Gallo Sr. during Prohibition. Joe and Mary Ann were enamored of each other as soon as they met, but her parents were less than thrilled about their daughter's blossoming romance. Mary Ann's father had married into the Coffee family, which was considered to be landed gentry in the region, and the Aratas were extremely wealthy by this time and highly regarded in the community. The Gallos, on the other hand, were still clawing their way up, and they still had some rough edges.

"I knew the Gallos when they didn't have a spaghetti pot to piss in," Mary Ann's mother said to her in an unsuccessful attempt to dissuade her daughter from marrying Joe.

Joe and Mary Ann were married in Denver on February 4, 1945, and no sooner had they consummated their union than Joe was shipped far beyond Ernest's reach—all the way to Luzon in the Philippines, where he saw combat with the 63rd Infantry Regiment. At the end of the war, Joe briefly joined the occupation forces on the Korean peninsula, and then he returned home for good early in 1946. Before he was officially discharged, Mary Ann gave birth to a boy on January 29, 1946. The couple named him Peter Joseph.

Now Joe was *really* back—back in the ongoing battle between his two older brothers. The winery war in Modesto was still in full swing. Julio approached Joe first and made him an offer that seemed too good to be true.

"I need your help down there in Livingston," Julio said to him. "I'll pay you $20,000 a year to be the vineyard manager, and you and Mary Ann can live in the ranch house on the property."

Joe was stunned. He had wanted to go into cattle ranching rather than winemaking, but he could hardly turn down an offer that would pay him twice as much as he expected to make. Ernest, however, had other ideas for Joe.

"I want you to become manager of the winery operations in Modesto," Ernest told him.

"But what about Charlie Crawford? That's his job, isn't it?" asked Joe.

"Charlie's a lying son of a bitch. I want you to take his place."

"I've already accepted Julio's offer in Livingston," Joe replied. "He asked me to be the manager down there." What was going on here? Why were his older brothers making him two separate offers? Ernest said something to the effect that he was worried about Julio's health. And then he said something else that set Joe back on his heels: "You know I built this winery, not Julio. So it's crazy for him to be talking like that."

Joe thought about the bind he was in, then gulped hard and made his decision.

"I've accepted the Livingston job. That's all there is to it," he said.

Crossing Ernest like that turned out to be something less than a brilliant career move, but Joe now had a job and a house to live in with Mary Ann and the baby. When he opened his first paycheck, however, he saw that Julio was paying him only half of what he had promised. His salary was $10,000 per year, not $20,000, and would remain at that level for the next few years. Now Ernest and Julio had him where they wanted him; the older brothers had been playing him like a violin. When Joe offered to buy the Livingston operation on his own and supply his brothers with grapes from the winery at a reasonable price, Ernest turned him down flat. He and Julio had no intention of selling a single acre of land they had acquired over the years. At the end of World War II, E. & J. Gallo Winery controlled nearly three-quarters of all the grapes grown in California, which allowed the brothers to virtually dictate prices when price controls were finally lifted on wine.

With the war over, Ernest was more determined than ever to close the gap between E. & J. Gallo Winery and the competition. "In 1946 I registered the Gallo trademark in most states," he said, "and started setting up distributors in state after state."

He was referring to his own distributors, who were dedicated to pushing the Gallo label exclusively. Then Ernest traveled to New York City to launch an advertising campaign that has to go down as one of the more memorable wine campaigns in advertising history. Ernest met with an ad executive who had come up with the slogan, "By Golly, Be Jolly, Buy Gallo." Ernest's advertiser in Los Angeles, John Freiburg, flinched when he heard it.

"I don't know," he said. "People might start thinking of the brand as 'Golly Wine.'"

Ernest directed him to come up with something better if he could. Freiburg returned to L.A. and proposed a billboard campaign featuring blood-red images of women's lips saying, "On Everybody's Lips: Gallo Wine."

Ernest loved it and decided to test it first throughout Southern California. The billboard campaign was moderately successful there, but Freiburg told Ernest that what he really needed to do was get the Gallo name out there nationally— turn it into a household name.

"How do you suggest we do it?" asked Ernest, who did not want to spend a ton of money on advertising.

Freiburg proposed throwing a party to celebrate that year's wine crush, with a pretty young woman taking a bath in a barrel of wine. "We'll call her 'Queen of the Crush.' We'll invite everyone in town and get *Life* magazine to photograph it. We'll have fantastic national exposure at no cost."

Once again, Ernest was enthralled. Free national exposure with a beautiful young woman bathing in his wine. It sounded just oddball enough to work, and it wouldn't cost him much beyond the expense of the party. But he was skeptical that *Life* would show up to photograph the event.

Freiburg was as good as his word. He rushed off to downtown Modesto and returned half an hour later with the pretty soda clerk from the local drugstore. Freiburg had promised that her picture would appear in the most popular magazine in the country, where Hollywood scouts were bound to see it and maybe put her in a movie, and that was all the enticement she needed.

Freiburg's wild idea turned out to be a stroke of marketing genius. The October 8, 1945, issue of *Life* devoted a full-page spread of the soda clerk in a two-piece bathing suit, climbing into a vat of sauterne. The caption read, "Queen of the Crush, Doreen Ronne, a twenty-one-year-old Modesto girl, who works as a secretary at the Gallo winery, crawls dutifully into a barrel for her coronation." Ernest had put her on the payroll as a secretary to avoid the image of exploiting a local soda clerk. The entire piece ran on for three more pages. Ernest printed up 30,000 copies of the article in attractive folders for his salesmen to take on the road when calling on their retail accounts. The campaign helped propel Gallo into becoming the leading wine brand in New York City within three years.

Ernest was more than satisfied with Freiburg's effort. It was successful and inexpensive. All told, Ernest had laid out $762,000 to generate $6,300,000 in sales revenue in 1946. As for Doreen—well, she didn't become another Lana Turner, but at least she had her fifteen minutes of fame, thanks to Ernest and his advertising maven.

Chapter Ten

In 1946, vintners throughout the United States crushed 1.6 million tons of grapes, forty percent more than any other crush in history. E. & J. Gallo Winery was well on its way to becoming a powerhouse in the U.S. wine industry, with a major share of the country's grape-growing capacity. But now a relatively small upstart had surfaced and attracted Ernest's attention—indeed, his wrath. A fellow in Ohio named Charles Gallo named his wine-bottling operations the Gallo Wine Company. The man was naïve enough to believe that a common family name would establish a bond with Ernest when he proposed that Ernest sell him bulk wines to be bottled under his own label.

Ernest responded with a lawsuit. It was a pattern he would follow for the rest of his life. He had trademarked the Gallo name, and anyone else audacious enough to use it would be subjected to the full force of Ernest's fury. Ernest sued the man to death—literally. Charles was so upset over the prospect of losing his family business that he suffered a heart attack and dropped dead on September 7, 1946. His son Rocco and wife, Mary, continued to fight, but they were up against a ruthless foe.

Ernest took the witness stand and declared, "The name of the brand 'Gallo' has been used since 1909 by the rest of my family; that is, my father. We used 'Gallo' in conjunction with the grapes during Prohibition. Millions of cases of grapes were shipped with that brand on it. Our company, the E. & J. Gallo Winery, then continued with the brand in 1933 when we started the business. We always sold wine under the brand name 'Gallo.'"

The judge rendered a decision worthy of King Solomon, acknowledging the proprietary claim on the Gallo name established by Ernest but allowing the defendant to continue using his own family name, as long as he used his first name with it. And so, the Gallo Wine Company was renamed the Charles Gallo & Son Wine Company. Ernest fumed at the decision, and he vowed that he would win the war in the end. It was the last time he would emerge as anything less than a clear victor when battling others for the exclusive use of the Gallo name.

Part of the pressure on all the U.S. vintners stemmed from the challenge of making inroads in a country that, by and large, had little interest in the product they were making. A distinguished vintner and author of the period, Philip Wagner (no relation to Rudy), put it succinctly after he served as a judge in a wine competition at the California State Fair.

"Here they were, these men and women," he said, "working themselves to the bone for something that the American public couldn't care about less, namely a decent glass of wine. The people at the fair were not even able to provide proper wine glasses; instead, the judges tasted their wines from receptacles that were more appropriate to a small milkshake or a gooey dessert. It turned out that in all of California it was impossible to find a supply of good, serviceable, all-purpose wine glasses of ample size and moderate price."

In 1947, one of E. & J. Gallo Winery's major competitors, Cribari Winery, flirted with bankruptcy. Bulk wine prices plummeted from a high of $1.75 a gallon to thirty-eight cents a gallon by the summer of 1947. Cribari was stuck with wine priced at $1.50 a gallon that it was forced to unload for about one-third of the price, and the company's entire cash reserve vanished. Cribari never fully recovered. E. & J. Gallo Winery, which had played its hand closer to the vest during the downturn, ended up buying Cribari on the cheap seven years later.

Ernest had more important issues to deal with than suing Gallos who were unfortunate enough not to be his own blood relatives. The major distilleries that had entered the wine trade by gobbling up failing wineries had deeper pockets than the independent winemakers. But they produced more wine than they could possibly sell and were hemorrhaging money—victims of their own earlier success. In 1947, Schenley lost sixteen million dollars attempting to keep its wine operations afloat. National Distillers ended the year with a loss of nine million dollars. E. & J. Gallo Winery managed to turn a profit in a generally disastrous year for vintners.

To suppress the supply of wine on the market, Schenley's CEO, Lewis Rosenstiel, proposed legislation requiring every bottle of wine produced in the state to carry a seal certifying that the wine was at least four years old. The company tried to present a united front to California lawmakers by convincing the directors at the Wine Institute that it was in their best interest to support the bill.

"As far as Rosenstiel's plan was concerned, I would not even consider it," said Ernest. "This was another fight for survival. If we lost, our winery might as well shut its doors. It would prove just as fatal to other small and medium-sized wineries that didn't have the financial wherewithal to hold their wine from the market for four years."

What Rosenstiel didn't know, and Ernest didn't reveal at the time, was that he and Julio were not sitting on a big inventory of wine. They managed to sell just about every gallon of wine they produced—an agricultural version of just-in-time manufacturing. Ernest defeated Rosenstiel by convincing other independent winemakers that it behooved them to line up with him and oppose the plan. Ernest and his cohorts, who included John B. Cella, A. R. Morrow, Walter Taylor, Jimmy Vai, Bruno Bisceglia, and Harry Baccigaluppi, beat Rosenstiel by a single vote—a nail-biter as it turned out, since Bisceglia misunderstood at first what a yea or nay vote signified. Ernest asked for a recount and got the confused gentleman to change his vote while Rosenstiel was in Europe, earning the enmity of Schenley's top executive for decades.

The big distilleries were not the only outsize competition for independents such as the Gallos. Beginning in the late 1930s, grape-growers throughout California started to band together in growers' cooperatives to share their risks. By 1950, California hosted twenty cooperatives with a combined storage capacity of more than seventy million gallons of wine, about one-third of the state's total. Louis Petri had founded California's largest cooperative, Allied Grape Growers, which had a membership of 275 growers with a storage capacity of nineteen million gallons of wine. Their clout was even greater thanks to low-cost government loans and tax subsidies extended by friendly legislators. Ernest and Julio refused to ride the bandwagon.

"The co-ops were an honest attempt by growers to bring some stability to the grape industry, and stability was badly needed," Julio said. "But co-ops were not the solution."

Ernest agreed. "One thing that worked against co-ops was the fact that their members had no sales or merchandising experience," he said. "By its nature, a co-op was primarily a producer, not a marketer. When the wine industry stepped up its efforts in marketing, advertising, and improved salesmanship, the co-op brands began to fade rapidly. In time, we were able to overcome the co-ops' built-in advantages. Several did remain in business through the years—mainly as suppliers of bulk wine, however, not as brand builders."

* * *

Ernest needed a rest. All his life, he had been working like a dynamo, following a routine with little time for vacations or leisure of any sort. When he did manage to take brief trips away from the business, away from the pressures of building his empire, he preferred to go deep-sea fishing with a few close friends. But in 1950 he decided to take a real break, and he boarded an ocean liner with Amelia to visit his parents' birthplace—his first journey ever outside the United States. Ernest and Amelia loaded a suitcase with a wide assortment of groceries to distribute to the villagers, who were still reeling from the aftershock of World War II. When they docked in Naples, Ernest looked on with anxiety as the customs agent boarded the ship and rummaged through his luggage, unearthing tins of tuna and sardines, salami, cheeses, and other items still in short supply throughout most of Europe.

"What are you doing?" Ernest asked.

"Figuring out the duty," the agent replied.

"The duty? We're going to give this food to people who are hungry, and you want to charge us duty?"

"That's the law, *signore*," he said.

"We're not going to pay their duty, not a damn cent," Ernest said to Amelia. The agent wanted to charge him a duty that was more than he had paid for the food. Ernest understood how the system worked. The agent would end up pocketing most of the money. If Ernest refused to pay and just left the food at the dock, the agent would sell it himself on the black market. On the spur of the moment, Ernest decided that he was not going to be victimized by a corrupt system. He picked up the suitcase containing his groceries and heaved it overboard into the waves lapping the side of the boat. The agent stared in horror, his eyes wide in disbelief as Ernest took Amelia by the elbow and guided her down the gangplank onto terra firma.

They drove north in a rented car to Fossano in the Piedmont region and found the inn where Ernest's father had been born. Ernest's uncle Bernardo, his father's brother, was still running a small shop there. From Fossano, they drove to Agliano di Asti, where his mother's side of the family, the Biancos, had hailed from. It seemed the locals expected to be wined and dined the way they were when Ernest's Uncle Mike had visited the area years before.

"Droves of townsfolk poured into the streets," Ernest recalled, "all of them apparently expecting me to invite them to a big dinner just like my Uncle Mike had some twenty years earlier. Out to impress my Aunt Celia's family and everyone else in town, Uncle Mike had acted like the typical rich American. On top of the world with big earnings from his bootlegging, Mike made sure he and his wife traveled in style, even shipping over his new Chrysler convertible to drive on the narrow roads through backwater villages."

That was clearly not Ernest's style. He had inherited his father's parsimony. In Italy, as at home in California, it was Ernest's way or the highway. Ernest and Amelia said their goodbyes and hastily made their exit, heading farther north into France to visit Lourdes. There, Amelia hoped to see visions of the Blessed Virgin Mary, who supposedly had appeared to a little French girl named Bernadette ninety-two years earlier. There is no record of whether Amelia was treated to the same vision as Bernadette. Ernest, for his part, was happy to be a distance removed from hungry relatives who expected more from him than a wedge of cheese and a long tube of salami.

The truth was, Ernest was getting antsy being away from work for so long. A two- or three-day fishing trip was one thing, but driving around Italy and France looking for miracles with Amelia was something else. He was anxious to return to California, to make sure Julio and Joe were doing their jobs properly in his absence. Were the wines being bottled on time? Were his salesmen pushing his Gallo label as hard as they could? What about his competition? Were they cutting into his market share while he was away? Just what the hell was going on back there?

It was time to go back to work.

Book Three

THY KINGDOM COME

Chapter Eleven

Every Christmas Eve, Joe and Mary Ann hosted a *bagna cauda* gathering for the entire Gallo family. They all arrived at Joe's house—Ernest and Amelia, Julio and Aileen, and their assorted children—to celebrate the holiday season in the traditional Gallo way. *Bagna cauda* in their Piedmontese dialect translated literally into "hot bath" or "hot sauce." In Florentine Italian, it would have been called *bagno caldo*. The hot bath or sauce was made with chopped garlic and anchovies sautéed in olive oil and butter. It was placed family-style in a big pan in the center of the table, and the Gallos ate it like a fondue, dipping roasted celery, cauliflower, artichokes, peppers, onions, and other vegetables in it. They washed it down with tumblers full of the finest table wine they were capable of making. But even here, in Joe's house, Ernest insisted on holding court like the lord of the manor. And the subject he insisted on discussing was business, business, always business. Nothing else interested him. It didn't matter if it was Christmas Eve or any other evening.

How many tons of grapes can we grow next year? He, Ernest, was selling everything Julio could produce, so Julio clearly had to find a way of getting more yield out of the vineyards. And Joe? What was he contributing? All of them had to work a little harder, a little longer, a little smarter. The women and the children sat around quietly as Ernest ranted, speaking only when he asked them a question directly. They had all accepted their roles in the Gallo family hierarchy—all of them, that is, except Mary Ann, who resented Ernest's bossiness and the way he dominated her husband. Rarely did Mary Ann challenge Ernest to his face, but she fumed inwardly, casting smoldering glances at her husband, wondering when he would find the gumption to speak up and defend himself, particularly in his own home. She would talk to him about it later, somewhat heatedly, in the privacy of their bedroom. There, at least, Ernest had nothing to say about what went on.

* * *

In 1950, Gallo wines were fully distributed in only six states: California, Kansas, Louisiana, New Jersey, New York, and Connecticut. Even in California they had yet to penetrate many of the markets outside of Los Angeles and San Francisco. Ernest had been the sales and marketing guru for the company, but he had to admit that he could not do everything on his own any longer. He needed a marketing professional if Gallo was going to conquer the U.S. marketplace. The person would have to be accomplished enough to do the job properly, hungry or crazy enough to put in long hours on the road, and tough enough to rise to Ernest's exacting standards. Ernest found his man in Albion Fenderson, a former salesman for a large distillery. Ernest lost little time in laying out his vision for the wine industry as he saw it unfolding.

"There are now about ten different wineries attempting to become national brands," Ernest told Fenderson during their interview. "They can't all succeed. In my opinion, within five years' time there will only be two or three of us left."

Fenderson told Ernest that he was up to the task of making sure E. & J. Gallo Winery was one of the few vintners left standing, and Ernest hired him in June 1952. Fenderson showed up for work only to discover that he had no office; indeed, not so much as a desk on which to do his paperwork. Ernest expected him to be out in the field hawking Gallo wines every minute of his working day. An hour spent in an office was an hour he was not out selling. If Fenderson was perplexed, he laughed it off and didn't let it show.

Fenderson was, if anything, overqualified for the job. He was thirty-six years old at the time. He had a degree in economics from Carnegie Tech, he had served as a whiz kid for President Roosevelt on the War Production Board, and most recently he had been a vice president of Armand Hammer's United Distilleries of America. He and his wife, Lynne, were art collectors, primarily of works with Native American themes, and over time they had established an impressive collection that they lent to museums. He found himself out of work when Hammer, under investigation by the FBI and the IRS for his pro-Soviet activities, sold his distillery to Schenley Industries. Fenderson was blond, good-looking in an Old Money, WASP-y manner, and he sported tweed jackets with leather elbow patches. He exuded an upper-class elegance that Ernest found appealing. It was the image Ernest was looking for to upgrade the Gallo name and label. Ernest abhorred facial hair on his salesmen or anyone else who worked for him. He frowned on heavy drinking, indiscreet sexual activities, and any other behavior that might cause a scandal for his company.

Fenderson went to work immediately, establishing new markets for the Gallos first on the east coast, then in Los Angeles, San Diego, Bakersfield, San Francisco, and other California towns where the competition had made deeper inroads. Al Fenderson quickly became a Gallo family loyalist, earning Ernest's respect and admiration. They were a study in contrasts, Ernest rough-hewn and swarthy with his Old World mannerisms, Fenderson fair and tweedy with his Old Money, well-bred American stylishness. But they made their partnership work. Fenderson had found his home for the rest of his working life, becoming a fixture at the Gallo winery for the next fifty years. Ernest even rewarded him, eventually, with a desk and office of his own when he promoted Fenderson to an indoor job overseeing a growing sales force.

Under Fenderson's tutelage, the Gallo salesmen began to adopt a more aggressive approach to positioning their wines in the stores they called on. Many were accused of tampering with competitors' products—back-screwing the twist-on caps to make the bottles impossible to open, puncturing the caps to hasten spoilage of the wine, putting vinegar or cigarette butts inside their bottles, and removing their brands from the shelves altogether and replacing them with bottles of Gallo.

"I had to keep a close eye on those guys when they came into my store," said one wine retailer at the time. "Otherwise, they would turn my store upside down and turn it into a Gallo outlet." This was a typical sentiment among store owners.

Ernest loved the results he was achieving under Fenderson's take-no-prisoners approach to marketing and gave him full rein to conquer the wine universe for Gallo.

Their compatibility was partly due to the sardonic sense of humor they shared. In addition to sales and marketing, Fenderson was in charge of advertising for the Gallos. When Ernest joined his new employee on the road from time to time, he peppered Fenderson relentlessly about concepts for new ad campaigns. Fenderson invariably preferred the edgier, over-the-top approach.

"If we don't produce this one, I would feel so bad about it I would want to shoot myself," Fenderson said to Ernest.

"Do you want to borrow my gun?" Ernest replied.

"It was like Nero. Thumbs up or thumbs down," recalled one of the advertising executives who dealt with them. "Ernest was the boss, the board, and the corporate culture rolled into one. But Al Fenderson was also an entrepreneur, a key decision-maker, rather than a marketing director trying to second-guess the CEO. You may not have agreed, but you knew what he wanted or didn't want."

So they got along splendidly. Ernest enjoyed spending time with the productive, quirky, old-line blue blood, and Fenderson took to Ernest as a surrogate father instead of a cranky old boss with impossible expectations for him.

Julio continued to deal with the frustration of producing wines that were not to his own tastes but were still in demand by his fellow Americans. One of the more successful wines at the time was a sickly sweet concoction sold as Vino da Tavola—wine from the table. It was made by Guild Winery of Lodi, which was able to sell oceans of the syrupy glop without resorting to expensive advertising. Julio tasted the stuff and spat it out. He would have preferred making the dry table wines that suited his palate, yet he couldn't ignore the demands of the marketplace.

"I sipped this popular new wine," Julio said, "swirled it around in my mouth, and in a nearby sink spit it out. I didn't like it. To make sure we didn't have a bad bottle, we opened up another. It wasn't any better. Part table wine and part dessert wine, Vino da Tavola was a common valley red wine sweetened with port."

Nevertheless, Al Fenderson asked Julio to make a wine just like it, only better if he could, since there was a huge demand for this type of plonk. Most Americans at the time considered dry table wines to be sour. "What we're looking for here is a red blend that is light and mellow," Fenderson said.

Julio winced and said that he would attempt to come up with something similar but more palatable. He went to work experimenting with different blends until he thought he had what Fenderson wanted. "We ended up making a very soft red wine," he recalled, "using some quality North Coast grapes in a blend that I liked better than Vino da Tavola. Fruitier and not so harsh, our wine did well in comparative tastings."

The Gallos called it Paisano—which meant countryman, usually from the same village—and they knew immediately that they had hit upon a winner. It went on to become the top-selling wine throughout the United States for the next few years—until the Gallos came up with a blockbuster that would land them squarely in the top ranks of American winemakers.

Julio was constantly under pressure from Ernest to make more and more wine, since Fenderson and his crew were selling everything the Gallos were able to produce. Toward that end, the brothers signed deals with other winemakers in the region, including the Napa Valley Cooperative, the St. Helena Grape Growers Co-Op (also in Napa), Frei Brothers of Healdsburg in Sonoma, Beaulieu Vineyards, Fountain Grove, Wente, Mirassou, and Seghesio. The vintners shipped their wines to Modesto, where Julio and his team experimented with blending different varietals before bottling the results under the Gallo label. No matter how much wine the Gallos contracted for, and how much they produced themselves, their aggressive sales force kept opening new outlets for it. Julio discovered a new way of filtering wine through membranes, called Millipore filters, which improved the shelf life of wine and provided the Gallos with an edge over their competitors.

"In our experimental vineyards in Livingston," Julio explained, "we had tried various methods of pruning—head pruning, cane pruning, cordon pruning—for each grape variety." Julio was referring to different types of pruning that vintners experiment with. Head pruning involves cutting back the shoots to the main stem; cane pruning usually means cutting every other cane; and cordon pruning leaves a horizontal extension of the trunk in place from year to year. He continued, "The only grapes a vine will produce well come out of the wood or cane that grew the previous year. Grapes will come from shoots or spurs growing off this 'fruit wood.' In pruning, you are planning just how much sunshine and aeration the grapes will get, decisions based largely on grape variety and local climate."

It was both art and science, and Julio was a perfectionist who demanded as much of himself as Ernest did. The pruning process commenced in the fall as soon as the sap stopped running, and it had to be finished before the buds began to open in the spring. While it was under way, Julio had to fight off a legion of pests that usually included cutworms and leafhoppers. Before organic farming, the best way to combat the pest invasion was by dusting the vines with sulfur. In June, he and his workers had to inspect each vine and thin out the ones that were "over-cropped" with too many grape clusters hanging on them. Over-cropped vines led to an inferior grade of wine—something Julio agonized over even if consumers cared little about quality. Julio oversaw the harvesting and crushing of the grapes in the summer, usually from about six in the evening until ten at night. He inspected each load of grapes before it was crushed and chalk-marked it with his own seal of approval.

Ernest was troubled. With all its success, E. & J. Gallo Winery still had not climbed into the top ranks of U.S. wineries. Roma was the largest, with a total storage capacity of forty million gallons of wine; the California Wine Association was second, with a thirty-million-gallon capacity; and Italian Swiss Colony was third, with the ability to store twenty-seven million gallons of wine. Ernest flew into a rage when E. & J. Gallo Winery failed to make *Time* magazine's list of the country's five largest wineries in 1953. The Gallos had sold more wine than all but two of their competitors that year, but the magazine's editors measured size according to a company's storage capacity, not sales. Ernest and Julio's capacity was around twenty million gallons, and Ernest had attempted to remedy the situation by buying Italian Swiss Colony in 1952, but the company ended up in the hands of another competitor, Louis Petri.

Another opportunity to increase storage capacity presented itself a year later, and Ernest pounced like a cat onto a wounded chipmunk. Virtually bankrupt after World War II, Cribari Winery defaulted on its bank loans and was forced to put its assets into receivership. Ernest had little interest in continuing the Cribari brand, but he lusted after the company's plant in Fresno with its huge, though antiquated, storage facility. In 1954, the brothers bought the facility with its dilapidated wooden cooperage for pennies on the dollar and set about converting it into a modern plant, fitted out with new glass-lined and stainless steel tanks. In time, the renovated Cribari plant would be able to store nearly 100 million gallons of wine.

* * *

The Gallos enjoyed good sales with their Paisano brand, but they needed another product with similar appeal that would allow them to outpace the competition. Ernest continued to make road trips with Fenderson and salesmen whom Fenderson had hired, to get a feel for what was going on in the various markets. Ernest loved hitting the streets more than anything else—interacting with people, sizing up his competitors, figuring out new ways to better position his brand in the retail outlets.

One of his most productive salesmen was a young fellow named Harry Bleiweiss, who specialized in selling sweet white port in predominantly black neighborhoods in San Francisco and Oakland. His marketing approach was so successful that Fenderson began to call him "White Port Harry."

Harry noticed that the liquor stores carried unsweetened lemon juice near the cash register, which they sold to their customers along with the white port they were buying. "What's that for?" he asked.

"They drink some port off the top, then fill the bottle back up with lemon juice," he was told. "They like the white port, but it's too sweet for their taste, so they add the lemon juice."

White Port Harry laughed about this innovation with Fenderson, but Fenderson saw opportunity where Harry saw only humor. Fenderson had long been aware that other citrus-flavored ports, such as Italian Swiss Colony's Silver Satin and Canandaigua Wine Company's Wild Irish Rose were flying off the shelves in black communities. When he returned to Modesto, he told Julio that they ought to try preblending the port and lemon juice themselves and selling it as a new product.

"Some guys are taking their white port," Fenderson said to Julio, "drinking four or five ounces out of the bottle, then filling the bottle to the top with lemon juice."

Once again, Julio tasted the concoction and spat it out. Foul. Here he was trying to upgrade consumer preferences so that he could make the type of wine he preferred, and both Fenderson and Ernest kept coming up with new ways to insult his palate. But he had little choice in the matter, not if the Gallo winery was to keep growing.

"The problem with white port is that it's too sweet," Julio agreed. "What they've done is correct the sugar-acid balance by adding more acid."

So back he went to the laboratory and came up with an approximation of what the customers themselves were doing. What he produced was a clear mixture of white port and lemon juice, fortified to an alcohol content of twenty-one percent, almost twice the strength of ordinary table wine. The next step was to test-market the result in a few Oakland liquor stores.

"They seem to like it," Fenderson said to Ernest.

"Not so fast," Ernest replied. "They're getting it for free. Let's see how much they like it when they have to pay for it."

Chapter Twelve

Now they needed a name for the white port–lemon juice mixture, a name that would resonate with their target market. The name had to be as seductive and memorable as Italian Swiss Colony's White Satin. Fenderson wanted to call the new blend Cockade.

"I don't like it," Ernest said.

Ernest sat on the product for more than a year; he understood that launching it without a dynamic advertising campaign would doom it to languish on the shelves. During a road trip through Texas, Fenderson noticed that Ford's new car, which the company introduced in 1954, was the most popular auto of the year. Americans were buying it as fast as Ford could make it. It was sleek, it was fast, and it connoted power and the latest in contemporary living.

"Ernest, I think I have the name for the new wine," Fenderson said somewhere around 15,000 feet in the air on the plane back to California. "It's a radically different kind of name for a wine."

"So what's the name?" Ernest asked.

"Thunderbird."

"That's it."

Thunderbird was launched at a time when the sales of Gallo wines had already climbed from four to sixteen million gallons per year, thanks largely to the popularity of Paisano. By 1955, the Gallo brothers accounted for ten percent of all the wine sold in America, even though they were distributed in only twenty states. More than any other place, Ernest wanted to make his mark in Texas, where Italian Swiss Colony controlled about eighty percent of the market. Italian

Swiss Colony was a sore spot for Ernest, who regarded it as his major competitor. He was still smarting over his inability to buy the company a few years earlier.

Ernest and Fenderson pounded the pavement harder than ever, going on whirlwind tours of Dallas, Houston, Fort Worth, San Antonio, and Odessa. They dropped the price of Paisano to where they were barely breaking even, just to get that brand into the Texas marketplace, to give it as much name recognition as the Italian Swiss Colony label. Ernest hired a new bottler and distributor based in Houston named John Saragusa, who was searching for a new national wine brand to expand his sales. Uncharacteristically, Ernest agreed to spend money on radio, TV, and newspaper ad campaigns to let Texans know that "Gallo Is Coming."

Now Ernest had a new wine, Thunderbird, with which to overwhelm his main competitors. Concentrating on four key markets—Houston, New York, Los Angeles, and Shreveport—Ernest introduced Thunderbird to the wine-drinking world (perhaps "wino-world" is more apt) with great fanfare early in 1957. He sold 19,000 cases of Thunderbird in Los Angeles in the first month, 9,000 cases in Houston, and similar numbers in the other test markets. Ernest was especially excited that Thunderbird was a huge hit in New York City, where his ad agency had introduced the wine in the form of "Princess Thunderbird," a beautiful model in a tight-fitting Indian outfit. Ernest and Fenderson were elated; if you can make it in New York, you can make it anywhere. Thunderbird was selling itself through word of mouth. They decided to distribute it throughout the country.

A new jingle was making the rounds: "What's the word? Thunderbird. How's it sold? Good and cold. What's the jive? Bird's alive. What's the price? Thirty twice." Sixty cents for a quart of high-test lemonade. Ernest and Fenderson knew they had a blockbuster on their hands when they drove through a slum in Atlanta, Georgia, on one of their trips. Ernest saw a disheveled wino on the sidewalk and rolled down the window of the car.

"What's the word?" Ernest yelled out.

"Thunderbird," the besotted man replied without missing a beat.

Ernest howled with delight. He loved it. Fenderson, with his finer sensibilities, recoiled a bit, but he was a salesman first and foremost. He wasn't about to let moral qualms interfere with the marketing opportunity of a lifetime. He could always indulge his finer sensibilities by acquiring another work of art. But this was *business*. In 1957, the Gallo brothers sold thirty-two million gallons of Thunderbird alone, rapidly overtaking Italian Swiss Colony and closing in on Roma for bragging rights as the number one wine seller in the country.

Julio was less than thrilled with the direction taken by E. & J. Gallo Winery under Ernest's leadership. Julio didn't need to be number one. He would have been content finding a niche as the purveyor of quality table wines, rather than rising to the top selling garbage like Paisano and Thunderbird. Always the moodier of the two older brothers, the more contemplative and introverted, he often kept his reservations to himself. But as sales of Thunderbird rocketed skyward, Julio tried to discuss his own vision for the family enterprise with his older brother.

Ernest would have none of it. The choice was crystal clear, as far as he was concerned. How could Julio even *think* of deliberately reining in sales when they had the opportunity to rule the wine world? That type of reasoning didn't make any sense to Ernest. He was a born empire builder, not a peasant farmer. Had he lived 2,000 years earlier, he would have striven to become the First Man in Rome while Julio tended his grapes on a Tuscan hillside. A top Gallo executive described Ernest as part Old World tyrant and part modern business buccaneer.

"He was an intimidating man," said the executive, "all five feet six of him. He could be brutal, but he was also a genius. He had to have an IQ up around one-sixty or so. People underestimated him by regarding him as crude and rough around the edges. The truth is, he couldn't have remade the American wine industry and built an empire in the process without a grand vision and the ability to achieve it."

The rift between Ernest and Julio widened. It reached a point where they couldn't be in the same room without arguing. It was easier not to speak to each other at all than discuss their radically different views of the company's place in the wine industry. They even stopped visiting each other at home. Ernest started inviting employees and locals to his house at 1712 Maze Road (Maze Boulevard today). The house still exists about a quarter-mile from the original Mediterranean villa, on the other side of the street hidden behind a phalanx of closely planted trees. Ernest's Sunday-afternoon barbecues continued the tradition started by his father-in-law many years earlier. Guests were perplexed to find that Julio and, more often than not, even Joe and their families were absent.

Meanwhile Ernest's sons David and Joseph—who was called Joey—were causing him some distress. Joey didn't appear to be the sharpest knife in the family's silverware drawer, although he managed to find his stride later in life. David was plain weird. He had graduated from Modesto High School by 1958 and started working in the family business. A couple of years older than Joey, David was bright enough, but he had been unpopular at school. He was given to hysterical outbursts for no apparent reason. When he thought no one was looking, and sometimes when they were, he had a habit of sticking a paperclip under each eyelid and prying them up so the eyeballs glared out. His peers described him as gawky and uncoordinated.

"He couldn't carry on a conversation," they said. "He really should have been Julio's son because he was very interested in winemaking, even in high school. But Ernest wouldn't let him get involved. He wanted him to go into marketing and sales eventually."

Much of his asocial behavior was undoubtedly from the way Ernest treated him at home. Not surprisingly, Ernest was nearly as hard on his first-born son as his own father had been on him—although he never resorted to violence.

"I never saw a man emotionally brutalize his son the way Ernest did," remarked a Gallo employee.

Joey, for his part, was more stable but not considered highly intelligent by his peers. He underperformed in school no matter how hard he studied in his effort to please Ernest. He idolized his father and tried to emulate him, but he just didn't have what it took to be a dynamic businessman in his father's mold. Despite this, he favored his father over his mother and was determined to follow in his footsteps, which he did, eventually becoming the winery's chief executive officer. David, on the other hand, turned to his mother to seek refuge from Ernest and his constant criticism.

"David inherited his father's temper," said a Gallo executive who worked closely with both boys. "Joey's temperament was more like his mother's." Ernest's sons had inherited the best and worst attributes of both parents. The genetic lottery had gotten scrambled, as it often does in any family.

Julio's first-born son, Robert, was five years older than David, and he was turning out to be the son Ernest would probably rather have had. This was yet one more point of contention between Ernest and Julio. Robert was tall, athletic, handsome, popular with his classmates, and by the time Thunderbird was rolled out, he had already graduated from Oregon State, served two years in the navy, and was planning to launch a career of his own.

Robert's choice of a wife befitted a young man who was destined to make his own mark in life. He fell in love with a pretty brunette named Marie Damrell, a graduate of Notre Dame and the daughter of a local judge and Democratic Party leader. Robert married Marie on July 5, 1958. She was Catholic like the Gallos, and everyone who mattered in town showed up for the wedding. Julio's daughter Susann had also turned out well. Born in 1936, two years after Robert, she had developed into a beautiful and intelligent young woman, popular with her classmates at Modesto High School. She attended Oregon State like her older brother, and along with her education she acquired a husband there, James Coleman. He converted to Catholicism at Susann's request and married her in a Catholic church on September 1, 1957. Coleman truly found his home with the Gallo family, in more ways than one. He went to work in sales under Fenderson's tutelage and, after a rocky start with Ernest, rapidly rose through the ranks on his own merits.

Julio's younger son, Phillip, who was born in 1939, was more like David with his flightiness and sensitivity. But unlike his older cousin, Phillip was more inclined to withdraw into himself than to throw temper tantrums in public. He was considered overly sensitive and "high strung." Ernest, who turned a blind eye to David's weirdness, complained that Julio and Aileen spoiled Phillip. Phillip locked himself in his room and wept when Julio scolded him for not being tough enough. Julio took him duck hunting and tried introducing him to other "manly" sports, but the boy was simply not interested. Although the family refused to think about the possibility at the time, in retrospect it appears that Phillip may well have been gay. In a family as male-oriented and power-driven as the Gallo family, homosexuality was regarded as a weakness, an aberration, a sickness that needed to be cured.

Joe Jr. was still odd man out within the Gallo clan. He and his wife, Mary Ann, and their children lived in a house he had built on property near the Livingston winery. Joe and Mary Ann had three children at this point—their son Peter, born in 1946, son Mike, who was born on November 11, 1950, and a daughter named Linda, who was born on May 5, 1952. They were content to be a distance removed from Ernest and his overbearing manner, particularly Mary Ann. She shuddered at the idea of going to Ernest's house for dinner.

Dinner with Ernest had never been a relaxed family affair. Both of Joe's sons remembered sitting around the dining room table as Ernest bombarded each of them in turn with questions about everything that crossed his mind. Even as little boys, they were forced to listen to Uncle Ernest hold forth on the intricacies of winemaking, politics, economics, and marketing strategies. Ernest interrogated everyone at the table, but his efforts to elevate his own two sons at the expense of Joe's fell flat. There was simply no comparison. Peter and Mike were bright and perceptive and well aware of their older cousins' oddities. When Ernest caught Peter in particular making fun of David, sometimes to his face, Ernest could barely control his temper. During those moments he saw David for what he was and responded by dressing him down unmercifully in front of everyone else.

Joe still put in long hours at the winery, dreaming of one day going off on his own to indulge his major love, ranching. He was a farmer to his marrow. He loved being around animals, getting his boots dirty in the rich, dark soil of the Central Valley. He bought a small herd of cattle and began to graze them on the uncultivated parcels of land at the Livingston winery. It was Joe that Julio turned to for support when he was especially depressed about his sour relationship with Ernest.

"If you want to split up the winery and go off to make your own wine, why don't you just do it?" Joe said to Julio. "Talk to Ernest about it."

"I did," Julio said. "He just gets upset and says he doesn't want to talk about it."

Julio always had half a dozen excuses for why his plans were not practical. In truth, he did not have Ernest's entrepreneurial drive, and he was afraid that he was destined to fail if he stalked off on his own. In that regard, he admired Joe for his willingness to indulge his own passion and branch off into livestock.

The other Mike in the family, *Uncle* Mike, the black sheep whom no one talked about, was long gone but far from forgotten. Mike was getting on in years, having turned seventy in 1955. After being shut down by the BATF toward the end of Prohibition, Mike opened a restaurant and hotel in Hawthorne, Nevada, where he established a reputation as a flamboyant character who loved to regale his customers with war stories about the Prohibition era. He was still a great storyteller. He sponsored card and crap games in his back room long before Nevada became a gambling mecca for the entire country. Mike ran into trouble with the law again during World War II when his establishment burned down, and he attempted to rebuild it with material stolen from a nearby military base.

His fortunes took a permanent nosedive after that. He roamed around with his third wife, Vivian, trying to get back on his feet with restaurants in places like Illinois and Minnesota. But the old magic seemed to have disappeared, this time for good. Vivian was about thirty years younger than the aging lothario. When she attempted to run off with a younger man, Mike stabbed her with a butcher knife—she survived with minor injuries—and he was sentenced to twenty-five years in jail. Mike was fortunate in one regard; a sympathetic judge viewed Mike's "divorce Italian-style" attack on Vivian against the mitigating circumstances of her infidelity, and Mike was paroled after a couple of years.

Completely down on his luck at this stage, Mike moved to Henderson, Nevada, outside of Las Vegas, where his son Mario was working as a pit boss and bouncer in a casino. Mike had had two sons with Celia, twin boys named Mario and Edward, who were the same age as Julio. Edward died in childhood of pneumonia; Mario became a rough-and-tumble roustabout like his father. Mike found a job as a short-order cook and lived in a shabby trailer until his death in 1971, estranged from everyone in his family except Mario, who visited him on occasion. But Mario had never achieved his father's success and was unable to help him with money. As so often happens with reprobates, Mike found religion when his other options had run out. His spiritual advisor was a young parish priest at the Holy Family Catholic Church, Father Benjamin Franzinelli, who was appalled to discover that his down-at-the-heels parishioner was the uncle of Ernest and Julio Gallo.

"I couldn't believe that these two wealthy men would let their uncle live the way he did," said Padre Franzinelli, whose own parents also hailed from the Piedmont region of Italy. "That trailer was a shambles. Mike didn't talk all that much about them. I think he was bitter that they had written him off and felt they couldn't forgive him for things he had done. I felt that while he may have been a bootlegger, and he may have taken up with a few floozies, in his heyday he was a real pioneer, an early entrepreneur. Look what he did up in Hawthorne with his casino. He was one of the first people to come up with the idea of shuttling customers on buses from California."

The Gallo family was aware of Mike's dire circumstances, Franzinelli knew, since the most valuable items in his trailer were cases of Paisano, which Ernest delivered to Mike regularly via Paul Merrigan, one of his sales managers. Merrigan, who was given the impossible task of grooming David for the sales team, dropped off Mike's supply of wine on his swing through Las Vegas.

"He was living in a rusted-out house trailer," Merrigan recalled, "and Ernest wanted me to make sure he had enough wine. I would visit him about once a month, bringing him his supply of his favorite cream sherry and Paisano, and I'd sit with him while he reminisced about the good old days and his successful nephews."

"My father remembered his uncle Mike," said Joe Gallo's son, who was also named Mike. "Ernest felt that he was an embarrassment to the family, and he didn't want him around. Privately, he stayed in contact with him, but he didn't want anyone in the family to be seen associating with him." Ernest continued to send his uncle wine, but he wanted to make sure he was separated from the family. "It was clear growing up," Mike continued, "that we weren't supposed to talk about him, or even about our ancestors in Italy. Ernest made it clear that he didn't want us talking about them and about them making wine back in Italy. If Ernest didn't want to talk about something, we didn't talk about it."

Ernest never went to visit Uncle Mike personally, but supplying him with wine and throwing a fistful of dollars his way once in a while was Ernest's way of staying in control. It was Ernest's way of keeping an eye on the old bootlegger and making sure that he didn't talk *too much* to strangers about the good old days when he and Ernest's father supplied grapes and wine to the Capone mob in Chicago.

Chapter Thirteen

Ernest decided that he needed a ship—a big ship, a tanker actually. He wanted one badly since one of his archrivals, Louis Petri, had just bought one and was using it to transport his wines to the marketplace faster than Ernest and Julio could. At first, Julio agreed with Ernest. The cost of shipping wine by rail had become prohibitive, and they needed to cut costs.

"Ernest and I were worried," Julio recalled. "We would be paying higher freight charges than Petri, putting us at a real disadvantage with our top competitor."

Ernest located three ships that were being auctioned in Southern California, and he and Julio flew down to check them out. Julio changed his mind as soon as he saw them. Their holds were rusted out, and Julio had heard stories about Petri's wines becoming contaminated en route because of impurities in the storage compartment. But Ernest was insistent. If Petri had a tanker, then Ernest would have *three* tankers.

"Maybe we should buy them," he said. "If we buy them now, we can probably get all three for under a million. If we don't buy them today, we could lose them at auction tomorrow."

"I'm not ready to buy ships," Julio argued. "What are we going to do with them, for Christ's sake?"

"We could always go fishing," Ernest said.

For once, Julio got his way. Ernest's basic business sense convinced him that Julio was right. When the brothers returned to Modesto, Ernest picked up the phone and called the president of the Santa Fe Railroad. He told him he intended to transport his wines by ship unless the railroad agreed to lower its freight charges. At the time, the rates were set by the Interstate Commerce Commission and were not at the discretion of the railroads.

"The railroad agreed immediately to seek ICC approval to lower its rates," Ernest crowed. He had solved his dilemma by exerting a little muscle where it counted the most.

Julio also managed to convince Ernest that they needed their own bottling plant. It would save them money, and Julio knew that the best way to get Ernest to agree to any proposal was by convincing him it would be cost-effective. At the time, Ernest and Julio had a bottling agreement with United Can & Glass Company, which was owned by Norton Simon, the wealthy businessman, philanthropist, and art collector. Ernest was pleased with the arrangement at first, but as United Can kept raising its prices, Ernest was determined to break his contract.

"You've talked to the bank and they'll lend you money to build a glass plant?" Simon asked him.

"Yes."

"What about a warehouse?"

"What warehouse?"

"You'll need a big warehouse for storing all your bottles before you fill them up," Simon explained.

"Then we'll build a warehouse."

"If you can get financing to build a plant and a big warehouse to store your glass," said Simon, "I'll let you out of our contract."

Ernest was stunned. Had their roles been reversed, Ernest knew he would have exacted a pound of Simon's flesh and then some to free him from their long-term agreement. Simon demonstrated that it was not always necessary to knee somebody in the testicles and then head-butt him into the next county to be a successful businessman.

The next step for Ernest and Julio was to find somebody to run the bottling operation, a different kind of business that required a completely different set of skills and know-how. Ernest wanted to keep their growing network of

A young Peter Brengetto and wife. Years later, Peter and his son found the bodies of their neighbors, Joe Gallo Sr. and Susie Gallo, in 1933.
(Photo courtesy of Gene Brengetto)

Gene Brengetto and his wife, Joyce, in 2008. In 1933, Gene's father and brother discovered the bodies of Joe and Susie Gallo. (Photo by Marie Winkler Tuccille)

The Brengetto farm in Fresno, three miles from the ranch where Joe and Susie Gallo were found shot dead. ((Photo by Marie Winkler Tuccille)

The Fresno ranch where, on the morning of June 21, 1933, Joe and Susie Gallo were found shot to death. (Photo by Marie Winkler Tuccille)

The white house with the balcony is the site of the Central Hotel in Jackson, the boarding house owned briefly by Joe Gallo Sr. around the time Ernest and Julio were born. **(Photo by Marie Winkler Tuccille)**

The Gallo operations building in Modesto. The main building is hidden from public view. **(Photo by Marie Winkler Tuccille)**

Cesar Chavez, leader of the United Farm Workers, shown here in 1975. He and Ernest locked horns over unionizing the farmworkers in California's Central Valley. **(Photo courtesy of Associated Press/Walter Zebowski)**

Oscar Renteria today manages about 1,700 acres in Napa Valley. His father, Salvador, was one of the first Mexican-American grape growers in the region and sold grapes to the Gallos.

(Photo by Marie Winkler Tuccille)

Ernest Gallo, shown here in 1993 conferring with delegates at an assembly of the International Office of Vine and Wine. **(Photo courtesy of Associated Press/George Nikitin)**

Joe Jr., right, with son and business partner Mike. Joe passed away in 2007. **(Photo courtesy of Joseph Gallo Farms)**

The odd, erratic David Gallo was to be Ernest's successor. He died mysteriously in his bathtub on March 2, 1997. **(Photo courtesy of Associated Press/George Nikitin)**

The entrance to the Sonoma winery. It is approachable only through a guardhouse, and the public is not welcome. **(Photo by Marie Winkler Tuccille)**

The author outside the Gallo tasting room in Healdsburg.
(Photo by Marie Winkler Tuccille)

The entrance to the Modesto house where Ernest lived until his death in 2007. The house is hidden behind a curtain of trees. **(Photo by Marie Winkler Tuccille)**

The Mediterranean-style house built by Joe Gallo Sr. on Maze Road in Modesto. **(Photo by Marie Winkler Tuccille)**

operations within the family, and they found their man in Julio's son Robert.

"Keep your company private," Ernest repeated throughout his life. "And if somebody buys it and takes it public, buy it back and take it private again." Ernest was clearly not the type of executive who would tolerate shareholders looking over his shoulder, second-guessing his business decisions.

Ernest had little choice but to acknowledge that Robert was the most qualified person within the family to oversee the bottling enterprise. Ernest's sons, David and Joseph, had just gotten out of high school, and Ernest still wanted David to make his way in the sales and marketing side of the business—regardless of what David wanted or was qualified to do. So Robert was the logical choice. He had already told his parents that he didn't want to go into the wine business, but when his father and uncle offered him the opportunity to run the bottling enterprise, he responded with enthusiasm.

"Within a few years, Bob was our in-house glass expert," Julio said. "He eventually became president of Gallo Glass as well as part owner. Ernest and I set up the plant as a separate entity not connected to the winery. We allotted our children equal shares of ownership."

Ernest demanded that David and Joey attend Notre Dame to further their educations. Ernest had donated considerable sums to grease the way for his boys, anticipating that they might have a bit of a problem getting in on their own. David entered Notre Dame in September 1957, and Joseph followed a year later. The next generation was now in the wings, getting ready to play their roles in the ongoing family operetta staged by Ernest—the men, at least. The women in the family would not be considered for key positions in the empire for another generation. And even then, only with limited authority.

* * *

Phillip's trajectory through life had continued downward until he could no longer cope. The youngster had packed a lifetime of misery into his nineteen short years. By the time he reached his last year of high school, his classmates tormented him unmercifully for his "swishy behavior," calling him a "fairy" and "homo" whenever he passed. Julio and Aileen sent him away for hormone treatments in an effort to cure his "effeminate ways," and the would-be cure caused him to surge in weight and break out in boils, which subjected him to further ridicule.

Ernest and Julio's cousin Stella Bianco, who lived in San Francisco and was connected to the art scene there, came to Phillip's rescue. Interested in music and arts rather than business, Phillip liked to visit Stella and her husband, Wilfred "Bill" Dorais, who was a writer working for public television. Phillip seemed to blossom in the City on the Bay, but whenever he returned home to Modesto, his father and mother criticized him for not being tough enough, for not responding to his hormone treatments as they expected him to.

"Just let Phillip be," Stella said to Julio and Aileen. "Stop trying to push him into the Gallo mold."

Her advice fell on deaf ears. There was no way a family as socially conservative as the Gallos could entertain the notion that their son might be a homosexual. The word never even came up when they discussed him. He was "different," "odd," "peculiar," perhaps "effeminate," and there had to be a cure for whatever ailed him. Hard work in the winery—manual labor in general—would make a man out of anyone, the family believed, as it had out of Julio and Ernest. But the cure failed to take. Phillip withdrew further within himself when he was in Modesto. He visited Stella and Bill in San Francisco as often as possible and wouldn't show up for work at the winery until Julio hounded him to start pulling his weight there.

At six o'clock one morning, Aileen knocked on his bedroom door to wake him up for a day in the vineyard.

When there was no response, she opened the door slowly and heard Phillip moaning inside. He lay sprawled in a pool of blood on the floor, with a shotgun beside him. Neither Aileen nor Julio had heard a gun go off during the night. Phillip lived a few moments longer, moaning desperately on the floor, but he was dead when the ambulance arrived shortly afterward. He had hemorrhaged to death from the hole he had blown in his stomach. The day was October 22, 1958.

"Phillip was undergoing treatment for a mental disturbance," Julio and Aileen told the investigators. "He had improved and was working as a laboratory technician at the winery, and he appeared to be in good spirits lately."

Julio and Aileen were crushed by Phillip's suicide, as any parents would be. The loss of a child is the most devastating loss of all, and the suicide of a child is all the more horrific because of the inevitable guilt that sets in afterward. It is a loss that sears the soul.

"Our youngest child was a sensitive and intelligent boy," Julio recalled later. "After graduating from high school, he had been working in our production lab. The previous summer, Phil had been Bob's best man. We buried him at St. Stanislaus Cemetery, not far from the grandparents he never met. Phil was nineteen."

Julio's brief reminiscence reflects a grief too overwhelming to talk about. Presumably, Phillip finally found peace there beside his grandparents, who had also met a violent end, buried in the earth along Scenic Drive east of Modesto.

A few short months before Phillip took his life, his sister, Susann, gave birth to a daughter named Christine in June 1958. Christine was the first of eight grandchildren—four boys and four girls—whom Susann and Jim Coleman would present to Julio and Aileen. Susann and Jim lost no time producing a second child, Gregory, who was born the following July. Robert and Marie were also busy bringing new Gallos into the clan, another eight altogether. Julie entered the world in 1959 and was followed by seven siblings, four brothers and three sisters, again a perfect division of the sexes. It seemed that, for a while at least, balance had been restored to the family after Phillip's suicide.

After Phillip's death, it was time for the family to get back to work. After all, that was how Ernest and Julio had learned to deal with all their family tragedies. They simply forged ahead and tried to put their difficulties behind them as quickly as possible.

* * *

Ernest and Julio had joined the Wine Institute in San Francisco after Prohibition, and Ernest was elected chairman in 1957. In his first report to the membership, he outlined the progress the American wine industry had made to date. They had all come a long way since the Noble Experiment, and Ernest was in a charitable mood, singing the praises of his competitors as well as boasting about his own accomplishments.

E. & J. Gallo Winery sold twenty-four million gallons of wine in 1959, putting it at number two in sales behind United Vintners, and one year later the Gallos ascended to first place with sales of more than thirty million gallons. Gallo wines were being distributed throughout thirty-one states by this time. The brothers had made inroads into Pennsylvania, buying the Bartolomeo Pio label, and they followed up with the purchase of Melody Hill in Indiana. Over time, they replaced those brands with their own.

But Ernest and Julio had yet to penetrate the Midwest as deeply as they wanted, despite their long-standing contacts in Chicago. Italian Swiss Colony was still the major presence there, so Ernest set up a distributorship called Edgebrook, named after the street in Modesto where several of his top executives lived. First he had to circumvent a law that prohibited wineries from owning distributorships in certain markets, so he installed Al Fenderson, Howard Williams, Ken Bertsch, and Jon Shastid as joint owners. Edgebrook was moderately successful, but it was clear that if E. & J. Gallo was to make serious headway in a deal town like Chicago, it needed to do business with the real players there and establish its presence as a winery, not a distributor.

Ernest and Fenderson approached Mike Romano first, an old associate of Al Capone. They got off to a bad start when Ernest tried to bulldoze Romano into carrying the Gallo brand. Romano recalled that two men stormed into his office, "a short, dark Italian and a dapper blond man, who looked very young but was older than he appeared." During their first meeting, Ernest started dictating terms to Romano, who was furious.

"What makes you think you can come in and just take over this market?" Romano screamed. "Who the hell do you think you are? This is my company, and nobody, I mean nobody, gives me orders!"

After Romano, Ernest turned to another old mobster in town, a bulldog of a man with a gravelly voice named Joe Fusco. By Ernest's admission, "Fusco had graduated from driving bootleg beer for Al Capone to managing his own large, legitimate wholesale liquor business." Ernest and Fusco hit it off better. They enjoyed sitting with their confederates in an Italian restaurant, swapping stories about the good old days during Prohibition when Eliot Ness was chasing them around town, trying to put them out of business. Fusco agreed to distribute Gallo wines in and around Chicago, but when he suffered a heart attack soon after, Ernest decided to see if he could make peace with Romano. This time, Ernest had a more receptive audience with Mike Romano's sons, Buddy and Mike Jr.

Buddy and young Mike flew out to San Francisco, where Ernest met them with his private plane and escorted them on the puddle-jumper over to Modesto. His attempt to intimidate their father had backfired, so Ernest, who could be charming when it suited him, treated the younger Romanos like family. When the brothers got a firsthand look at the sprawling Gallo facilities, the ultramodern bottling plant and warehouse operation, they were able to convince their father that a deal with Gallo made good business sense.

"Ernest has the reputation for being ruthless, demanding, and even vicious, which he can be," Buddy reported. "But he's also generous, and if you're loyal to him, he's loyal to you."

The carrot approach worked better than the stick, in this instance. The Romanos returned home with a deal to be the de facto Gallo wine distributor in the hard-to-crack Chicago market. But Ernest ran into an unexpected problem when Joe Fusco, who had been written off as a dead man, abruptly recovered and sprang back into action. When Fusco learned that Ernest had replaced him with the Romanos—and was demanding $350,000 from him for the Gallo products stored in Fusco's warehouse—Fusco threatened to kill Ernest the next time he saw him. Ernest took the threat seriously enough to discuss business with the Romanos at the airport instead of downtown, where he was an easier target for Fusco's henchmen. Fusco accommodated Ernest by dropping dead for real after suffering another heart attack, thereby taking the contract he had put out on Ernest's life to the grave with him.

"Nothing gave Ernest greater pleasure than outliving his enemies," said one of his former executives. "One by one, they fell away like flies over the years."

Chapter Fourteen

Joey got his MBA at Stanford, another university to which Ernest had donated generously. In addition to giving money to the business school, Ernest made an annual appearance there, bragging about how he and Julio could bottle their own wines within forty-eight hours after crushing the grapes. The students were usually appalled by his comments and made fun of the crusty rube who looked more like a used car salesman than a tycoon, but their laughter always gave way to astonishment when they found out how wealthy he had become thanks to his marketing acumen. Ernest was delighted that Joey had earned an MBA, but he was disappointed when David failed to make the grade at Stanford. Bright as David was, he was a poor student, unfocused, and essentially lazy. He seemed to believe that he had a natural right to rise to the top because he was Ernest's son.

Ernest asked Al Fenderson to teach David the ropes in the sales and marketing division. Fenderson gave David the assignment of promoting the new Gallo champagne brand, Andre, a sweet and fizzy mass-produced wine fermented in tanks instead of individual bottles. Andre tasted more like soda pop than a bona fide sparkling wine, but it was more suited to the American palate of the time than expensive French champagnes. The Gallos expanded the Andre label, producing a malt beverage version called Andre Cold Duck, Andre Pink Champagne, and Andre Sparkling Burgundy. These brands were so successful that the Gallos inflicted yet another low-rent champagne on the populace, Eden Roc. Fenderson pushed these products gallantly. He was infuriated at being made to babysit Ernest's impossible son, although he had little choice but to grit his teeth and make the best of the situation.

Fenderson's job was all the more difficult because Ernest insisted that David sit in on key meetings in which major marketing decisions were made. David was a disruptive presence around the conference table, still sticking paperclips under his eyelids as he had been doing for years, tipping his chair backwards so far that he sometimes fell over, echoing his father's thoughts on advertising campaigns, and generally making a nuisance of himself. Ernest sent his other son, Joey, on the road, first to Florida and then to the Romano brothers in Chicago for initiation into the workings of the wine industry and E. & J. Gallo's presence in it. Ernest was critical of David, but he was especially rough on Joey, from whom he seemed to expect more. He quizzed him in front of other employees and constantly dressed him down if he failed to come up with the answers Ernest wanted to hear.

"You know, Ernest, perhaps Joe would be more willing to learn if you weren't so hard on him," said a Gallo executive who took the liberty of expressing himself candidly.

"You don't understand," Ernest explained. "It's the most difficult thing in the world to raise a successful son if you have money." That was Ernest's final word on the subject. It was something he firmly believed, and no one would be able to change his mind.

Following Phillip's suicide, Ernest and Julio began to draw closer to each other. Julio had decided not to branch off on his own, and now he applied himself to the family enterprise with renewed fervor. Julio and his family started to show up at Ernest's Sunday-afternoon barbecues, and it appeared to everyone that the brothers were a team again. Joe Jr. expanded his herd of cattle, named his business the Gallo Cattle Company, and continued to grow grapes at the Livingston winery. He, Mary Ann, and their family also showed up at the barbecues, completing the appearance of familial harmony.

But all was not peaceful. From the beginning, Mary Ann had resented Ernest for intruding into every aspect of Gallo family affairs, as well as her husband for acquiescing to Ernest's constant bullying. In addition, she had also grown tired of Amelia's and Aileen's nosiness and provincialism, and she was exasperated by the way they tried to take over her kitchen when she invited them for family dinners. Mary Ann wanted more out of life than the rural tranquility the valley had to offer. She wanted to travel, to get away from the ranch more, to spend time in San Francisco and soak up the city's cultural attractions. Joe, on the other hand, was essentially a farmer and a rancher with little interest in exploring the world outside the San Joaquin Valley. Feeling that she would go mad if she didn't break out of her stultifying existence, Mary Ann started going to San Francisco to take in shows with Aileen's daughter, Susann Coleman, who had similar interests.

In effect, Mary Ann had begun to act out the role of an American Madame Bovary.

"My mother was never enamored of Gallo family life," said Mike Gallo, Joe's son. "She particularly hated the way Ernest monopolized the conversation and the way everybody kowtowed to him. Mom was very independent and feisty. She had her own ideas and liked to express them, but Uncle Ernest never listened to anyone else, especially women. He wanted people to think he knew it all. Mom finally had enough. She left dad and moved back to her family in Modesto."

When Ernest heard about the split, his first reaction was to call Joe and tell him he would arrange for a good lawyer. This was not just a case of Ernest being Ernest; he was concerned that the financial fallout from any pending divorce would affect his and Julio's interests as well as Joe's. While Joe was not a partner in E. & J. Gallo Winery, the brothers did have some overlapping business interests. The old slop or tartar company had been dissolved after the war, ending that business relationship. Joe claimed that he never got more than his original investment back, but he continued to manage one of their vineyards, and he owned stock in a glass bottling plant with his brothers—an arrangement that would cause Ernest considerable grief following Joe's divorce proceedings. Ernest found a lawyer named John Whiting who had established a solid presence in the valley, and Whiting agreed to represent Joe at the divorce hearing.

"We liked each other almost immediately when I started working on his divorce," Whiting said. "I could see that he was really upset by the whole thing. I don't know if he and Mary Ann could have gotten back together, since she was seeing another man by then. I think at one point Joe wanted to try, but his pride kept getting in the way." The other man in Mary Ann's life was a Modesto internist named Sam Klor, whom she married shortly after the divorce.

Joe was not anywhere near as wealthy as his brothers, but he was still considerably well off by almost anyone else's standards. The proceedings progressed smoothly, considering the circumstances; both Mary Ann and Joe were close to their children and eager to make their split as amicable as possible. After their divorce, Linda went to live with her mother in Modesto, and Peter and Mike stayed with their father to learn his business from the ground up, so to speak.

It was around this time that Ernest was arrested for attempting to break into a liquor store—at least that's what it looked like to the arresting officers. Ernest was a nonpareil hands-on executive, involved in every aspect of his company's operations. He enjoyed going out into the field with his sales managers to get a firsthand look at how his wines were displayed in retail outlets. One evening, while Ernest and Fenderson were driving through Beaumont, Texas, some seventy miles from Houston, Ernest asked his driver to stop in front of all the liquor stores in town. A few were still open, but others had closed for the night. So Ernest pressed his face up against the windows to check out the shelves in the darkened stores. After he had done this a few times, two squad cars pulled alongside him with flashing lights. One of the officers ordered the driver, who couldn't produce a driver's license, to slide over to the passenger seat while he climbed behind the wheel.

"Look," Ernest complained, "I'm Ernest Gallo, president of the Gallo winery. We're here on business."

"And I'm John Wayne," the officer replied.

At the station house, Ernest pulled all sorts of identification out of his wallet trying to convince the cops that he was who he said he was. But they remained skeptical.

"When did you arrive here in Beaumont?" asked a police officer.

"We flew into the airport about an hour ago."

When the officer smugly informed him that there had been no flights into town that afternoon, Ernest said, "We came on my private plane."

It was not often that visiting hoodlums made such grandiose claims. The officer placed an obligatory phone call to the airport, convinced that he had a real con artist on his hands. It took only a few moments for the traffic controller to confirm Ernest's story, thereby sparing both him and Fenderson the discomfort of spending the night in the clink, courtesy of the local taxpayers.

Ernest's close encounter with the Texas law enforcement authorities came at a time when the sales of table wines were closing in on dessert wines in the U.S. marketplace. Ernest and Julio's main entries in the table wine segment were their so-called "Gourmet Trio"—Chablis Blanc, Pink Chablis, and Hearty Burgundy—which allowed them to cover the oenological color spectrum, everything except plaid. While these table wines were not of the caliber that Julio had in mind, they were at least a step in the right direction. He had to accept that his fellow countrymen were not ready for the dry whites and reds favored in Italy, France, and Spain. The American market still had a long way to go to catch up with Europe. Annual wine consumption in most of Europe, for example, approached fifty gallons per capita in 1961, while in the U.S. it was still under a gallon.

To Julio's frustration, Americans not only preferred their wine on the sweeter side but they also liked it carbonated. To satisfy that requirement, the Gallos developed Ripple, a bubbly blend of Thompson seedless grapes and fruit juices, trimmed back to an alcohol content of ten percent. Ripple hit stores in late 1959, just before Gallo launched it with an advertising blitz beginning in January 1960. It was pleasant-tasting for what it was—a substitute for Coca-Cola or iced tea on a warm afternoon, but with enough kick to produce a bit of a buzz.

"Get ripped on Ripple," comedian Redd Foxx joked on late-night television.

Sales of Ripple took off, thanks to comedians who picked up on Redd Foxx's stab at street poetry, and to an aggressive advertising campaign primarily in Los Angeles and New York, which Ernest unfortunately had to pay for. Ripple eventually replaced Thunderbird as the Gallos' most popular product, peaking out at 7.5 million gallons before sales nosedived a decade later.

* * *

Two years after his divorce, Joe visited the family's headquarters in Modesto to see one of Ernest's top executives, Jon Shastid, the executive vice president who doubled as the company's financial expert and legal adviser. Shastid was a former Modesto councilman who was considered to be "one of the sharpest men to read a financial statement I've ever known," according to the town's former mayor, Peter Johansen. He went on to become an inveterate Gallo family loyalist over his thirty-five-year career with the company.

An attractive blue-eyed blonde sat at a desk near Shastid's office. Joe traded pleasantries with her while he waited to visit with Shastid. Her name was Patricia Gardali; she was a divorced mother of a boy named Sam. Within a few days, she and Joe began to date.

"I worked as an executive secretary at the winery for Charles Crawford at the time," said Patricia. "That's when we met, in 1965. Joe and I had an instant attraction to each other. It didn't take us long to realize that we would be happy together. He accepted Sam right away too. In short, he was handsome, great company, and I was in love with him."

Joe made it clear to Patricia from the start that he was not a partner in the winery. "I just work for my brothers," he told her.

Joe and Patricia got married on February 13, 1966, but Ernest felt a need to set their wedding date. The couple had planned to be married the day before in a small ceremony at the San Francisco apartment of Joe's attorney, John Whiting. But Ernest told Joe that he needed him to make up a golf foursome on the 12th with some grape growers they did business with, so Joe postponed his marriage for a day— the 13th. Fortunately, it was not a Friday.

What happened next set the stage for the rancorous feud that erupted two decades later over control of the family business. Ernest wanted to merge the glass company with the winery now that the law permitted it. The fly in the ointment, as far as he was concerned, was that ten percent of Gallo Glass Company stock was owned by Joe and Mary Ann, who were acting as trustees for their three children. Ernest proposed that Joe and Mary Ann sell him their shares for a bit more than $8,000, an offer that was preposterously low considering the value of the facility. Joe wavered, but Mary Ann refused to accept the offer. This was one time she was not going to allow her despised former brother-in-law to get away with his trademark bullying. Mary Ann hired an independent analyst to assess the value of the shares. The fair market value he came up with was $650,000.

"The glass company stock was owned by my brother, my sister, and me," said Mike Gallo. "Ernest wanted to get us out of the company by folding it together with the winery. My father thought it was worth more than Ernest offered. It was eventually valued much higher than Ernest's figure, which outraged [Ernest]. Ernest didn't like anyone questioning his authority, and he was incensed that my father didn't give in."

Ernest found himself in a royal snit. He fumed; he exploded. Joe had always been pliable, but now his first wife was getting even for all the years of bad feelings between them. Mary Ann had backed Ernest into a corner. He had little choice but to come up with the money, payable to Joe and Mary Ann's three children over the next few years. Ernest was anxious to keep total control of his company's assets within the family. Joe's divorce changed all that, since Mary Ann was still in the picture, hovering in the background with an interest in his business. Ernest achieved what he wanted, but his victory cost him dearly, more than eighty times the amount he had offered.

With that issue behind them, the feuding was still not over. Ernest convinced Julio that it was in their best interests to cut Joe loose from his duties at the Livingston ranch. This time around, Julio was the emissary who would deliver the bad news to their kid brother.

"At the same time as his cattle operations grew," Julio recalled, "Joe was expanding his vineyard holdings to more than five thousand acres by the mid-1960s. As his holdings and outside interests increased, I began to notice that Joe spent less and less time at our vineyards. It had gotten so that he was never there when I went to inspect the vineyards. I went to see Joe. 'I can see you're very busy with your own ranching business, and that's fine. That's what you've always wanted to do. It's just that we need a full-time ranch manager down there.'"

According to Ernest and Julio, Joe agreed that a complete separation of their business activities was best for everyone concerned. Joe, however, had a different take on the incident. "I felt it just came out of the blue," he said.

Patricia said that Joe had been extremely upset by his brothers' decision to replace him with another vineyard manager. And Joe's son Mike confirmed his stepmother's interpretation of events.

"My father was very disturbed when his brothers told him he couldn't work for their winery anymore," he said. "It was his nature not to let it show, however. He always buried his feelings and went on as though nothing had really changed. But it was obvious that he was upset and confused about why they were doing this to him. My father had worked for them for many years."

Joe had little choice but to expand his cattle business, which he wanted to do anyway, while continuing to grow his own grapes for various wineries in the region. He built a new adobe-style house for his extended family on West Vineyard Road in Livingston and renamed his business Joseph Gallo Vineyards—something that would become another point of contention between him and his brothers. Joe branded his cattle with the initials JG and purchased another 1,900-acre parcel in Merced, where he grew crops as well as grapes. In short order, he bought more land in Atwater, just south of Modesto, and other property nearby.

While Joe seemed to be recovering from the body blows delivered by Ernest and Julio, a new tragedy struck the Gallo clan, this one involving Joe's son Peter. The war in Vietnam was beginning to heat up in the middle of Lyndon B. Johnson's first elected term as president. It had been an unpopular conflict from the start, and now it was growing worse by the day. It was going so poorly, in fact, that LBJ declined to run for reelection.

Along with millions of his countrymen, Peter was facing the prospect of being drafted soon after his eighteenth birthday, in January 1964. He entered the army—as his father had years earlier—in February 1966 and earned his commission as a first lieutenant. Just after Christmas 1967, Peter got assigned to a tank division in Vietnam. He served honorably, earning a bronze star and two purple hearts for injuries sustained in battle. But his life ended there, on the blood-soaked battlefield of an Asian hellhole. The family got word that he was missing in action and later learned that he had been killed by enemy fire on March 30, 1968.

"Pete was such a special kid," said John Whiting. "Joe had always dreamed of Peter and Mike working with him as a team, and now that dream was shattered. His death was just so tragic for everyone."

"It was hard for me to accept that my brother was gone," said Joe's son Mike. "He was almost five years older and I looked up to him. He was athletic and outgoing, with a great sense of humor. My father was devastated by the news. We all were."

It was up to Mike now to join his father in the cattle and ranching business. Instead of going off to a four-year college as he had planned, Mike got his associate's degree at Merced Junior College before studying oenology and viticulture at Fresno State. After class, he worked at the ranch with Joe. Unlike Mike's grandfather Joe Sr., who had promised his sons equal partnerships but never delivered on it, Joe Jr. made good on his promise to Mike. Father and son worked together as a well-knit team until Joe's death in 2007. Mike became a full partner with his father over time, something Ernest and Julio had only dreamed about a few decades earlier.

Chapter Fifteen

"Do you think you can work for somebody who has absolutely no appreciation for human values, who is a pure autocrat, who will drain you of everything you've got?"

A headhunter posed that question to Neil Sweeney, who was contemplating taking a marketing job in Modesto working directly for Ernest.

"I met Ernest in December 1968," said Sweeney. "He was dressed very formally in a conservative, three-piece pinstriped suit. My impression was of an intense, neurotic man. He exuded a basic dissatisfaction with the status quo. He seemed driven, overdriven, and conveyed a sense that nothing was ever good enough."

At this time in his life, Ernest had packed another twenty pounds onto his five-feet-six-inch frame, and he still wore large, thick, horn-rimmed eyeglasses to correct his lifelong myopia. Julio, too, who stood about three inches taller than his brother, had put on weight around the middle and still wore identical glasses. Despite their different heights, the brothers looked more alike than ever as they grew older—even losing their hairlines at the same rate.

With some misgiving, Sweeney took the job in Modesto and was immediately dispatched to Ernest's second home, as it were, in Chicago. His assignment was to spend time with the Romanos and create a training program for new Gallo salesmen. He hung his hat in the Romanos' new headquarters, with its adjoining warehouse that Buddy Romano claimed had been built with a million-dollar interest-free loan extended by Ernest. With input from the Romanos, Sweeney toiled away and came up with a manual that became "the bible" for all Gallo salesmen.

"We created the first Gallo sales manual," said Sweeney. "We put quizzes at the end of every chapter, which later became famous among recruits, who attributed them to Ernest and his desire for military-like training. This became the famous 'Big Red Book,' the manual that all Gallo trainees have to memorize."

Sweeney respected Ernest's intelligence and drive, but he also recoiled at many of his cutthroat tactics and overall ruthlessness—the very traits the headhunter had warned him about. When Sweeney discovered that his duties also included firing employees who had earned Ernest's displeasure, many of them loyal and hardworking family men, he realized that his own days at Gallo were probably numbered as well.

* * *

As the fortunes of the American wine industry improved throughout the late 1960s, those of E. & J. Gallo Winery soared. Ernest and Julio were rapidly running out of space. In 1967, they built an enormous new facility in Modesto modeled after North Carolina's state capitol building, complete with fishponds bordered by palm trees in the central atrium. Towering columns with arches graced the front of the building, but they served as bars to keep people out rather than porticos to welcome them. The name Gallo was conspicuous by its absence. Visitors to the area had no way of knowing who owned the building or what purpose it served. The structure was surrounded by forty acres of rolling hills—hills created on the formerly flat land by Ernest's landscape architects. He had them put there for additional privacy, like a Roman field commander protecting his forces against barbarian invaders, or in this case, the prying eyes of a curious public. In addition to being the headquarters for E. & J. Gallo Winery, the building was a mausoleum for all the family secrets hidden behind the façade, along with the skeletons of the family's past that Ernest forbade anyone to talk about in his presence.

Sales of Ripple continued to soar, encouraging the brothers to introduce similar products into the marketplace. If the American public craved sweet carbonated grape juice with a bit of a kick, why not produce a similar product made from apples? The Gallos had introduced such a product a few years earlier, but it had failed to gain traction. In 1968, however, a distributor in Delaware reported a sudden spurt in demand for the Gallos' cider-like beverage called Boone's Farm Apple Wine. Within a few months, E. & J. Gallo Winery was dispatching railroad cars full of Boone's Farm to such diverse regions as Delaware, Texas, and Michigan. Ernest sent Fenderson on a national tour to find out what was happening. The dapper blue blood reported back to Ernest that Boone's Farm was flying out of the liquor stores at an unprecedented rate despite the lack of any advertising push. There was no apparent reason for the phenomenon, other than word-of-mouth momentum across the length and breadth of the country. Sales of Boone's Farm Apple Wine skyrocketed from 90,000 cases in 1968 to 2,400,000 cases (about six million gallons) two years later. By 1970, it was the best-selling wine of any type in the country.

Ernest and Julio extended the line to include different flavors, such as Boone's Farm Strawberry Hill, of which 7,400,000 cases were sold in 1971. A year later, sales of the Boone's Farm spectrum hit sixteen million cases, and *Time* magazine dubbed Ernest and Julio the "kings of pop wine" in a November 1972 cover story. The magazine's researchers reported that Gallo, with its mind-boggling array of sweet bubbly beverages, accounted for ninety percent of the six million gallons of so-called pop wines sold in the United States.

"Certainly the most difficult and maddening part of the reporting," the article stated, "was the pursuit of the elusive Ernest Gallo, who guards his private and business life only slightly less zealously than Howard Hughes."

In the midst of all this success, Ernest and Julio fretted about the image they had earned on the way to becoming the most powerful winemakers in the country. Julio had long resented all the Thunderbird jokes that had made the rounds since the product's rollout, and now Ernest was concerned enough about his own reputation to do something about it. He had his brand managers conduct a survey that concluded that Gallo products, popular as they were, had a lower image in the marketplace than that of Almaden, Paul Masson, Inglenook, and Taylor—none of which were highly regarded by wine aficionados.

"We had a major problem overcoming this perception," said one of Gallo's top lieutenants. "Other wineries had begun to promote their table wines by this time. We were trying to move our own wines into better shelf positions, but the retailers resisted our efforts and didn't want to include the pop stuff with better-quality wines. Ernest was making a fortune, of course, selling this sweet pop wine with a high alcohol content, and he didn't want to admit that it was basically rotgut. In fact, he and Julio both insisted that they were making the best-quality wines in the country, which was totally absurd. Ernest seemed to believe that what we really needed to do was change people's perceptions instead of upgrading the products. In reality, he was afraid that a boost in quality would hurt his market share."

Still, even Ernest admitted that the Gallo label was causing problems for the company's image. "It seemed that even though consumers preferred our table wines in blind tastings," he claimed, "once the label and price were showing, they often preferred other brands. Pricing, advertising, packaging, and public relations all contribute to the image of a product."

Ernest's solution: instead of embarking on a campaign to upgrade the quality of his wines, he directed his production department to develop a more upscale look for the labels they slapped on the bottles.

"The new labels were more sophisticated," Ernest said. Case closed.

The Gallo clan continued to expand. David had been on the lookout for "a nice Catholic girl who wanted to raise a family," according to a family confidant, and he found her in Mary Costa, a farmer's daughter who lived in the region and was from a Portuguese background. At the same time, Joey started to date a twenty-year-old Nicaraguan named Ofelia Carrasquilla, the younger sister of a girl he had known at Stanford. Gallo employees at the time claimed that Ernest was less than thrilled by his sons' choices for wives, and only a brief note about his daughters-in-law and their children appears at the end of Ernest and Julio's joint autobiography. In any event, both sons got married within weeks of each other in 1970, and over the next few years they would present the family with a total of five new grandchildren. Mary delivered a girl named Theresa in 1972 and a boy, Christopher, in 1974. Ofelia gave birth to two boys, Ernest and Joseph, and one girl, Stefanie Amelia.

Joe's children with Mary Ann entered into serious relationships too. Linda fell in love with her brother Mike's roommate at Fresno State, Kenny Jelacich, the son of a Croatian immigrant. Mike met a local girl from Merced, Sherrie Spendlove, on a blind date arranged by one of Sherrie's friends. Kenny was studying viticulture and Sherrie was pursuing a degree in French literature. Marriage for both Linda and Mike was still a few years off, however, and brother and sister continued to see their future mates while they all completed their educations. Both couples married in 1977.

* * *

Paul Merrigan continued delivering wine once a month to the rusted old trailer where Mike lived, in the desert outside Las Vegas. On a Monday evening in 1971, Merrigan was about to pack up his usual box of supplies for Mike when the Las Vegas distributor stopped him.

"Mike was buried on Saturday," he said. "Father Franzinelli told me about it. Didn't the family know?"

Merrigan confirmed what he had just heard with Franzinelli and then called Ernest in Modesto. Two weeks later, having heard nothing from Mike's family, Franzinelli telephoned Merrigan, exasperated. "I can't believe they haven't acknowledged his death," he said to Merrigan. "Didn't you tell them?"

Well, yes, Merrigan *had* told them, but neither brother had yet acknowledged their uncle's death. Merrigan took it upon himself to deliver a few cases of wine to the church as a goodwill gesture, but the silence from Ernest and Julio continued. Once again, Merrigan called Ernest to tell him that the priest was upset because of the family's disregard for poor old Uncle Mike. Again, nothing happened for weeks. Finally, Ernest relented and sent his son David on a mission to make amends with Father Franzinelli. Merrigan arranged a meeting between the priest and David, with a couple of Gallo employees along as David's attendants, at a restaurant in Las Vegas.

"Your great-uncle was a prominent member of our parish," the priest said to David. "He always told people how proud he was of his family. So we were wondering if you didn't want to do something more for his grave site. We thought the family might want to put up a stone, some kind of memorial."

"You're talking money, aren't you?" David said, his voice shrill and edgy.

"Just a few hundred dollars, enough for a suitable headstone," replied Franzinelli.

"God damn it!" David shrieked. "He wasn't a close member of the family, and you get me down here to hold me up for cash! Who the hell do you think you are?"

Franzinelli, understandably, jolted upright in his chair, as though a lightning bolt had blasted him from the great vault of the heavens. He sat there in silence, stunned, as David flew into a tirade about how all that anybody ever wanted from the Gallo family was money. Money! Money! Money! That's what it was all about.

Merrigan, who was scarcely taller than Ernest, felt himself shrinking into his chair, wishing he could disappear. The others at the table exchanged horrified glances. The whole restaurant grew still as the diners, table by table, turned to observe the priest and this wild young man who berated him unmercifully. After a few moments, Father Franzinelli simply rose from his chair and walked out of the restaurant, bewildered, a man of God inexplicably condemned by the Almighty. David ranted for a few more minutes until, finally, Merrigan and his colleagues gathered the pieces of the disastrous dinner meeting and hustled David back to the airport, back to his father's private airplane on which he continued to froth at the mouth on the long bizarre flight back to the Central Valley, back to Modesto, back to the barricaded headquarters of the most successful wine company in the United States and eventually the world.

Poor old Uncle Mike lay in his grave, presumably in peace, there in the Nevada desert, with a simple grave marker to memorialize his days on earth. This renegade son of the Italian soil, who had come from nothing and risen so high before he plummeted to earth again, left little more than a trailer filled with cheap wine, courtesy of his nephews, to measure his accomplishments through eight and a half adventurous decades of life in America. He also left behind his only surviving son, Mario, who was destined to become nothing more than a footnote in the sweep of Gallo family history.

Book Four

DELIVER US
FROM EVIL

Chapter Sixteen

Route 99 slices an arrow-straight slash north and south through the Central Valley across some of the flattest agricultural land the U.S. has to offer. Tractor trailers chug like behemoths up and down, up and down the highway, twenty-four hours a day, delivering grain, fruit, and heavy cargo. The vineyards, ranches, and dairies are surrounded by chain-store America—a vast sprawl of Wal-Marts, Subways, McDonald'ses, and middle-class retail outlets carpeting the land for as far as the eye can see. The ranch where Joe and Susie Gallo were found dead in 1933 is a prosperous sea of raisin grapes many times its original size, spread out there along Whitesbridge Road a few miles west of town.

Modesto is a company town owned lock, stock, and barrel by the Gallo family, who supplies half the jobs in the region, funds the city's art center, curries favor with the area's movers and shakers, and extracts favorable coverage from the local media. On the surface, Modesto is unremarkable; a tidy reflection of Middle America in California's San Joaquin Valley, a friendly place to live and do business as long as you don't challenge the local power structure. Yet, in all its blandness, the town was destined to become the focal point of a celebrated labor dispute as life got under way in the 1970s.

In the beginning, peace reigned in the valley. "When Cesar Chavez tried in 1967 to organize our farm workers—already the best-paid in the state—he found nothing standing in his way but the Teamsters, who also wanted to represent our laborers," Julio wrote. "The dispute between the two unions over our farm workers was soon settled. State officials oversaw an election in 1967, and our farm workers elected Chavez's union, organized under the AFL-CIO as the United Farm Workers of America, as their bargaining agent. We signed a three-year contract with the UFW—one of the first growers to sign with Chavez's new union."

Chavez was a charismatic Mexican-American labor organizer who was born in Yuma, Arizona, on March 31, 1927. He began his career with a Latino civil rights group, the Community Service Organization, urging Latinos to get out and vote for candidates who vowed to support the rights of laborers. In 1962, he and a colleague named Dolores Huerta founded the National Farm Workers Association, which later became the United Farm Workers or UFW after it was merged with an AFL-CIO affiliate. Chavez and Huerta began to organize Latino grape pickers throughout California. In the fall of 1965, their organization launched a strike to agitate for higher wages, then staged a 250-mile march from Delano, where they had protested against the growers in the region, to the state capital in Sacramento a few months later.

Delano was a dusty, nondescript valley town with only twelve thousand inhabitants. The strike was originally called by the Filipino-American members of an AFL-CIO affiliate, the Agricultural Workers Organizing Committee. They were quickly joined by the Mexican-American contingent led by Chavez and Huerta. The strike spread rapidly to other vineyards throughout the state, and the Gallos were among the first vintners to come to terms with Chavez and the UFW. Ernest claimed that his farmworkers were the highest paid in the state, but he would later have strong reservations when Chavez insisted on a union hiring hall. Ernest wanted to maintain control over his hiring policies. For the moment, however, Ernest backed legislation giving farmworkers the right to bargain collectively with employers. For Ernest, it was a business decision, something that would buy him goodwill, considering the shifting social and moral climate of the country.

"Ernest admired Chavez at first," said Neil Sweeney. "Ernest saw Chavez as much like himself, driven, disciplined, inspiring loyalty and hard work. So in 1967, when he announced that the winery would allow its vineyard workers to vote for unionization, he let other growers know that he was supporting Chavez."

Ernest and Julio renewed their contract with Chavez for another three years. But relations between the wineries and the farmworkers soured when Chavez ratcheted up his protests. The strike had little overall impact until strikers launched a grape boycott three years later, which achieved global fame as "La Causa." La Causa grew into a broader social coalition, joined by other unions, churches, civil rights organizations, and mostly Democratic politicians, including Bobby Kennedy. The spectacle of farmworkers climbing into beat-up old buses and traveling to major cities across the country to agitate for better living conditions mesmerized the entire nation. The workers picketed thousands of markets and exhorted shoppers not to buy grapes until farmworkers received union contracts guaranteeing them a living wage. They convinced schools and other institutions to remove grapes from their menus and got longshoremen to refuse to load grapes destined for foreign markets.

John Giumarra Jr., a lawyer who represented the grape growers in announcing their agreement to sign union contracts, conceded that boycott pressures were threatening to "destroy a number of farmers." Giumarra's family owned and operated some of the state's most important vineyards, but he realized that the world was watching closely to see if social justice would prevail.

"If this works here," he said, "it will work well throughout the rest of the world."

Chavez himself was optimistic. "Today is really, truly, the beginning of a new day," he said. "We give hope to millions and millions of farmworkers, and we will not disappoint them."

But his initial victory was short-lived. Grape growers refused to renew their contracts with the UFW when they expired three years later. Giumarra believed the union had gone too far, and he urged the wineries not to "buy into the union's promises anymore."

Ernest, too, thought Chavez and his minions had gone too far. "I'll lose the ranch before I knuckle under to that son of a bitch!" Ernest yelled, banging the table in his Modesto office. He decided at that point to dig in his heels and fight Chavez. Their honeymoon was over. It was time to revert to form. No more Mr. Nice Guy from that moment onward.

When Ernest's contract with the UFW expired in 1973, he decided to sever his relationship with Chavez and sign up with the rival Teamsters Union under the leadership of Frank Fitzsimmons, whom Ernest considered easier to do business with. The major sticking point with the UFW, aside from Chavez's general grape boycott, was his insistence on a union hiring hall, which essentially stripped the wineries of their right to hire their own workers. Fitzsimmons was more pliant on that issue, so Ernest and Julio signed with him on July 10, 1973. At that point, the dispute between Chavez and Ernest got personal, and Chavez urged a boycott of Gallo products across the country. What ensued was a battle royal that devolved in no time flat into a three-ring media circus.

Chavez claimed that Ernest had evicted vineyard workers from their homes and replaced them with scab laborers, who were instructed to vote for the Teamsters. Ernest denied it, and he refuted UFW charges point by point: he didn't pay substandard wages—quite the contrary, he maintained that he had always paid his workers more than the market rate for their stoop labor in the fields; he didn't expose his grape pickers to pesticides; he didn't exploit child labor; he did provide toilets and potable water in his vineyards.

The excesses abounded on both sides. To prove his point about child labor, Chavez had one of his lieutenants produce photos of a child bent at his task under a blistering summer sun. The child, however, was stooped over in an onion patch—someone else's onion patch, since the Gallos didn't grow onions. For his part, Ernest encouraged the Teamsters to hire goons to attack Chavez's workers on their picket lines, thereby treating the public to an unfortunate display of laborers for two different unions pummeling one another with clubs and fists.

Chavez's boycott began to bite. He warned the public not to be fooled by the absence of the Gallo name from products like Boone's Farm, Andre, Ripple, Thunderbird, and other popular beverages; if the label said "produced and bottled in Modesto, California," that was code language for Gallo and, therefore, the products should be shunned by consumers. Sales of Gallo products plunged, and Ernest was terrified that the E. & J. Gallo Winery might lose its top position to one of his major rivals, Almaden, another purveyor of mass-produced wines in gallon jugs. Ernest felt a need to abandon his CIA-like obsession with privacy and go on a public relations offensive. The only problem: he chose himself to be the spokesman for his own cause. His appearance on *60 Minutes* in 1974 was a PR disaster. Sitting under the glare of Mike Wallace and confronted with the newsman's pit-bull reporting style, Ernest looked like a "complete villain," admitted Paul Merrigan.

"He came across as the heartless owner of a big, impersonal, uncaring corporation that was eager to enslave the poor Mexican-American migrant workers," said Merrigan. "Gallo became to the farmworkers' struggle what Dow Chemical was to the antiwar movement."

Students at the University of California, Berkeley, who revered Fidel Castro as the model of revolutionary moderation, staged a mock trial that found Teamster president Frank Fitzsimmons and Ernest and Julio Gallo guilty of "crimes against the people."

Then Chavez did the unthinkable, in Ernest's mind: On March 1, 1975, Chavez had the audacity to invade the

Gallos' home turf in Modesto, the seat of the Gallo fiefdom. Chavez converged on Gallo headquarters with 10,000 supporters, some of whom had begun their march all the way from Union Square in San Francisco. Chavez delivered an oration designed to fire up his forces and the public at large. For his talk, Chavez picked his spot carefully. He made the impassioned speech in Graceada Park, a graceful stretch of greenery a few blocks from Modesto Junior College, to make sure the town's youth would turn out in force. The park was Modesto's oldest, developed in 1907 by John McClaren, the man who had designed Golden Gate Park in San Francisco. Chavez thundered before an overflow crowd, accusing the Gallo dynasty of everything short of murder and mayhem.

Ernest felt as though he had been personally violated, as though he had returned home after a tough day laboring in the winery only to find his underwear strewn across his living room floor. This was *his* territory, and now the barbarians had breached the barricades. Ernest held a press conference, his first ever, at the Chuck Wagon restaurant a few blocks from the park, where he faced a phalanx of out-of-town reporters looking for blood—Ernest's. He was naïve enough to assume that the press would give him a fair hearing if only they heard his side of the story. But the reporters had a field day with the Gallo patriarch. They asked him loaded questions for the most part: Did he *still* exploit child labor? Did he *still* pay substandard wages? Did he *still* expose poor grape pickers to pesticides? Not *had he ever* committed crimes against "the people," or *were the allegations true* in the first place? The assumption was that Gallo was guilty as charged, and the only issue remaining was whether Gallo's evil practices continued.

"We believe we have turned the other cheek for too long," Ernest said to no avail. "This has subjected us to vilification and character assassination." He might as well have been howling into the wind.

Ernest admitted afterward that his media battle with Chavez taught him a valuable lesson. "He was a master propagandist," Ernest said, "with great skills in shaping public opinion. Truth was not the issue. In this respect, it probably wouldn't have mattered what we did to defend ourselves. What mattered was public perception. Chavez understood this more clearly than I did at the time." Quite clearly, it was not in Ernest's nature to come across as a sympathetic figure. The tough old rooster was incapable of it.

In the end, both sides simply got tired of fighting each other. Chavez had won the public relations battle; he had also won a legal victory when the California Agricultural Relations Board ruled that E. & J. Gallo had "illegally supported the Teamsters Union" and "harassed UFW organizers." But both Fitzsimmons and Chavez determined that ongoing warfare was not in the best interests of either union, and they agreed to drop their disputes and let workers decide for themselves which union they wanted to represent them. The media began to lose interest, and the forest of microphones and TV cameras grew thinner as the public became bored with the show.

It was time to change the program. While the public craved a steady diet of bread and circuses the way a junky needs a fix, its attention span was short. The great American multitudes demanded that the old, battle-scarred gladiators be replaced by new ones. When the spotlight of public attention moved elsewhere, Chavez ended his boycott and turned his attention to other battles. His efforts had resulted in the enactment of the California Labor Relations Act, which protected the rights of unions to organize farm laborers. Ernest and Julio, for their part, went back to doing what they did best, making and selling wine.

Chapter Seventeen

By the early and mid-1970s, the Gallos were buying about fifty percent of the bulk wine grapes grown in Napa Valley to blend into their concoctions of Hearty Burgundy and Chablis Blanc. But varietal wines had finally begun to catch on in the United States, and Julio believed that Sonoma Valley north of San Francisco produced some of the best strains grown anywhere. Sonoma Valley had the right climate and soil base—gravel, limestone, and soft shale—for the production of better-quality varietals. Julio liked Sonoma's warm days and cool nights, its closer proximity to the coast than Napa, and its abundance of rivers and streams, all of which were necessary for the ideal combination of acidity and sugar characteristic of premier wines. He and Ernest had been buying grapes and wine from several growers, including the Frei Brothers Winery in the Dry Creek Valley region of Sonoma, but the bulk of their purchases until this time had been in Napa Valley.

The Gallos and the Freis went back a long way together. A furniture store owner named Andrew Frei had bought his small winery in 1895, and his sons Walter and Louie started to sell virtually their entire output of grapes to Ernest and Julio beginning in 1948. Louie's son Andy was running the family operation in 1971 when he sold the Gallo brothers a half-interest in his winery after he and his brother had a falling-out. Six years later, in 1977, Ernest and Julio bought the rest of Frei Brothers from Andy, completing their first major acquisition in Sonoma County. Julio finally achieved a major goal in his life. After four decades of selling substandard products to satisfy the unsophisticated tastes of his countrymen—a business decision that earned E. & J. Gallo a fortune—Julio believed the time was right to make the kinds of wine he had dreamed about all his life. And this time around, he and Ernest were in accord.

"Sales of beverage wines peaked in 1972," said Ernest. "We needed a variety of new products on the market when consumers were ready to move up. Whether we would be able to keep them as wine consumers depended upon making certain that the right products were on the market at the right time."

Before they got going with their upgrade into varietals, however, the Gallo brothers had some housekeeping problems to deal with. The one that concerned them most was the unwanted attention focused on the company by the Federal Trade Commission. "The FTC had become interested in the wine industry in 1969," Ernest explained, "when Heublein, a giant in the distilled spirits business, acquired United Vintners, the nation's second-largest winery. Franzia had been purchased by the Coca-Cola Bottling Company of New York in 1971. Coke–New York also purchased the popular Mogen David label. This operation, called the Wine Group, became the fifth-largest wine marketer in the United States."

Ernest's comments were a bit disingenuous to say the least. It was true that the FTC was interested in the sometimes incestuous relationships between wine producers and distributors, many of them involving sweetheart deals favoring one brand at the expense of others. But the federal regulatory agency had singled out the Gallos' marketing practices as particularly onerous. Among the charges against E. & J. Gallo Winery was that it canceled contracts with various distributors if they failed to hire more Gallo-trained salesmen.

The FTC delivered its laundry list of legalistic broadsides in language that only a government bureaucracy and its legal staff are capable of spewing: "Gallo has used its dominant position, size, and power to lessen, hinder, or restrain competition in the sale and distribution of wines in the United States by engaging in various unfair acts, practices, and methods of competition, including, but not limited to, the establishment and maintenance of exclusionary marketing policies and their enforcement through coercion of distributors."

The Gallos signed a consent order in 1976 regulating E. & J. Gallo Winery's relationships with distributors for the next ten years (an agreement that Ernest regretted and later got revoked with the help of some close political friends in California and Washington, D.C.). Among other provisions in the agreement, the Gallos could not prevent distributors from taking on competitors' wines, could not require them to handle less popular Gallo products if they wanted to handle the more popular Gallo wines, and could not extend loans to distributors or subsidize their capital expenditures. In 1981, Ernest and Julio's political allies convinced the FTC that the order was unfair. The FTC fell in line, stating that "the broad scope of the order's prohibitions appears to hinder unnecessarily Gallo's ability to utilize many of the marketing devices that are freely employed by its competitors."

"Ernest understood the art of making political contributions," said one family member. "He understood that it was better not to give money to politicians all at once. You waited until they really needed it for something, and then you doled it out little by little. I remember one time when he screamed at Pete Wilson before he became governor of California. He was still a senator at the time. I never heard anyone yell at a powerful politician like that. After that, Wilson voted the way Ernest wanted him to vote, and then Ernest made a sizable contribution to his campaign."

Ernest and Julio also dealt with growing dissention in the ranks of their top executives. When one of them, wondering about his future at the company, asked Ernest what kind of succession plan the brothers had in place, Ernest was visibly startled.

"You don't understand. You're a very capable guy," Ernest replied. "But forget about taking over. You have the wrong last name."

Ernest made no secret of the value he placed on nepotism. Gallo was a family company, plain and simple. He respected the talents of his chief lieutenants, but if their last names weren't Gallo, they were just hired help. Despite the shortcomings of his sons, which he was hardly reticent about enumerating in excruciating detail in the presence of other employees, Ernest was determined to see David and Joey acquire the skills necessary to lead the business. As Ernest promoted them to positions of greater responsibility, the tension between David and Joey on the one hand and Ernest's chief lieutenants on the other reached its breaking point. Joey, the more capable and stable of the two sons, surrounded himself with a network of loyalists, men closer to his own age who created a barrier between the Gallos and Ernest's long-standing executive staff. The writing was on the wall. A New Guard was forming, and the Old Guard was being pushed out. One by one, Ernest's handpicked apparatchiks tendered their resignations.

"Joey and his circle perceived us as threats to them," said Paul Merrigan. "It became more and more difficult to get our jobs done. At that point, I was burnt out, what with Chavez, the FTC, and the challenges of expanding the winery. Things had become too hectic and chaotic," he said.

While those leaving the ranks received generous severance packages for their years of service, they were also advised that it would be in their interest if they found new jobs outside the wine industry. They knew too much. Most of them knew the details of the company as well as Ernest and Julio did. Their knowledge could benefit Gallo competitors if put to use. They knew about the skeletons in the family closet; they knew where the bodies were buried—almost literally. Most heeded the advice and went on to other fields.

If there was one lesson Ernest and Julio had taken away from their encounter with Chavez, it was the value of good publicity. Ernest's inclination was to use a stick rather than a carrot to get what he wanted. Chavez had taught him that a stick doesn't always work best; public perception can be a far more effective tool than intimidation in advancing one's cause.

Beginning in 1976, the Gallos embarked on a mission to establish a reputation as good corporate citizens. Julio bought a Victorian mansion in Modesto and donated it to the city to be used as a museum. Ernest followed a year later with a $400,000 gift for the construction of a medical research center at Modesto Hospital. The brothers stepped up their pace of charitable giving with substantial donations to the viticulture and oenological programs at Fresno State, where they also built a football stadium. Other charitable donations flew out from the Gallo treasury in short order to various universities, including Stanford's medical and business schools and Notre Dame. Years later, they would build the Gallo Center for the Arts in Modesto, a structure modeled after the Colosseum in Rome, complete with graceful arches and towering columns—but no lions or gladiators on the premises—for staging plays, musicals, and concerts. The center sits like a jewel in the midst of the Central Valley's sprawl of vineyards and shopping malls.

At the same time, Ernest and Julio did not abandon the power of the stick—the political stick, as it were. Ernest worked the Democratic side of the fence, while Julio courted Republicans—but the "juice" they gave politicians of any stripe came out of the same vineyards. Alan Cranston, a Democratic senator from California, was a particular favorite of Ernest's. The elder Gallo brother had helped Cranston get elected to the U.S. Senate in 1968, contributed to his campaign coffers over the years, and ten years after Cranston was first elected, he returned the favor with a controversial piece of legislation that gave special tax treatment to the Gallo family.

A Washington law firm with Democratic Party connections designed a bill allowing the Gallo family to spread inheritance tax payments over fifteen years instead of having to pay the tax bill in the year it came due. On June 17, 1978, Cranston helped push this new tax rule through the Senate on a rare Saturday session, just as Congress was about to adjourn for its summer recess. When crusty Republican senator Bob Dole heard what had happened, he famously labeled the bill "the Gallo Wine Amendment."

An interesting footnote to this episode took place years later, in 1986, when the Democrats were in the process of putting the nation's godforsaken tax code through one of its many reincarnations. The Gallos decided that an amendment on the table could lower their inheritance taxes even further, so this time they bought the support of none other than Senator Bob Dole of Kansas, who supported the Gallos and dropped any allusions to "Gallo Wine Amendments." Dole became one of the Gallo family's favorite Republican politicians; his political action committee initially received four separate $5,000 checks, one from Ernest and one each from Ernest's wife, Amelia; Julio; and Julio's wife, Aileen. Over the years, the Gallos became Dole's primary financial supporters.

"It's kind of interesting to pull together the numbers and see who's given Bob Dole the most money over the years," said Robert Krulwich, a PBS journalist. "Number one, at the very top, are the Gallos. Now why would Ernest and Julio, who have a vineyard in California, give $381,000 to a senator who lives next to cornfields in Kansas? What's the connection here? Well, the Gallos treat their politicians kind of like grapes. They plant their seeds early, and then they wait. And they are very patient. They planted money all over the political landscape to help pave their way—Alan Cranston, Leon Panetta, Jerry Brown, Pete Wilson. When a family like the Gallos tries to ask for a favor, how do they do it?"

"They never approached me, so I don't know what their style is," said Bill Bradley, former Democratic senator from New Jersey and unsuccessful presidential candidate, who was being interviewed by Krulwich in 1996. "I don't know what their strategy is. Most people who want to affect legislation work through high-priced Washington lobbyists who insulate them from direct involvement."

The Gallos' largesse was broad and bipartisan. It spread to the presidential arena when they formed a cozy relationship with the former Arkansas governor, President Bill Clinton, to resolve a dispute about the importation of foreign wines onto the hallowed shores of the United States.

* * *

Julio's dream of launching a new line of higher-quality varietal wines failed to come to fruition according to plan. Once again, the main problem was Gallo's reputation as a mass producer of "inexpensive, lower-quality wines," according to industry experts. Ernest admitted as much when he recalled, "Our varietal line simply did not meet with the kind of acceptance I had hoped for." But abandoning the project was not an option the brothers wanted to consider. "Julio and I didn't even consider the possibility of failure," Ernest said. "He would go back to work on the products, and I would keep working on the marketing. Whatever changes we ended up making, the name on the label had to be Gallo."

Well, not really. Their eventual success in the quality varietal market was achieved by bottling wines with other labels, such as Frei Brothers and Louis Martini, where the Gallo name is nowhere in sight.

In a last-ditch attempt to launch a quality line of varietals under the Gallo label, Ernest and Julio put together an advertising campaign featuring the well-known actor Peter Ustinov in a series of television commercials. "Ustinov was a wine lover himself," Ernest said, "and he had raised wine grapes in Switzerland."

Ustinov captured the European bonhomie and courtliness better than anyone else. An elegant man with Russian, German, French, and Italian blood in his veins, he spoke six languages fluently and was proficient in two others. In the commercials, Ustinov appeared in a dimly lit study dressed in a well-tailored blue suit and polka-dot tie, with the portrait of a bottle of Gallo wine on an easel and a glass of wine raised aloft in his right hand. Ustinov was portly and gray at this stage of his life. In the finest British accent he could muster—he was a master of many dialects, having worked with British intelligence during World War II—he stared into the camera and intoned:

"Let me invite you to enjoy Chenin Blanc from Ernest and Julio Gallo. It may be one of the finest wines you've ever tasted."

It was the closest brush with elegance the Gallo label would ever experience. But, alas, Ustinov's velvet tones fell on deaf ears. The wine in particular, and the Gallos' attempt to upscale their image, flopped.

For the moment at least, Ernest and Julio had little option except to keep pushing the products that worked best for them.

Chapter Eighteen

The name Rossi had been a household name in wine going back to Prohibition. It had a ring to it that resonated with old-time wine drinkers, particularly those who remembered the days when some of the best wines available were made in damp cellars by Italian immigrants. Charlie Rossi, who was an old sidekick of Ernest in the wine trade but unrelated to the Rossis of Italian Swiss Colony fame, had married a cousin of Ernest's wife. Charlie had been working for the Gallo family since 1953. He was a loyalist who did double duty as one of David's chaperones and overseers, helping to mop up the mess Ernest's son often left in his wake. After Charlie's more than two decades of dedicated service to the Gallo clan, Ernest decided to make him a star.

The Gallo brothers had been marketing a low-rent table wine called Red Mountain, named after the first winery established in Stanislaus County. Until this time, they had distributed Red Mountain only in California, but in the mid-1970s the Gallos decided to launch it nationally. They needed a hook, something as memorable as the name Thunderbird to catch the public's attention, perhaps a personality to serve as a spokesman for the brand. Ernest had a brainstorm. His wife's cousin's husband had been working for him in various capacities lo these many years, and his laconic, down-to-earth personality struck Ernest as just right for the kind of spokesman he wanted. His first name, Charlie, however, didn't have any panache. He needed a name with an Old World flavor. Charlie. Carlo. Why not rechristen Charlie with a new name? From now on, his name was Carlo. Carlo Rossi.

Any confusion with the Martini & Rossi label wouldn't hurt either. Ernest told Charlie—Carlo—that he wanted to put him on radio and television.

"I'm not an actor," Charlie/Carlo said. "I can't go on radio or television."

Ernest had more faith in Carlo than Charlie had in himself. Ernest hired a media coach, someone to teach Carlo how to smile and say a few words about this wonderful red wine that he had presumably stomped out in his basement. Then Ernest had Carlo record a thirty-second commercial at a local radio station, which Ernest ran during a San Francisco Giants baseball game at Candlestick Park. During the break in the fifth inning, all ears were glued to the radio as Charlie's voice burbled over the airwaves, introducing himself as little old Italian winemaker Carlo Rossi. The next step was to put the act on national television. They gave Charlie a script, and he muffed it, coming across as stiff and amateurish. Ernest, however, refused to accept failure. He knew he had a hit if only Charlie would just relax and be himself. Let Charlie be Charlie—or Carlo be Carlo. So Ernest hired another media professional, Hal Tulchin, a well-known director and television producer, to coach Charlie on how to come across on the boob tube. "Relax, be yourself," Tulchin advised. Charlie read his script, but he couldn't nail it. Finally, embarrassed and exasperated, Charlie just stared at the wine and said spontaneously, "I'd really rather drink it than talk about it."

"The next day on the set," Ernest said, "Tulchin put Rossi in a back-porch scene, handed him a glass of wine, and rolled the cameras. The result was advertising history."

"Hi, I'm Carlo Rossi," Charlie said. "You know, to make really good-tasting wines, you need to know exactly the right time to pick the grapes, and that's when experience makes the difference. We get the grapes to the winery when they're at their peak. That's why folks like our Carlo Rossi wines, like our Burgundy. It's soft and mellow. I'm sure you'll taste the difference experience makes. I like talking about Carlo Rossi Burgundy, but I'd rather drink it."

Carlo Rossi quickly became a household name, and Charlie Rossi a celebrity. Old and young, male and female, Carlo Rossi enthusiasts approached him at shopping center openings and asked him for his autograph. Ernest featured him in parades throughout the Central Valley, where Charlie sat up on a float in his overalls, waving at the crowds, and sipping from a glass of the red wine he had helped craft for two and a half decades as a jack-of-all-trades in Ernest and Julio's winery.

* * *

The late 1970s marked the beginning of the intensely litigious phase of Ernest's and Julio's careers. Ernest, in particular, had begun to take a proprietary interest in the name Gallo everywhere it appeared in public. It jumped out at him one morning in 1979 when he opened the business pages of the *San Francisco Chronicle* and read a story about Consolidated Foods, which had recently acquired an outfit named the Gallo Salame Company. Consolidated Foods was the parent of Sara Lee and a behemoth in the food industry. Ernest and Julio knew of Gallo Salame's existence; Ernest had spotted a tube of the company's salami in a San Francisco delicatessen. But the company was local then, a small enterprise that had been around since 1941, based in the city's North Beach neighborhood with limited distribution outside the area. It was a different matter entirely now—Consolidated Foods had bought this local family business with the obvious intention of distributing it nationally.

"What would this giant conglomerate want with a small San Francisco salami manufacturer if they didn't intend to capitalize on the Gallo name?" Ernest wondered.

Ernest picked up the phone and called Nathan Cummings, Consolidated's chairman, who assured him that his company had no intention of exploiting the Gallo brand.

Ernest had met Cummings during a trip to Greece, and the two men had established a cordial relationship. Cummings was one of those Renaissance businessmen, equal parts profit maven and philanthropist who had made substantial contributions to hospitals, universities, and the arts. He was an art collector who had established an endowment that created the Nathan Cummings Arts Center at Stanford University and the Joanne and Nathan Cummings Art Center at Connecticut College in New London. He contributed significantly to the National Gallery of Art in Washington, D.C., to the Metropolitan Museum of Art in New York City, and to the Art Institute of Chicago. Ernest admired men with that kind of complexity, and he attempted to emulate them in his own ham-handed way.

At one point, Cummings had casually asked Ernest if he would ever consider selling his company, a suggestion that Ernest shot down immediately. Cummings's interest in the wine business created a blip on Ernest's radar screen. Food and wine went together like a hand in a glove. Ernest's guard was already on high alert when he stumbled upon the article about Consolidated's Gallo Salame acquisition. He was skeptical of Cummings's assurance there was no interest in exploiting the Gallo name, and he believed that Cummings was out to raid his business one way or another. Ernest insisted that Consolidated take the Gallo name off the product.

"Consolidated refused," Ernest said, "and started to expand the line and its distribution."

He set his attorneys in motion and filed a lawsuit against the food conglomerate. Neither side wanted a protracted legal battle, which was bound to cost each company tens of millions of dollars in legal fees and lead to unwanted publicity. So, during a period of intense negotiation, Ernest and Consolidated crafted an out-of-court deal that gave E. & J. Gallo Winery the trademark rights to the Gallo Salame brand in return for Consolidated's exclusive right to market and distribute food products using the Gallo name for four years; after that time, Consolidated agreed that it would not distribute Gallo Salame beyond eleven western states. It was a milestone victory for Ernest, establishing a precedent that gave the Gallos quality control over products other than wine that bore their surname, according to the terms of Ernest's agreement with Consolidated.

With that issue resolved, Julio went to work digging up the ground a few hundred yards southeast of their Modesto plant to create an underground storage facility. The cavern ran the length of two football fields, reinforced with concrete walls a foot thick and ceilings twenty feet high. Julio packed six feet of soil on top of the cave and planted a two-and-a-half-acre field of grass and trees above it, so that the entire structure was hidden. Visitors could stroll across its entire expanse without having the faintest idea what was in the ground beneath their feet.

The underground temperature remained a constant sixty-five degrees, within a range of two or three degrees regardless of the season—an ideal environment for wine storage. Over time, it would cost less than constructing an aboveground storage building with heating and air conditioning to maintain the right temperature range, particularly during the energy crunch of the mid- and late 1970s. Wines that were aged in oak came into vogue at this time, and the brothers decided to import forests of French and Yugoslavian oak to build casks.

"We had enough European wood for six hundred and fifty big, upright casks shipped by train to Italy to be constructed there," Julio said. "At the time, the wine trade called it the largest purchase of imported oak cooperage ever recorded in U.S. wine industry history."

It took two years to complete the project, and when it was finished, it could store more than two million gallons of wine, initially oak-aged red varietals including Zinfandel and Cabernet Sauvignon. The wines were filtered into tanks in a sterile environment to prevent contamination by bacteria. The casks were filled to the top to keep air from seeping in, and then the wines were aged from one to three years in the oak, plus another six months in bottles before they were shipped to retailers. Julio was now making the kind of quality wine he had dreamed of from the time he and Ernest had started their business.

If only they could find a way to sell it with the Gallo name on the label.

A new competitor surfaced from an unlikely quarter. This time it was not one of the venerable wine companies that emerged to challenge the Gallo brothers' position in the U.S. wine hierarchy, but a giant with global dominance in the soft drink industry.

"In the mid-seventies," Ernest lamented, "Coca-Cola bought the Taylor Wine Company of New York, followed by Sterling Vineyards and Monterey Vineyard. Coca-Cola grouped these wineries together in what they called the Wine Spectrum, which immediately became the fourth-largest U.S. wine company."

The brothers knew they were in for a battle when a spokesman for the Wine Spectrum stated plainly, "We don't want to be second to anyone in this market." The Gallos went into combat mode, determined to win the coming conflict. Coke aired a television commercial, the first of its kind, showing so-called tasting groups sipping Taylor California Cellars wines—the Coke-owned label—alongside wines made by Almaden, Paul Masson, and Inglenook, and claiming to prefer Taylor. The commercial did not include Gallo in the staged taste test, but Ernest knew that the battle lines were drawn. Coca-Cola had spent hundreds of millions of dollars informing the public that "Coke tastes better than Pepsi." Now it was telling everyone that Taylor wines taste better than Almaden, Paul Masson, and Inglenook. It was just a matter of time before Coke got around to telling people that Taylor tastes better than Gallo.

Ernest's hackles were up. Coke had taken him on, and now he was spoiling for a fight. Julio was equally determined to keep Coke out of their vineyard. "This business is a lot different than putting syrup and water together," he maintained. Julio understood that making wine was an agricultural business, not chemistry, and he was first and foremost a farmer. "You can't sit in some office in Atlanta," he said, "and set up a program for buying grapes and crushing on a certain date. You have to be ready to make an instantaneous switch, if need be. We're dealing with Mother Nature here. Every growing district is different from the standpoint of quality. This takes experience to deal with. You've got to put your boots on and go out and take a look."

Coca-Cola lasted about six years in the wine business before it threw in the towel and sold the Wine Spectrum to Seagram in 1983. It did so at a time when U.S. wine consumption was accelerating at a pace not seen before. In 1934, Americans drank thirty-three million gallons of wine, but by 1980 that number had shot up to 480 million gallons. The Europeans spotted the trend and wanted in on the action. Shipments of wine from France, Italy, Germany, Spain, and Portugal rose significantly, until they accounted for twenty-five percent of U.S. wine consumption by 1984. Ernest and Julio feared competition from the Europeans far more than they feared competition from Coca-Cola—or Seagram for that matter. The Europeans had been making wine from time immemorial and realized the importance of weather and soil conditions better than the whiskey and soda pop companies did. The Gallo brothers also had concerns about other factors beyond their control.

"Most of these countries subsidize their wine industries," Ernest claimed. "At the same time, the U.S. government was permitting these foreign wines to come into this country with very low tariffs, while foreign governments retained restrictive tariffs for U.S. wine products. It was not a level playing field."

Over time, Ernest and Julio would take their battle into the political arena as well. For the moment, however, they fought the wine wars the best way they could, stepping up production, intensifying their marketing efforts, and shaving their profit margins. Their strategy produced measurable results during the next few years. The sales of European wines in the U.S. peaked at 142 million gallons in 1984 and began to decline over the next eight years. At that point, less expensive good-quality wines from South America, most notably Chile and Argentina—and later from Australia— began making inroads into the American marketplace.

By then there was a new president, a smiling charmer from Hope, Arkansas, named Bill Clinton. Ernest sized him up and decided he could do business with Bill. FOBs, Friends of Bill, got special treatment. Ernest would enlist Bill as an ally in his efforts to control the flow of foreign wines onto U.S. shores. But that was still a long way into the future.

First, he and Julio had a serious bit of litigation to deal with—litigation that would consume much of their energy throughout the 1980s and create an unbridgeable rift within the ranks of the Gallo family.

Chapter Nineteen

June 12, 1983, broke warm and sunny across the valley. Joseph Gallo had gone his own way since being fired by his brothers. At this time, he owned a sizable spread along Route 140 west of Atwater, a combination cattle ranch and dairy farm with a two-story white house that would soon be his administration building. On this particular afternoon, Joe and his son Mike invited about 100 family members, employees, neighbors, local dignitaries, and members of the press to a barbecue to celebrate the launching of his new cheese business. Father and son had built a cheese-processing plant on the property a year earlier, and now it was time to let the world know about their latest enterprise.

The guests assembled beneath a large tent on the property, where the tables were laden with cuts of meat, a forty-pound block of cheddar cheese, salads, and a prominent display of the finest Gallo wines. Ernest arrived by helicopter mid-afternoon, after most of the guests had assembled, accompanied by Amelia. Julio and Aileen were off on vacation and couldn't attend. Joe greeted his brother and escorted him around the property, showing Ernest his new plant with its glimmering array of state-of-the-art equipment. Joe and Mike explained how they were able to eliminate transportation costs by having the plant right there next to the dairy. They channeled milk to the plant through an underground pipeline, processed it into cheese in 3,500-pound vats, and pressed the molds into forty-pound blocks, which they then shipped to commercial wholesalers in cardboard boxes stamped "Joseph Gallo Cheese Co., Plant No. 06-77, Atwater, CA."

"I've never seen my father happier than he was that day," said Mike.

Ernest was concerned when he spotted the Gallo name on the boxes of cheese, and he grew even more alarmed later when a crop-dusting plane flew overhead pulling a banner that read, GOOD LUCK, GALLO CHEESE. According to Ernest, he asked Joe about how he intended to market his product. "You're selling it wholesale?"

"Forty-pound blocks to customers who cut it into smaller pieces and package it for retail sale under their own brand names."

"So you won't be selling to consumers under the Gallo name?"

"No, I sell only to commercial buyers. Chain stores mostly. They package it under their house labels."

"Good. We can't have consumers thinking the winery is in the cheese business."

Joe's recollection was different. He remembered telling both Ernest and Amelia during a dinner in San Francisco a few months earlier that he intended to sell his cheese under the Joseph Gallo label. When Amelia asked him why, he responded, "Because that's my name."

The difference in these accounts set the stage for a bitter, protracted legal battle that would ensnare the Gallo family for years to come. Joe's case wasn't helped by a television news report the night of his barbecue featuring shots of Joe and Mike celebrating the opening of their cheese plant, with the reporter saying, "Gallo, already known as the largest winemaker, may soon become a big name in the cheese business. Wine and cheese—a popular combination. The Gallo wine folks may think so as they open their own cheese factory. Why not? Wine and cheese go hand in hand."

Joseph Gallo, as it turned out, would incite his oldest brother's wrath, thanks in part to the sloppy reporting of an empty suit on TV.

The issue festered in Ernest's mind, but he ignored it for the moment to deal with a more pressing problem at the winery. With the failure of Gallo varietals to strike a chord with the wine-drinking public, Ernest and Julio needed to regroup and find a new way to improve their market share. Ernest racked his brain to come up with suitable spokesmen for a new Gallo product. He wanted to launch another line of pop wine beverages, a wine spritzer contained in a single bottle so that time-pressed Americans didn't have to go through the trouble of pouring seltzer into their plonk. A couple of fellows in Lodi had achieved considerable success by concocting a beverage they called California Cooler in their garage. California Cooler was composed of fruit juices, wine, and carbonated water, with an alcohol content of seven percent. Ernest figured he could go them one better, and his ad agency found spokesmen for his product in the personages of two folksy gents he named Bartles and Jaymes.

Hal Riney, E. & J. Gallo's advertising maven, told Ernest that he wanted to film "two old codgers who look like farmers sitting on a porch talking about wine coolers." The porch theme had worked so well with Carlo Rossi, why not try it again?

Riney had bought the San Francisco office of Ogilvy & Mather in 1976 and turned it into his own agency, which put San Francisco on the advertising industry map. He was considered a stickler for details who had produced some of the most successful ad campaigns of his era. "Getting it right is like painting the Golden Gate Bridge," was one of his favorite sayings. "You can never stop doing it." His perfectionism and inspired approach to advertising were what Ernest was looking for in his own marketing campaign.

"Riney wanted 'real people' instead of polished actors for the commercial," Ernest said. "He sent his wife, Liz, who ran her own casting company, around the country looking for our spokesman, Frank. She eventually found a local fellow hanging around a grange in Alfalfa, Oregon. His name was

Dave Rufkahr, and he was a small-time cattle rancher. Rufkahr became Frank. Ed was cast closer to home: Richard Maugg, a construction contractor from Santa Rosa, California, and an old school chum of Riney's."

"We looked at nine hundred different people," Riney said. "We had people all over the West Coast looking for some farmer. I was never so scared in my life. The reason Dave was so good as Frank Bartles was that he didn't have a clue about what he was saying. Ernest never really understood the humor in those spots either."

Within weeks, Frank and Ed were expounding on the virtues of Bartles & Jaymes wine coolers, a bubbly, inoffensive spritzer flavored with lemon, strawberry, and other flavors sold in four-packs of twelve-ounce bottles. After a successful launch in Phoenix, Arizona, where the coolers rapidly captured fifty percent of the cooler market, Ernest and Julio decided to go national with them. Within the next twelve months, Bartles & Jaymes rang up sales of 7.5 million cases, establishing the brand as the number-two wine cooler in the country. One year later, sales of Ernest and Julio's new liquid confection skyrocketed to seventeen million cases, capturing about twenty-five percent of the market for that type of product. Bartles & Jaymes managed to outsell Seagram's Golden Wine Cooler brand, which employed movie star Bruce Willis as its spokesman. Imagine that: two old gents on a porch, who many television viewers thought were actually Ernest and Julio, wrestled action hero Willis to the mat and pinned him.

Ernest and Julio were delighted, and presumably Charlie Rossi was relieved that he no longer had to sit up there on a float dressed in overalls in parades staged by Ernest.

In August 1984, a bit more than a year after Joe and Mike's open house celebrating the opening of their cheese factory, a small block of cheese landed on Ernest's desk with the impact of a bomb. Ernest was a vigorous seventy-five years old, still putting in fourteen-hour days on the job and planning for the next war on the horizon. Julio was a year younger, also undiminished by age or serious health problems. Their brother Joe was ten years younger than Ernest, a healthy and energetic sixty-five-year-old on the verge of launching a major new enterprise of his own. Joe's son Mike was thirty-three, a full partner with his father in their business.

Ernest stared at the eight-ounce package of Monterey Jack cheese that had been placed on his desk by one of his minions. He read the label: Joseph Gallo. Something in him detonated. A winery employee told Ernest that he had found the cheese at a supermarket in Modesto, alongside a display of Gallo wines. Ernest picked up the phone on his desk and called Joe immediately.

"I've got a package of your cheese here," he barked in his gravelly voice. "I'm surprised—shocked, really—to see this consumer packaging. You assured me you weren't going to sell in this manner under your name."

"Yes?" Joe said. He couldn't understand Ernest's attitude. Joe and Mike had been marketing their line of cheeses in retail outlets for about five months now. Sales of their retail label had reached almost five million dollars, and sales for their forty-pound blocks of bulk cheese had already soared to thirty-five million dollars.

"We have a real problem with your label," Ernest continued, "because of that agreement we made with Consolidated regarding Gallo Salame. You'll be creating great problems for us because it will seem we're permitting our brother to sell cheese under the Gallo brand after we've licensed it exclusively to them for salami and cheese."

"What does that have to do with me?" Joe asked. "It's my name too. I have a right to use it."

"Trademark law is very complicated and does not give anyone the automatic right to use his name," said Ernest. "Our agreement means we have to protect our trademark." According to him, E. & J. Gallo Winery was required to notify Consolidated about any infringements on the Gallo food trademark.

"We've been making this cheese for a while now, and you must have known about it," Joe replied. He denied that he had ever told his brother that he would sell cheese only in bulk to wholesalers, without the Gallo name on consumer products.

"We need to meet," Ernest insisted. "You and Mike come up here, and we'll discuss it."

Joe and Mike agreed to go up to Modesto the next day. Ernest and Julio were both in Ernest's office when they arrived. Ernest had positioned two chairs side by side in front of his desk, and two others facing them. Ernest and Julio sat down next to each other, and Ernest directed his youngest brother and nephew to sit down opposite them. Ernest outlined his case, that he had no problem personally with Joe using his name on his cheese, but he was concerned about Consolidated Food's reaction when they heard about it.

"It's all Gallo Salame—that's the real problem. If you use the name, you have to ask our permission. If you don't, Gallo Salame might force us to sue."

"The license doesn't change the fact that Joseph Gallo is my name," Joe responded, "and I can use it on my own products."

Mike Gallo said nothing, observing his uncle and his father as they deliberated, reiterating their conflicting views of the matter. Julio, too, remained silent, growing increasingly ill at ease as his older brother pressed their case. Ernest finally concluded the meeting, saying he would have his lawyer contact John Whiting, Joe and Mike's lawyer, to see if they could arrive at a mutually acceptable agreement.

Ernest and Julio's chief counsel, Jack Owen, called Whiting a few days later. Owen essentially laid out the case that Ernest had been making all along, while Whiting listened carefully. At the end of their conversation, Whiting asked Owen to send him a copy of the winery's licensing agreement with Consolidated Foods. After reading it, Whiting was convinced that his client had a legal right to use his own name on his cheese. As far as he was concerned, that right was a basic principle of law protected by the First Amendment.

"It appeared to me that Joe was on solid legal ground," he said. Joe and Mike had no interest in exploiting the winery's brand, he maintained; their concern was that they should have the right to use Joe's name on their products. When Whiting reported his opinion to Owen, the winery's lawyer called for another meeting in Modesto to discuss it in greater detail.

Once again, on October 15, 1984, the brothers and Mike met in Modesto, this time in a conference room with their lawyers. Ernest and Julio sat across from Joe and Mike, and the two lawyers took up their positions alongside their respective clients. Whiting was an affable round-faced man in his mid-sixties with thinning hair; Owen was thirty years younger than Whiting, tall and paunchy, with long blond hair combed straight back from his forehead. Julio opened the meeting this time, with Ernest nodding as he spoke. Julio did little more than repeat Ernest's assertion that they had no problem personally with Joe using his name on his cheese; the issue was the Gallo Salame licensing agreement with Consolidated. Whiting and his clients took it all in, and the meeting broke up cordially with both sides agreeing that it was in everyone's interest to avoid a lawsuit that could result in negative publicity for the family.

Whiting told Joe and Mike that he would seek a second opinion with lawyers who were more practiced in trademark law than he was. On October 25, Whiting received a letter from Al Herzig, a respected copyright and trademark lawyer based in Los Angeles. The letter stated, "It is our opinion that Joseph Gallo has the right to utilize the name 'Joseph Gallo' on or in connection with packaged cheese products." Citing precedent, the letter went on to say "that the right to use one's personal name in connection with a trademark and trade name is protected by the courts and in the absence of fraud or intentional deception, the courts will permit the utilization of a trademark or trade name which is a person's real name in his trade or business."

So there the matter stood, a stalemate, until Ernest decided on another tack. This time, instead of demanding that Joe stop using his name altogether on his products, Ernest offered Joe and Mike a deal similar to the one he had worked out with Consolidated.

"After many discussions and considerable persuasion on our part," Ernest recalled, "we succeeded in getting a green light from Consolidated to prepare a licensing agreement for Joe." In effect, if Joe and Mike agreed to turn over the Joseph Gallo trademark to the winery, as Consolidated Foods had done with the Gallo Salame label, the winery would agree to allow Joe and Mike to market their consumer products under Joe's name without paying a royalty to the winery. Julio, playing the good cop to Ernest's bad cop, added a sweetener, hoping that their youngest brother would take the bait.

"We can also work something out on your grapes," Julio told Joe. "We can set a guaranteed price on your vineyards that aren't under contract."

Joe was tempted. This sounded like a sweetheart deal for him, given the vagaries of the grape market with its wild swings in prices from season to season. He was tempted, that is, until he read the fine print in the licensing agreement Ernest wanted him to sign. A red flag of betrayal went up immediately, and any possibility of an amicable agreement between the warring brothers evaporated like wine fumes.

Chapter Twenty

On April 19, 1985, Owen sent Whiting a copy of the licensing agreement in which Joe and Mike would transfer the Joseph Gallo trademark to the winery. "Our attorney included a clause that forbade Joe from selling his brand name with his company to outsiders," Ernest said, "thereby ensuring that the name would stay in the hands of his heirs, the extended Gallo family." That was bad enough, as far as Joe was concerned. He had no intention of selling his business to anyone, let alone a stranger, but he reserved the right to do so as any business owner would. But the deal-breaker was the last clause in the agreement, which granted the winery the right to inspect the cheese plant at any time and shut it down if, in the inspectors' judgment, it failed to pass muster.

Whiting and Herzig were both alarmed. "The quality condition and inspections," said Herzig, "meant that Ernest could close Joe down."

Joe was particularly upset that his brothers would try to strangle him this way instead of leaving him in peace to sell his cheese under his own name. Julio's insistent plea that "we would never shut you down, Joe" failed to reassure him. Ernest maintained that he wanted to keep the Gallo trademark within the family, and he also claimed that he was concerned about quality control, citing a *Los Angeles Times* article about bacteria contamination in a cheese plant in Jalisco, Mexico. The more that Joe, Mike, and their lawyers analyzed the situation, the more it appeared as though Ernest and Julio were determined to keep total control over all things named Gallo. It had become an obsession with Ernest, and apparently with Julio as well. When Whiting tried to reason that it was in the winery's interests to create a firewall between itself and any risk of contaminated cheese, instead of linking itself to the cheese business with a licensing agreement, Ernest changed the subject. They were at an impasse, and the breach between Ernest and Julio on one side and Joe and Mike on the other grew wider.

The dispute dragged on into the following year, when Ernest wrote Joe a letter on February 16, 1986, threatening him with a lawsuit unless he accepted the winery's terms. When Joe refused to yield, Ernest invited him and Mike to another meeting with their lawyer. On March 21, Joe, Mike, and Whiting made the all-too-familiar trek up Route 99 to the winery's headquarters in Modesto. There they met again in the conference room with the lawyers for both sides. Again, Ernest reiterated the same demands he had been making for well over a year, and Joe refused to sign any licensing agreement that called for regular inspections by the winery and denied him the right to sell his business to whomever he wanted. The meeting was a total waste of time. Nothing was new, no new proposals were forthcoming, and it appeared to Joe that the entire exercise was just a last-ditch attempt by Ernest to bend his youngest brother to his will—with Julio's silent complicity. Finally Joe stood up and informed everyone present that he was leaving. Mike followed his father out the door, while Whiting gathered up his papers and hurried to catch up with his clients, who were storming out of the building toward the parking lot.

On April 17, 1986, Whiting was sitting at his desk in his office in Merced, just outside of Atwater, when his phone started ringing off its hook. Reporters from all over the country were calling him for comments about the lawsuit that E. & J. Gallo Winery had just filed against Joseph Gallo Farms in the U.S. District Court in Fresno. This was the first Whiting had heard about any lawsuit, which mentioned him as the defendant's attorney. Among the charges were trademark infringement, trademark dilution, and unfair competition. Most stunning of all, however, was the assertion that Joseph Gallo cheese was manufactured under unsanitary conditions. Any question that perhaps Julio was being dragged into the lawsuit reluctantly was dispelled by his own comments on the situation.

"We later found out just how unsanitary his operations were," said Julio. "State inspectors found a lot of things at his cheese plant that weren't up to standard, including excessive 'insect and fly problems.' This certainly didn't surprise me. Who ever heard of building a cheese plant so close to a few thousand cows?"

It was true that the U.S. Department of Agriculture had found mold and other "deficiencies" in Joe's plant shortly after it opened. Another attorney whom Ernest and Julio hired, Patrick Lynch of O'Melveny & Myers in Los Angeles, stated, "I don't think any person in litigation would knowingly ignore the issue of quality when you're trying to stop somebody from using their name. We had heard that the cheese plant had failed state inspections, and we felt it was important to bring this to the court's attention, even though we were talking about a brother's company."

But according to Whiting, the quality issue was just a smokescreen spewed by the winery's legal team to conceal the real issue: Joe's right to use his own name on his cheese. "At one point I asked Lynch why he had made all these baseless charges against Joe's cheese," Whiting recalled. "That's when he told me, 'I'm not so naïve to think that a jury of twelve people would want to take away a man's name.' He knew that the ordinary person off the street has an instinctive feeling about the right to your own name."

Joe was crushed when he learned that his brothers, whom he had loved and respected all his life, were accusing him of distributing contaminated cheese to retail outlets. Whether he had a right to use his name on his product was one thing, but this was hitting below the belt. And it wasn't just a case of Ernest playing hardball; Julio was joined in combat with him.

"I think Ernest and Julio were both in sync," said Mike Gallo. "Julio had the reputation for being the more affable one, and Ernest for being the more hard-driving businessman. But Julio was equally driven. The difference was that while Ernest would look you in the eye and speak directly, Julio would smile and pat you on the back."

Mike's sister, Linda Jelacich, agreed. "Ernest was a hardworking man, driven, obviously a hugely successful businessman who built an empire," she said. "Julio was just like him in many ways—not in everything, but he was also driven to succeed."

The lawsuit coincided with another Gallo family tragedy. Joe's first wife, Mary Ann, had been suffering from cancer for about a year at this point, and she passed away in May 1986. Ernest chose not to attend her funeral on May 16, although his wife and sons did go to the church but not to the family reception afterward. Julio, Aileen, their son Bob, and his wife, Marie, went to both the funeral mass and the reception but kept mainly to themselves, creating a widening breach between both sides of the family.

"The few times I saw my dad with Julio," recalled Linda Jelacich, "they seemed very tense and strained."

A few days after the funeral, Whiting obeyed an impulse and drove to the Stanislaus County Courthouse in Modesto. Joe had never been aware of a will left by his parents after their deaths in 1933, or whether they had left any sort of an estate that had gone through probate. Throughout his life, he had listened to Ernest and Julio talk about how their father and mother were close to financial ruin when they died, and how Ernest and Julio had built their winery from scratch after Prohibition. A cloud of doubt surfaced in Whiting's brain now that the brothers were engaged in legal combat, and he decided to pursue the matter on his own. What Whiting unearthed at the courthouse set him back on his heels. He presented his findings to Joe, who was his close friend as well as his client. The information he discovered was nothing short of devastating.

"The court records indicated that Susie left a will stating that Joe was entitled to a one-third share of his parents' estate, which included the winery," said Whiting. "He was a ward of Ernest and Julio in perpetuity. That doesn't end until it's dismissed by the court. Joseph had never seen the will. He had no idea that he was entitled to an equal share, and he was devastated that he had been deceived by his older brothers. He worshiped them. He trusted them. They were like parents to him."

Mike Gallo recalled, "John Whiting did some background checking and discovered that my grandfather, also named Joseph like my father, had made wine and used the name Gallo. My father wondered why he was not entitled to use the family name like his brothers did. While investigating all this, Whiting uncovered some amazing things that really affected my father. My father was raised by his brothers, so they became parents to him. It turned out, that from day one, Ernest and Julio manipulated things to serve their own needs. Whiting learned that Ernest and Julio used my father's assets, the one-third of the farm that should have been his, for their own interests. If they needed to borrow money to buy grapes until they sold their wine, they borrowed against my father's assets. Ernest was a brilliant man, and he put together a court hearing to address all these issues before they became a problem."

The court had decided when Joe turned twenty-one that Ernest and Julio had to pay him a nominal sum of money to account for his share of the inheritance. "That's the way they did things," said Mike. "Even after they fired my father, Ernest and Julio were smart enough to have my dad use their accountants and attorneys so that nobody else would come in and raise any questions."

The bottom line: the three brothers were each entitled to a one-third share of the winery they inherited from their parents, and the winery that Ernest and Julio established as E. & J. Gallo Winery when Prohibition ended was a continuation of the one the three brothers inherited. Ernest and Julio, in effect, admitted as much in their own petition to terminate the guardianship, filed when Joe turned twenty-one, when they listed among Joe's assets "an undivided one-third interest in E. & J. Gallo Winery." To get Joe out of the picture at the time, Ernest had the court value his interest at $16,492.26 when he turned twenty-one in 1941. Ernest had hired an attorney named Fowler to represent Joe at the time, and the court documents revealed that Fowler was able to secure an additional $20,000 from the winery for profits on the loan of Joe's stock.

"I never heard of Fowler," Joe said when Whiting presented him with his findings. "I never sued my brothers. I've never seen or heard about any of this. I'm damned sure I never hired a lawyer and went to court against Ernest and Julio."

"On paper it looked as though Joe already had his day in court," said Whiting. "The record indicated that he received a settlement for the loan of his stock to the winery, so any future claim by him would not have been justified. The only problem was, Joe didn't know anything about any of this."

The evidence indicated that Ernest and Julio had fleeced their youngest brother out of his share of their parents' inheritance by paying him a nominal sum of money for his interest, and then arranging a lawsuit brought by him against themselves to ostensibly settle the matter for all time.

"All of this hit him like a ton of bricks," said Whiting, "especially the part about his supposedly suing his brothers. He had never seen his mother's will, either. It was in her handwriting, and I know that really affected him."

What hellish confluence of events would incite two brothers to deprive the third of his fair share of their parents' property? It appeared as though Joe had been victimized by treachery of biblical proportions. The wheel of time spins on and on, revealing one thing more clearly than all others: humanity's capacity for evil is boundless, and no treachery is greater than the treachery of kin against kin, blood against blood.

Book Five

GALLO BE
THY NAME

Chapter Twenty-one

"Shouldn't we get to my third of the winery before we get any older?" Joe asked Ernest and Julio.

The three brothers faced one another across the conference table at the Modesto winery on May 28, 1986. Ernest stared intensely at Joe. The moment that he had feared all his life had surfaced. He had always been able to manipulate his youngest brother and bend him to his will. Joe was more like a son than a brother, like the son Ernest had been to his own father a half-century earlier, the son whose father had denied him and Julio their own fair shares in the family business an eternity ago.

"Joe, where did you get such a crazy idea?" Ernest asked. "You don't own any interest in this winery. You know that. You've had nothing to do with building the winery."

"My lawyer has found papers in the Modesto courthouse," Joe said. "They indicate a one-third interest in the winery."

"Where did you get the idea that you own a third of the winery?" Ernest repeated.

"It's all there in black and white," said Joe. "Right there in the courthouse in Modesto. It's as plain as day. The records of the guardianship proceedings prove that I own a third of the winery. Send somebody down there and they'll find it."

"There's got to be a mistake," said Ernest. "You know I offered you an interest in the winery, and you turned it down."

"You never offered me a third," said Joe. "After I got out of the army, you said I could *work into* an interest. You certainly never indicated that I should have inherited a third from our father."

"This is ridiculous," Julio spoke up for the first time. "It is pretty well known who the hell built up this business."

"Send somebody down to the courthouse," said Joe. "Have them look at the guardianship files. Then maybe you can tell me what it all means."

Joe stood up and stared at his brothers, his surrogate parents, the two men whom he had loved and trusted the most all his life. He was looking into the faces of strangers. What evil had they committed against him? He could not believe the evidence that his own attorney had unearthed. It was beyond the pale that his brothers would have done this to him. Joe looked into their faces and felt like crying. He turned around abruptly and left the conference room, left them sitting there side by side in their shared guilt, their partnership in deceit and financial fratricide.

Ernest had one of his lawyers check out the documents at the courthouse, and according to Ernest, his chief financial and legal adviser Jon Shastid told him, "It took me a while, but I finally figured it out." Referring to the First and Final Account of Guardians document, listing Joe's undivided one-third interest in the family winery, Shastid said that the money paid to Joe was "an account receivable. The winery had been buying the estate's grapes every year. This was the amount the winery owed Joe for his one-third interest in the estate's grape crop. He was credited with this amount and it was included in the assets he received when the guardianship terminated."

On June 19, Shastid met with Whiting to discuss his interpretation of what the Modesto courthouse finding actually meant—that the money paid to Joe was an accounting procedure to give Joe his one-third share of what the winery owed to the Gallo Brothers' partnership for the sale of grapes.

Whiting saw the matter differently. Why did the document list a one-third interest in the winery as one of Joe's assets? Why did a court assign an additional sum of $20,000 as a settlement for profits earned on Joe's loan of his stock to the winery? None of this made any sense to Whiting. At Joe's request, Whiting contacted other lawyers who corroborated Whiting's opinion that Joe should have inherited a one-third interest in the winery and the Gallo trademark.

A few weeks later, Ernest called his youngest brother and said, "I want to have a meeting."

"When?"

"I'll be right down."

Ernest drove down to Joe's ranch through an early summer rain, and when he arrived, Joe took him outside to the porch where they stood under the eaves, protected from the rain, looking out over the swath of greenery that sloped away toward the parking lot and the road beyond. Joe was about an inch taller than his oldest brother. Ernest was paunchy and balding, Joe trimmer, frowning beneath a full head of graying hair, unsettled by recent developments.

"You and your attorney are all wrong," Ernest began. "That one-third interest did not mean you had a one-third interest in the winery, Joe, but that your guardianship account was due a third of the money the winery owed the estate for its grapes."

"I don't agree," said Joe grimly. "I don't see it like that. If it just meant that, why didn't it say so? Why did it say one-third interest in the winery? Our father's estate included his business. The business that the court document says you continued, and which I should have inherited one-third of."

"You know that Father was only in the wine business in a limited way before Prohibition," said Ernest.

"I remember he told us that he bought wine in barrels and sold them to restaurants," said Joe.

Ernest repeated his own version of family history, that their father had ceased selling wine during Prohibition, that there was no winery to speak of when he and Susie were killed, that Ernest and Julio had built E. & J. Gallo Winery from scratch after Prohibition ended in 1933. "When it looked like Repeal was coming, I was all for going into the wine business, and I discussed the idea with him several times," said Ernest.

"I don't remember that. We were down in Fresno, but you and Julio were still up in Modesto. I don't remember you coming down to talk to Father," Joe replied.

"You remember how sick he was," Ernest plowed ahead, "how upset he was about his financial losses. So he couldn't make a decision."

"I don't think he was that bad," Joe countered. Even in Ernest's revisionist view of history, he conceded that their parents were making and selling wine during Prohibition—albeit on a limited scale, by Ernest's account—and it was apparent that the winery that Ernest and Julio developed was a continuing operation from what their father had started. "I just don't understand," Joe continued, "why you told the court things you never told me when I was growing up. I always trusted you, and I never asked questions even though I always wondered why I wasn't a partner in the winery."

"This is outrageous!" Ernest howled, suddenly reverting to form. "It's extortion! But you're bound to lose. Lawsuits cost a lot of money. You know you don't own an interest in the winery. You're going to end up losing, and you'll have to pay attorneys' fees."

"My lawyers will take this case on contingency," Joe replied. "I've got nothing to lose." His face was set. His mind was made up. He was the one who was outraged, convinced that his older brothers had been swindling him throughout his entire life. There would be no backing down this time.

Ernest glowered at Joe, and then he bolted down off the porch and stormed toward his car in the parking lot.

On July 31, 1986, Joe filed a lawsuit against his brothers, claiming that he was entitled to a one-third share in their winery amounting to more than $200 million in damages over the years. Joe's second wife, Patricia, was cognizant of the emotional strain the trials were bound to have. There was a good chance they would drive an unbridgeable wedge between everyone concerned.

In all probability, some members of the family would never speak to one another again.

"I liked Ernest and Julio before the trials," said Patricia. "All three brothers were quite alike. Joe had a more relaxed personality because Ernest and Julio worked from the time they were little. They were driven very hard, working with the winery. Their social contacts were mostly business-oriented. Joe had been in the service, and he met a lot of other people. He liked to play bridge, and he liked to go hunting. He took time for those things. The other brothers didn't take that much time for them."

Joe may have been the more easygoing brother, but the next few years would change all that. In addition to the toll the trials would take, they would inevitably draw unwanted attention from the media. Ernest had always been fanatical about his privacy, but now the spotlight would be shining directly on him and the family business with relentless intensity. There was a chance that all the family skeletons would be disinterred for public scrutiny. And as Ernest had demonstrated in the past, he was less than a sympathetic figure when called upon to defend himself in the court of public opinion. He was not a man known for his charm; his warts and rough edges were all too prominent. A sample of what was to come appeared in the trade magazine *Wine Spectator*, which illustrated an article about Joe's lawsuit with a photograph of Susie's handwritten will.

The ordeal had its impact on Julio as well, and his health took a turn for the worse. On February 11, 1987, Julio and his son Bob met Joe at the Clift Hotel in San Francisco. There, the three men huddled together in the dining room, Joe sitting between his brother and nephew.

"This is hard on my dad," said Bob. "We have to work this out."

Julio was visibly ill. The day before, his doctors had petitioned the court to excuse Julio from testifying at the trial because of medical reasons. Bob acted as a mediator, trying to find a reasonable way for the brothers to drop their litigation against each other. After some heated discussion in the dining room, they retired to Joe's room in the hotel to see if they could hammer out an agreement in private.

"Here's our offer, Joe," said Bob Gallo. "Ten million dollars plus a license for your trademark. In return, you'll drop the counterclaim."

"Maybe you don't realize it, Bob," Joe replied, "but I was offered that same amount just so Ernest and Julio could avoid publicity."

"We've already had the publicity," said Bob.

"So that's it?" asked Joe. "That's the end of it. No more talk about it."

"Wait," said Julio, standing up and pacing the floor. "Would you take twenty million?"

Joe thought it over for a minute. "As long as we can work out the trademark agreement and figure out the tax questions and lawyers' fees," he said.

At that point, the meeting broke up, with both brothers thinking they were close to a settlement. A week later, however, Bob told Joe over the phone, "Ernest has rejected the deal. He doesn't want to go along with it."

The damage had already been done as far as Ernest was concerned. The media were all over the Gallo family conflagration, which was past the point of being brought under control, and any hope of reconciliation and avoiding publicity had been lost. Joe had already gone too far. Ernest was not in a peacemaking mood; he was in combat mode and set to go for Joe's jugular.

The Gallo brothers' lawsuits proceeded at the federal courthouse in Fresno. All brothers, including Julio, were called upon to testify, notwithstanding his health concerns. The court listened patiently to Ernest's and Julio's complaints about Joe using his name on his cheese, and to Joe's counterclaim that he was entitled to a one-third share of the winery. One issue that came up during the hearings was the assignment of judges to the case who were reputed to have strong ties to Ernest and Julio's side of the family.

"You're not going to beat Ernest in court," said Mike Gallo. "He had very deep pockets, and he was instrumental in getting the federal court justices who heard the case appointed."

On August 29, 1988, Joe's case against his brothers was decided by Judge Edward Dean Price. He ruled that the additional payment of $20,000 to Joe for his share of the family estate had already been settled by a judge. Therefore, Joe had no basis for claiming that he was entitled to a one-third share of the winery. His lawyers, according to the decision, had failed to establish facts that would support their assertion that Ernest and Julio had defrauded Joe out of his inheritance. In a second finding, Price ruled that E. & J. Gallo's suit against Joseph Gallo should move forward.

Round one was over. Joe's offensive against his brothers had failed. Now it was time for round two to begin, with Ernest and Julio charging across the ring hoping for a knockout blow that would put their brother down on the canvas for the count of ten.

Chapter Twenty-two

"Ernest was convinced that the Gallo trademark, and all their trademarks for all the wines they came out with, had value," said Mike Gallo. "So he would go to great lengths to defend those trademarks. Ernest went all over the world defending them against anyone using the name Gallo. He wanted to protect the name Joseph Gallo because someday, he thought, maybe he would come out with a wine named Joseph Gallo." Mike was alluding to Ernest's son Joseph, or Joey. Mike continued, "He wanted to protect it at the time because, after a period of years, you can't win in court if you let a situation continue.

"I don't know that Julio felt the trademark was quite that important. Nevertheless, they were partners in their business, and Ernest wanted to do it. They fought against each other, but when it came to fighting somebody else, they were united. That's the way it was throughout their history. Julio clearly wasn't going to side with my father, even though he might have felt it wasn't that much of a problem with my father using his own name."

Judge Robert Coyle was assigned to hear Ernest and Julio's lawsuit against their brother after Judge Price recused himself following his earlier decision. Again, the deck appeared to be stacked in favor of the winery. Coyle's former law firm had helped negotiate the Gallo Salame trademark case with Consolidated Foods, and Coyle still had financial ties to the firm. He called the trial to order shortly after 9 a.m. on Tuesday, November 22, 1988.

"Joe's sales representatives, who had been warned not to officially connect 'Joseph Gallo Cheese' to the winery," Ernest recalled, "couldn't resist doing so. Some even wrote to prospective customers implying that Joe's product was produced by a division of the winery. Similarly, Joe's retail customers promoted Gallo cheese as another Gallo product, tying it not only to our table wines, but to Gallo Salame's products as well."

Ernest and Julio's attorneys asserted that Joe was attempting to get a "free ride" on the reputation of the Gallo wine brand. Joe's attorneys, for their part, tried to make their case that Joe was entitled to use his own name on his products under the First Amendment. But when Judge Coyle began to focus the case on the trademark infringement issue, Joe's attorneys took a different tack. "The winery is carefully distancing itself in this litigation from Thunderbird, Bartles & Jaymes, pop wines, and Gallo street wines," they countered. The winery was putting out wine with the Gallo name omitted from the labels, since Gallo had become associated with cheap wine, otherwise known as street wine.

"What do you mean by street wine?" Ernest asked defiantly.

"Cheaper wine used by winos," said one attorney.

"And what do you mean by wino?"

"People who drink excessive amounts of wine."

During recesses in the trial, Ernest stalked the corridors with his hands clasped behind his back, asking everyone he encountered, "Now do you see why I can't have my name on that cheese?" He was referring to an article in the *Los Angeles Times* about wedding guests who had gotten sick after eating Joseph Gallo's Monterey Jack cheese—even though the article went on to report that the cheese had not been refrigerated, which was the real cause of the contamination. Ernest admitted as much when he later wrote, "Happily, no one was seriously ill, and Joe's cheese was not to blame."

But outside in the hallway during the trial, he was going for the kill. "Do you realize how many tests that cheese failed?" he asked members of the media in his rhetorical manner. "You wouldn't let your name be put on such terrible stuff, would you? I thought you people in the media were supposed to be smart. Does the government have to tell you not to eat garbage?"

Julio remained absent from the proceedings until December 22, one month after the trial began and one day after Joe's lawyers rested their case for the defense. Julio took the witness stand, downcast, appearing somewhat ill and glum. According to Julio, Joe had asked him, "What would you do if you were in my shoes? Wouldn't you want to use your own name?"

"I would use another name just starting out with a new product," Julio testified that he had told Joe, "unless you intend to capitalize on all the effort and amount of money we've spent building up our trademark."

Joe sat there stunned listening to Julio. He had expected as much from Ernest. But now here was Julio, with whom Joe had sympathized to some degree, and whose health problems Joe had been concerned about, making Ernest's case in his low-key manner. On cross examination, Joe's attorneys managed to get Julio to admit that he had always considered Joe to be an "honest person" who "tells the truth," but that was all they got out of him. Julio stepped down from the witness stand, somewhat slumped, and left the courtroom immediately, never making eye contact with Joe.

The matter hung in abeyance, with Joe's lawyers disagreeing about whether they should try to resurrect the First Amendment argument for Joe's right to use his own name. In March 1989, Al Herzig, the trademark attorney from Los Angeles, filed a motion stating, "To preclude an individual from using a given surname would be, as a 1942 Second Circuit Court decision put it, 'to take away his identity; without it he cannot make known who he is to those who may wish to deal with him; and that is so grievous an injury that courts will avoid imposing it, if they possibly can.'"

But another of Joe's attorneys withdrew the motion on the grounds that it would just muddy the water and lead to further delays. And so, on March 29, 1989, Judge Coyle ruled that "because the pretrial order does not assert any legal issue involving the First Amendment, the court holds that the issue is not before it in resolving this action."

On June 19, 1989, Judge Coyle delivered his coup de grace to Joe Gallo, enjoining him from using his name as a trademark. Joe could use the name on his bulk cheese, and also on his retail cheese as long as it was printed in no larger than twelve-point type and appeared below the trademark and variety of cheese. The judge further ruled that his name could not appear on any published material, nor could it be "audibly communicated" on radio or television.

"Do you realize what this means?" asked Whiting. "Joe can't mention his own name on radio or television. He can't stand up and say, 'My name is Joe Gallo and I make cheese.' If that isn't a violation of Joe's right to free speech, I don't know what is."

"Ernest always gets what he goes after," said Mike Gallo. "It's always been like that, and it will never change."

Ernest was jubilant in victory. "The judge gave Joe one hundred and twenty days to stop infringing on our trademark," he said. "On his label, Joe would be allowed to show himself as the producer of the cheese, but his name would have to be smaller and placed below a new brand name.

"When I left the courtroom for the final time, Joe was also on his way out," continued Ernest. "Without looking at each other, we went our separate ways. I headed down the hallway in one direction, and Joe went the other way. Time heals all, I used to think. Now I am not so sure."

Ernest and Julio's victory became final on February 7, 1992, when the U.S. Court of Appeals for the Ninth Circuit upheld the earlier decision that Joe did not have any ownership claim on the winery. It also upheld the ban on the trademark use of his name—although the court slightly modified the injunction against the audible broadcast of his name on the grounds that it was "overbroad" and might have "unforeseen" consequences on his heirs.

Ernest was right when he doubted that time would heal all. The wounds he and Julio had inflicted on their brother were fatal. The end of litigation marked the beginning of the end for Joseph Gallo Jr.

"During the course of the trial, we could tell there was something wrong," said Mike Gallo. "My father probably had a stroke shortly after the trial. It took some time to diagnose. At the time, there was a drug out there called Halcion, and there was a suggestion that it had some side effects. We thought at the time that this may have been causing the problem. It turned out that wasn't the problem. He actually had a stroke. His life after that degenerated. There was nothing that could be done. It got worse throughout the rest of his life. We went through a period when he couldn't remember certain words. It was frustrating for him, because he would try to think of a word for something but couldn't remember it. He reached a point where he couldn't speak at all. He developed a problem with one of his arms, then the other arm, finally his ability to walk. Toward the end he couldn't talk at all. There was a time when we didn't know whether he understood us. He couldn't write, so we had no way to communicate with him. At the end, which was pretty typical of this sort of thing, he even had trouble chewing food."

Joe Gallo's life was essentially over after the trials, although he lingered in a debilitated state for many years afterward.

"My husband had a series of small strokes during the trial that we weren't aware of," recalled Patricia Gallo. "He was under a lot of stress, naturally. It was heartbreaking for him. He loved his brothers. In all honesty, we really thought you could use your own name. We didn't say Gallo Cheese, we said Joseph Gallo Cheese. He was out on his own, trying to establish his own business. He did not want, by any means, for people to think there was any connection, and that's what they were accusing him of."

A chasm developed between the warring sides of the Gallo clan that would only grow wider.

On January 2, 1990, Julio and Aileen were driving home from their second home in Pebble Beach, up the road from Carmel. Aileen was behind the wheel, navigating their large Lincoln Town Car eastward over the narrow twisting road across the Pacheco Pass on the way to Modesto. The mountain pass is in the Diablo Range in southern Santa Clara County and is the main road through the hills separating Silicon Valley and the Central Valley. A single lane runs in each direction.

Suddenly—there was some debate later about which car crossed the center divide into the opposing lane—Aileen slammed head-on into a small Honda Civic heading west. Julio and Aileen suffered broken ribs and bruises, but the driver of the Civic was not as fortunate. Twenty-seven-year-old Sharon Kauk was killed in the collision. Her husband suffered a concussion, and their three-year-old son suffered serious head injuries.

Witnesses for both sides claimed they had seen the other vehicle swerve across the center divide, but the California Highway Patrol concluded that it was Aileen's fault. She pleaded no contest to a count of vehicular manslaughter and was sentenced to a $2,000 fine and 350 hours of community service—although driving under the influence was ruled out. Aileen was heartbroken by the other woman's death and the injuries to the child. She and Julio settled quickly with the Kauks, who withdrew their claim against the Gallos in December 1990.

Patricia Gallo had always liked Aileen and was troubled by the rift that had arisen between herself and members of the family with whom she wanted to remain friendly. Patricia attempted to commiserate with her sister-in-law after the accident, hoping that the olive branch she extended would help bridge the divide separating them. But her effort was unrewarded.

"Aileen had a wreck coming home from Carmel after the trial, and a lady in the other car was killed. I wrote her a nice letter, but I never heard from her," Patricia said sadly.

Her other attempts to communicate with Ernest and Julio's side of the family would also fall on deaf ears over the ensuing years.

After the trials, business continued as usual for Ernest and Julio. Julio's son Bob and Bob's son Matt had been looking to expand the family's holdings in Sonoma, and in 1989 they bought the 1,000-acre Asti vineyard that had once been the property of Italian Swiss Colony. Together with the Frei Brothers ranch the Gallos had bought earlier, plus other properties they owned in Sonoma Valley, Gallo Sonoma now owned about 4,000 acres in the region, more than any other winery in Sonoma.

It was around this time that eighty-year-old Ernest began to turn more and more of his responsibilities over to his son Joseph, who was in charge of sales. Ernest still went to work every day and continued to put in long hours behind his desk and out in the field, checking the retail outlets to make sure his products were well positioned on the shelves. But he was realistic enough to know that time was running out for him and Julio, and they both wanted to make sure that the succession plan they had in mind would move ahead seamlessly, without a hitch in the closely held family business. Ernest had hoped that David would take his place alongside Joseph and Julio's offspring, but David had grown even more erratic over the years and was a laughingstock in his role as director of marketing among other executives at the winery.

Julio, too, was as active as ever in the family's grape-growing operations, but he had been grooming his son and grandson to assume more of his responsibilities in Sonoma.

"My son Bob, along with his twenty-seven-year-old son Matt, went out with our engineering experts," said Julio, "and figured out how best to shape the terrain so we could expand our grape acreage into the hills. Bob and I visited Asti every week during the summer, taking the helicopter over from Modesto. Though we had rolls of schematics drawn by engineers, we liked to climb over the hills ourselves. My grandson Matt usually accompanied us. In fact, Matt was now in charge of vineyard land development in Sonoma."

Julio's son-in-law Jim Coleman, who had been with the winery for thirty-five years at this time, was another key player in the business. Bob and Jim jointly assumed the day-to-day grape-growing operations that Julio gradually ceded to them. The next generation was also moving up the family ladder in both the marketing and grape-growing operations. Jim Coleman's son Greg, who had earned a degree in viticulture, managed the family's vineyards in Madera. His brother Brad, a graduate of Fresno State, managed vineyards in Livingston and Modesto. And the distaff side of the family had recently begun to penetrate the patriarchal structure that Ernest and Julio had nurtured from the beginning. Greg and Brad's sister Caroline worked in the advertising and communications department in San Francisco.

The woman who was destined to become the most visible female Gallo of all was the brilliant and gorgeous Gina, Bob's daughter, who had graduated from the College of Notre Dame, Belmont, and who at twenty-six years of age was well on her way to becoming an accomplished winemaker, respected throughout the industry. Over time, more than fifteen members of the family would begin to operate the levers of control at the winery that Ernest and Julio had been running on their own, after their parents' death, for close to six decades.

And as the extended Gallo family ascended in power, one by one the top-tier executives who were unfortunate enough to have the wrong last name slowly dropped away, floating off to other industries in their golden parachutes. They were well compensated for all the years of service they had devoted to the winery, but they were less than pleased with the brick wall that awaited them at the end of their long tenure in the Gallo empire.

Chapter Twenty-three

In May 1991, Ernest spoke to members of the Young Presidents' Organization, an international group of presidents and chief executive officers under the age of fifty, when they visited Gallo headquarters in Modesto. He told them that his board of directors consisted of him, Julio, Bob, Jim Coleman, David, and Joseph.

"We want things done right away," said Ernest. "No waiting, no dawdling. As soon as we make a decision, we do it and do it now, before a competitor gets it done." He ended with his trademark advice to all budding entrepreneurs: "If you have a private firm, stay private. If you are public, buy it back."

E. & J. Gallo Winery was firmly ensconced in the catbird seat within the wine industry, by far the largest winery in the world, selling about forty percent of all the wine produced in California and accounting for nearly one of every three glasses of wine consumed in the U.S. Ernest and Julio were ranked by *Forbes* among the 400 richest people in the country. They had achieved the very pinnacle of success, and they intended to remain there by every means possible. One way to ensure that their dynasty would not come undone was by continuing to nurture their political alliances in California and Washington, D.C. The list of politicians who were regular recipients of their largesse included the biggest household names on both sides of the political divide: President George Bush, senators and representatives Bob Dole, George Mitchell, Barbara Boxer, Tom Daschle, Lloyd Bentsen, Diane Feinstein, Leon Panetta, John Seymour—and on and on. Anyone who had anything to say about how wine was made, distributed, marketed, and sold throughout the nation, and which foreign wines were allowed to enter our shores, was worthy of a donation.

Those worthy of support included the new president of the United States, William Jefferson Clinton, elected in November 1992, who made Ernest cochairman of a fund-raising lunch in San Francisco in September 1993. Ernest raised $100,000 in a matter of days, only weeks after he had met privately with the president to discuss Chilean wine imports, according to the *Los Angeles Times*. Ernest's support for both President Clinton and Republican majority leader Dole paid off handsomely. Not only did Congress delay any action to increase Chilean wine imports, but it passed funding for a wine promotion program that gave the Gallo family millions of dollars to promote its wines overseas. Despite opposition to the legislation from a bipartisan group of senators, who derided the program as a crass example of corporate welfare, the program survived.

"Remember that five-city campaign trip that President Clinton took on Air Force One?" asked PBS's Robert Krulwich, who appeared on the January 30, 1996, episode of *Frontline*. "Well, one of his stops was in San Francisco, and the occasion was a fund-raiser at the Fairmont Hotel. Money came to town for a chance to catch a glimpse of the president. And here he is. Just behind him, there's Vice President Gore. The president now will stop and have a few words with his supporters. But now, who's the guy with the bald spot? Ernest Gallo, Bob Dole's single biggest contributor, the man who gave over one million dollars to the Republicans. He's here. It seems that in just three days, Ernest Gallo raised $100,000 for this event. And at this point, he is number five on President Clinton's list of all-time givers.

"But why? How does the president know this wine guy? Let's go back a bit. It turns out in the last election, Mr. Gallo had not given to the Clinton campaign until days before the election, when he gave some money to the Democratic

National Committee. He'd given heavily to Bush and the Republicans. But the nifty thing about our system is it's very forgiving. There are lots of ways to give. So Ernest Gallo gave $40,000 to the Clinton transition. But what could Washington do for Gallo?

"Gallo is the biggest wine producer in the country, nearly a billion-dollar-a-year business, and their market share is big and stable. So they need to expand worldwide, and that means marketing their wines to other countries. And guess who helps them pay for commercials? The Gallos received thirty million dollars under the market promotion program, a piece of legislation pushed by California agribusiness and originally sponsored by Senator Pete Wilson and Representative Leon Panetta, both longtime Gallo political favorites. But not everybody in the wine business is happy about this because it is structured to reward the biggest producers."

"I had to look at the bill as a rebate for Gallo basically," said Bill MacIver, another guest on the show. MacIver headed the far smaller and infinitely more upscale winery Matanzas Creek, tucked away a few miles south of Healdsburg in the rolling hills near Santa Rosa. "I mean, they get forty-eight percent of the funds, and it's really of virtually no use whatsoever to small wineries."

"Last Labor Day," said Krulwich, "when President Clinton came to town, he stopped for a few hours in California's Central Valley. He met with workers, and with his chief of staff Leon Panetta, he met with ranchers and farmers. Then he went behind closed doors for a private meeting with Ernest Gallo. We don't know what they talked about except for official statements that they discussed NAFTA and the threat of low-cost Chilean wines. But the next month, the ad promotion program was reauthorized with President Clinton's enthusiastic support and, for good measure, with an increase of thirty percent."

"Frankly, it infuriates me," said the less fortunate MacIver, "that the American people are giving that money to Gallo, which has revenues of almost a billion dollars a year, that the taxpayers would fund something like this. It's a travesty, as far as I'm concerned."

Travesty or not, it was politics as usual, and Matanzas Creek was not big enough to benefit from taxpayer subsidies. Only the biggest players with the deepest pockets need apply.

* * *

The Gallo family had an anxious moment on February 11, 1993, when Ernest's son Joseph and his wife, Ofelia, were among the ninety-four passengers held captive for more than eleven hours on a plane hijacked from Europe to New York. Lufthansa Flight 592, which was scheduled to fly from Frankfurt to Cairo and Addis Ababa, was hijacked at gunpoint by a lone Ethiopian man. The A310 initially flew to Hanover for fuel before flying to New York's JFK, where the hijacker surrendered after brief negotiations.

"He called in after they landed to say he and his wife were on the plane and were safe," said Gallo Winery spokesman Dan Solomon. Neither Joseph nor Ofelia was injured during their transatlantic ordeal. "They were just traveling in Europe, I guess. I have no idea of their scheduling."

After the gunman surrendered, Joseph, his wife, and all other passengers were released unharmed.

The near tragedy was quickly followed by other traumatic events affecting the Gallo family. Ernest's victories in the legal and political arenas were tempered by ongoing tragedies in his personal life. On May 2, 1993, he lost the person who was closest in the world to him, except possibly for his wife, Amelia. His brother, his confidant, his friend and partner from the time they were children, was involved in a fatal accident; this time, Julio was behind the wheel.

"Julio died driving a Jeep up in the mountains near the coast range," said Mike Gallo. "They had family get-togethers up there on property Bob owned. Julio insisted on driving after Aileen's accident, and he did not like to wear a safety belt. The Jeep rolled over with other family members in it. Julio was killed, but the others came out of it okay without life-threatening injuries."

Julio's death was a crushing blow for Ernest.

"We had always worked well side by side," Julio once said of his long partnership with Ernest. "Our personalities seemed to complement each other."

Ernest felt the same way. Despite their differences in style and personality, their partnership had been a formidable one. Julio's passing, however, was not the only tragedy Ernest would suffer that year. Amelia suddenly became ill in the fall of 1993 and slipped away quickly, just before Christmas, on December 22. Ernest was rocked by her death as well. Through a spokesman, he issued the simple statement, "Amelia was a great wife, mother, and grandmother, and a truly great lady. While her loss is very, very difficult for me, I feel fortunate and thankful I have had her for sixty-two memorable years."

The old guard was moving on and the new one slowly beginning to take over. But Ernest's career in the wine business was not yet finished—far from it.

Under his guidance, the Gallo empire continued its blitzkrieg across Sonoma Valley. Its army of bulldozers, earthmovers, and mammoth dump trucks, which had been bought from the builders of the Alaska pipeline, gouged their way over a swath of terraced hills blanketed with rolling vineyards. Their onward march was relentless, ripping apart hundreds of acres, erecting dams, and creating man-made lakes to facilitate the process of growing and harvesting tons of varietal grapes.

"It is very hard to reshape something that Mother Nature has spent thousands of years making the way she wanted it," said Phillip Freese, a winemaker based in Healdsburg in the heart of Sonoma County. "But if anyone can take on Mother Nature, they can."

Only Ernest and his legions had the power to redesign the land to their own liking in their push to dominate the market for reasonably priced varietal wines—the only growth area remaining in the U.S. market.

"They have been behemoths for longer than most people have been alive," said a former Gallo salesman. "Sometimes bullies, sometimes geniuses, usually right, but always bigger, faster, and more determined. When it came to selling wine, Ernest was like a bulldog with its teeth in your ankle."

In 1994, George Davis, owner of the tiny Porter Creek Winery in Healdsburg, pointed with distaste to a tall hill crowned with towering redwoods on land adjoining his thirty-five acres. Davis's winery specialized in organic, hillside-grown varietals.

"E. & J. Gallo owns that hill and plans to cut it," he lamented. A constant deep-throated rumble broke the quiet of an otherwise balmy afternoon as mechanized mammoths clambered up and down the road toward Gallo's gigantic spread of land, which dwarfed Davis's small vineyard.

"Their huge D-9s are the biggest thing you can transport on the roads," Davis said. "What Gallo is doing has been a disaster. See that pile down there. Those were once living oaks. Now it's like an oak Auschwitz."

Notwithstanding the damage inflicted on the landscape by the Gallo earth-eating machines, Davis and other local farmers opposed government intervention, preferring instead voluntary guidelines and a hands-off approach to existing winery operations. "If we make too many regulations for hillside vineyards, only Gallo will have the money to afford them," said Davis. Davis helped organize Friends of the Twin Valley, which advocated pressure from the region's agriculture community rather than government controls. "There has been enough pressure that Gallo is attending meetings on the matter," he said. "We need to reward sustainable forestry practices and offer incentives to do the right thing."

Davis and his organization favored hillside plantings in pastures and other existing farmland to counter the loss of forests and wildlife habitat. "You get the best fruit off the hills, more concentrated," he said, "but we are losing critical areas where such animals as bobcats and pumas move through. We need riparian corridors that are not fenced, so that animals can get to the water. With extensively recontoured vineyards, you get a cartoon landscape rather than a natural one."

Wineries in the area making environmentally friendly wines grown without chemicals included Davis Bynum, Adler Fels, and Benziger. Among those producing certified organic wines were Coturri and Sons, One World, Kenwood, Mark West, Wild Hog, Michael Brody, and Topolos. Mendocino's wine industry was much smaller, but it produced half the organic wine sold domestically at the beginning of the 1990s. "Approximately half of Mendocino's grape growers are certified organic farmers or practice sustainable farming techniques," claimed an article in *Wine Business Monthly*. Among the environmental leaders in both Mendocino and Sonoma were Fetzer, Hop Kiln Winery, Matanzas Creek Winery, and Sam Sebastiani at Viansa Winery, all of which were concerned about protecting wetlands.

Years later, George Davis spoke of the change of direction taken by the younger generation of Gallos. "Gina and Matt had a great learning experience," Davis said in 2008. "We've made peace, especially through Matt. We worked with him to correct the lot line, and he's made very significant changes in the way Gallo does business.

"Bob Gallo started the transition process. He was shocked when we had a direct confrontation, and we were able to save a lot of forest land. Matt has a strong ethic about the environment and has taken a more enlightened approach to winemaking.

"Julio, too, deserves a lot of credit for the innovations he made in this industry before he died. Thanks to him, the Gallos funded valuable research at the University of California in Davis, and they made it available to everyone."

* * *

Vintners were attracted to Sonoma Valley by the liquid gold that the soil and the conditions in the region made it possible to create. Millennia of submersion under water, dense forestation, and favorable microclimates resulted in an environment that allowed the wine industry to command higher and higher prices for its products. When big agribusiness moved in, it turned much of the terrain into bombed-out craters with bulldozers and earth-recontouring machines. Then the winery giants fumigated the soil with toxic methyl bromide, which polluted the creeks and the nearby Russian River when the spring rains washed the pesticides into ditches that emptied into the waterways. Hillside vineyards rapidly took over and evolved into the region's most prosperous industry, attracting the attention of environmentalists like George Davis and other small, family-operated vineyards.

The price of acreage throughout the valley skyrocketed. "In eighteen years of my business, I've never seen such a feeding frenzy," said John Statzer of Agricultural Properties in the area. Undeveloped vineyard property cost up to $30,000 an acre in 1996, up forty-five percent from 1990. Over the years, the price for an acre of land in Sonoma Valley would ascend well into the six-figure range. Sonoma County vineyards and wineries rapidly became sizzling-hot investment properties, affordable only by the wealthy. Family farms and boutique wineries started to fall along the wayside, replaced by corporate-industrial agribusinesses, many of whose owners lived outside the county. The land was transformed from a region boasting diverse crops into one with a single crop—grapes—displacing much of the homegrown food, as it had already done in Napa Valley across the mountain range to the east.

Small, organic Sonoma wineries like Taylor Maid Farms were among those affected the most by Big Corporate wine. Taylor Maid's manager, Michael Presley, observed, "Some people are planting vineyards who want the prestige and are hobbyists. They are investors rather than farmers."

Gallo was not the only corporate target in his gun sights. Kendall-Jackson was another major player in Sonoma, having bought eighty heavily forested acres of land, clear-cut it, and turned it into a vineyard. On balance, there was no question that the wine industry overall was an economic asset to Sonoma County. Wine advertising alone jumped twenty-three percent in 1996. The vineyards expanded the county's open space and attracted tourists with credit cards and deep pockets to the premier "wine country" in the nation. Another major benefit of the invasion of Sonoma by big vintners from other areas was the production of high-quality varietals at affordable prices.

"When I started growing grapes, you could put ten bottles of California wine on a table, and five would not be drinkable," said legendary grape-grower and vintner Charlie Barra, who had been growing grapes in the area surrounding Mendocino for more than half a century. "Today you put fifty wines on a table, and they are all drinkable. They will be different, but there will not be a bad bottle in the lot."

But the price paid for better quality wine and growth was recontoured hills and slashed heritage oaks, exposing the dark, shadowy side of the wine industry, with its insatiable appetite for ever-increasing market share.

Of the top fourteen Sonoma County wineries in 1996, measured by annual revenue, only Sebastiani was owned by a historic local wine family. Gallo, of course, had invaded the county from the Central Valley. Four were owned or partly owned by people with deep roots in Sonoma County: Jordan, Korbel, Geyser Peak, and Kenwood. The others were either foreign-owned or dominated by large corporations, while others yet were controlled by silent, sometimes carefully concealed partners. Clos Du Bois was British-owned; Piper Sonoma and Simi, French-owned; Buena Vista, German-owned; Domaine St. George, Thai-owned; and Gloria Ferrer and Marimar Torres, Spanish-owned.

The Australians, too, were getting in on the act, including that continent's giant Southcorp, whose Penfolds subsidiary bought fifty percent of Geyser Peak from local owners. Swiss conglomerate Nestle owned Chateau Souverain and other Sonoma wineries. Texas Pacific Group and Silverado Partners bought Wine World Estate, which included Chateau St. Jean, Beringer Vineyard in Napa, and other wineries in both counties. Oil mastodon Chevron owned a couple of brands in Sonoma. Great Britain's Guinness bought Rodney Strong—and on and on it went through a mind-boggling array of vertically integrated corporate and foreign-controlled wineries with no ties to the region.

"Recent trends indicate that, in coming decades, only the big wineries and distributors will survive," wrote Glen Martin and Jay Stuller, authors of *Through the Grapevine*. "The big fish are already eating the little fish; in a few years, only whales may remain. Seagram sells about 150 brands of wine worldwide, and after Gallo, had been the second-largest marketer of wine in the United States, until the Canandaigua buyout of Taylor and Masson."

It was increasingly inevitable that more and more small wineries would have to sell out to large corporations. Throughout Sonoma, the vineyard acreage of the top ten wineries and growers more than doubled in a span of five years. Kendall-Jackson, for example, had virtually no Sonoma County acreage before 1990, but by 1996, it was second only to Gallo. When wineries are bought by large corporations, they often retain their labels. Kendall-Jackson owned over a dozen premium estate vineyards at the time, managed under the umbrella of Artisans and Estates, and its battles with Gallo reflected an intense struggle for turf throughout the region.

But the battles weren't restricted to the region. Globalization was rapidly becoming the name of the game. In 1996, Sacramento hosted a wine industry trade conference, "Vineyards and Vintners: A Global Perspective." The chairman of the symposium, Ed Weber of the University of California Cooperative Extension, commented, "Thinking of ourselves as the California, Oregon, or even American wine industry is too limiting. We have no choice but to view this business globally." His theme was adopted by the Sonoma County Wineries Association and United Airlines when they announced a major marketing agreement to increase the visibility of Sonoma County wines on United Airlines flights.

"This is the largest marketing program that any association related to the wine industry has ever achieved," said Jaimie Douglas, a wineries consultant.

The idea was to promote Sonoma as a key tourist destination as United pushed Sonoma County wines across the friendly skies. The downside was that the valley's economy increasingly depended on the health of a single industry, with its fiscal eggs in one basket rather than diversified among many baskets, exposed to the risk of disease, changes in tastes, and the inevitable boom-and-bust cycle of the wine industry. Wine in the United States was more about agribusiness than farming. Kenwood Vineyards president John Shella summed it up succinctly when he stated, "The wine industry in Sonoma County has changed from a sleepy, jug-wine business to a highly technical, capital-intensive premium-wine business."

For better or worse, the economic landscape of Sonoma Valley was irreversibly altered along with the physical landscape, thanks to the onslaught of Gallo and the other giants who now firmly controlled the rapidly evolving U.S. wine industry.

Chapter Twenty-four

Ernest had described himself as a warrior many years earlier, and now the march of time was taking its inexorable toll on the tough old patriarch and his family. Ernest was still standing on the field of battle, but on March 2, 1997, his son David became the next Gallo family member to fall victim to a tragic, premature end.

"David passed away some years back," said Mike Gallo. "It was suggested that he died of a seizure or a stroke in the bathtub." The details surrounding David's death remained a closely guarded family secret, like so many secrets hidden away in the family's vault at Ernest's insistence.

Julio's widow, Aileen, followed David to the grave in 1999, thinning out the ranks of the older generation even as new Gallo offspring rose to take their place in the empire. But the passing of the old guard failed to heal the wounds within the family; on the contrary, they had only worsened since the internecine trials of the previous decade.

"When Ernest's son David died, I wrote them a note but never heard from them," said Patricia Gallo, trying once again to build a bridge across the divide.

Thanks to the efforts of the youngest Gallos, primarily Matt and Gina, Kendall-Jackson had begun to replace E. & J. Gallo Winery as the bad boy of the industry, at least in Sonoma. By the end of the 1990s, Gallo's farming practices had become a modified organic regime, and the new generation of Gallos was included among the industry leaders dealing with soil erosion and the reuse of wastewater. To its credit, Gallo seemed to be taking a long-term view of the industry.

The environmentalists began to turn their wrath on Jess Jackson at Kendall-Jackson, the Gallos' main competitor for premium Sonoma County wines. The former San Francisco trial lawyer shifted his battlefield from the courtroom to the grape fields in the 1980s, spending more than sixty million dollars to build new wineries in Sonoma, Napa, and Monterey counties. Later in life, Jackson would expand into Thoroughbred racing, earning the enmity of the established gentry in the field. Kendall-Jackson owned over 2,000 acres in Sonoma County and about 10,000 acres throughout the state, as well as substantial holdings in Latin America and Europe. The company's 1996 revenues of $240 million from its local vineyards were the highest of any winery except Gallo, whose estimated annual revenues at the time were $1.5 billion. Gallo's revenues soared to $3.5 billion in 2007, putting Kendall-Jackson a distant second.

Kendall-Jackson's neighbors were less than pleased by Jackson's growing presence in the area. County resident Laura Goldman, who lived next to the winery's Sonoma vineyard, complained, "Where I live outside Occidental is fast becoming a sprayed and sterile vineyard heaven, and to hell with the neighborhood and the environment."

Another neighbor described Jackson as "a wine baron in the tradition of the 19th-century railroad barons."

Gina Gallo, meanwhile, had replaced Ernest and Julio as the public face of E. & J. Gallo Winery. She had become an expert at getting good press for the Gallos while establishing a reputation as a consummate winemaker.

"I share my grandfather Julio's two biggest passions: family and our family's wine business," she said, her long reddish-brown hair cascading across one side of her face as her perfect teeth flashed brilliantly for the camera.

The public image had changed, but Gallo still offered no public tours or tastings as other wineries did, nor did the company put up signs to identify its presence at any of its facilities. As Ernest turned over more and more responsibility to his son Joseph and the extended Gallo family, he occupied himself with the business of protecting the family name from any and all would-be interlopers. Ernest, whose own father had called him *l'avvocato* (the lawyer) when he was still a teenager, now devoted much of his energy to safeguarding the franchise that he and Julio had spent their entire lives creating.

A young woman in Plano, Texas, was unfortunate enough to attract Ernest's attention in 2001, just as the new century, the new millennium, was beginning to unfold. Jennifer King had decorated her home with hand-painted plates, vases, and pitchers resplendent in iridescent red, green, gold, and blue. Along one wall in her house were shiny steel racks supporting cups, teapots, plates, and individual ceramic tiles embellished with rooster patterns. Her house served as the showcase for a tiny Internet importing company that Jennifer had launched in February 2001, from which she derived about $10,000 per year to help support herself and her young daughter, who suffered from diabetes. King, who also worked as a piano teacher, had the misfortune of falling in love with Italian ceramics when she lived in Rome a few years earlier. She never dreamed that labeling her ceramic roosters *gallo rosso, gallo verde, gallo dorato,* and *gallo blu,* which were the literal translations of her products in Italian, would raise the hackles on the back of Ernest's deeply creviced neck.

Ernest responded with a legal fusillade the likes of which the entrepreneurial Texas homemaker could never have imagined. The legal beagles, representing the world's largest winemaker, fired a series of e-mails expressing Ernest's displeasure with her expropriating the Gallo logo for her enterprise. Surely, this was some sort of joke. Everyone knew the word *gallo* meant rooster in Italian. How could anyone object to her using a word commonly used among Italian ceramics enthusiasts for rooster patterns on tiles that had been stamped out in a small village in Umbria since the early 19th century?

"When I got the initial e-mail," she said, "I didn't even respond because I thought, 'This is a joke.'"

But Ernest wasn't laughing. A month later, Jennifer King got another e-mail from Gallo lawyers threatening to slap her with a trademark infringement lawsuit if she didn't strip her Web site of all uses of the word *gallo*. At this point, the flabbergasted importer sent back an e-mail of her own explaining that the label on her products was a historically accurate and generally recognized descriptor for what she was selling. She couldn't understand how a man named Ernest Gallo didn't know what his name meant in Italian. But, then again, poor Jennifer just didn't understand the nature of this man.

"I understand that Gallo means rooster in Italian," replied an associate general counsel for E. & J. Gallo Winery. "Italian is not the official language in the United States, so it plainly is not a generic term." He demanded that she remove the offensive word from her Web site immediately.

Again, Jennifer thought this had to be some sort of ludicrous mistake. But a couple of weeks later, when she received a notice that the winery was filing a lawsuit against her in a California U.S. District Court charging her with trademark infringement, trademark dilution, and unjust enrichment, she finally understood that the joke was on her.

"I think it's a little bit of hardball myself," said her attorney, Jeffrey Look. "The unusual fact is that you're talking about a case where the central issue turns over art history, a particular form of art. We're just trying to use this term on this art."

King and her lawyer were up against a mammoth. A year earlier *Forbes* had ranked the winery the 141st largest privately held company in the United States, with annual revenues totaling $1.6 billion. It employed an entire staff whose sole purpose was to scan the globe for potential trademark incursions. In its complaint against King, Gallo claimed that it had already forced others to stop using the word *gallo* on products ranging from salsa, beer, and rice to hosiery, poker chips, and Thoroughbred racehorses. A few years earlier, Gallo had sued San Antonio artist Joe Lopez for silk-screening a rooster profile on T-shirts and selling them under the names *Puro Gallo*, *Gallo Fino*, and *Gallo Indio*. So the Spanish version of gallo (pronounced *gah-yo*) was not immune from prosecution either. A Latino maker of ceramic roosters marketed as *Gallo de Oro* was also sued for infringing on the E. & J. Gallo trademark.

A more egregious case of trademark infringement occurred in February 2000, when someone in Houston tried to patent the domain name "ernestandjuliogallo.com" and force the winery to buy the name from him. E. & J. Gallo Winery prevailed in that case, as it had in most of the lawsuits it had launched over the years. One exception was a trademark infringement suit Gallo had leveled against a tobacco company in the Philippines, which marketed a brand of cigarettes under the name Gallo. An appeals court dismissed an earlier decision prohibiting the tobacco company from using the name, on the grounds that it had been doing so for twenty years, and no unfair competition was intended.

But the winery would prevail against Jennifer King. Gallo attorneys cited a 1990 case in which Gallo successfully sued the Consorzio Del Gallo Nero, an Italian trade association that promoted Chianti Classico under the rubric *gallo nero* in its U.S. marketing efforts. A U.S. district judge blocked the consortium's use of the term, even though a black rooster had been the symbol of the Chianti region for 800 years.

Others thought Jennifer King's case was entirely different. It was possible to believe that using the word *gallo* within the wine industry could lead to some confusion, but how could that be true in the case of ceramics? "That would seem to be quite a stretch," said Frank Vecella, a Dallas trademark lawyer. "That would strike me as quite an uphill battle to show actual infringement. Is somebody looking at that Web site and mistakenly thinking that the Ernest & Julio Gallo Winery is behind this?"

No matter. Jennifer King had little choice but to cave in to the power of Ernest's corporate muscle. Before the case went to trial, the Texas housewife removed all references to *gallo* from her Web site and replaced them with *galleto*, which means *little* rooster in Italian. Presumably, the little rooster, the pugnacious bantam fighting cock who still presided over the largest winery on earth nearly seventy years after taking it over from his father, had no objection to Jennifer King calling her ceramics little roosters.

"I have a small daughter who requires a lot of care," she explained. "I have a family. I'd like to not have to deal with this for the next however many years of my life."

"In the end, Jennifer decided to put the interests of her family ahead of the lawsuit," said Look. "She had to decide whether or not it was worth the trouble of going up against a big corporate giant like the Gallo family. That's what it came down to."

* * *

The Gallo reach extended farther out across the country, over the oceans, into other regions of the globe. Shortly after the turn of the century, E. & J. Gallo's imported wines accounted for between twelve and fifteen percent of the company's sales in the United States.

"The import category of wine in the United States has been growing for many years, and that's true for Gallo as well," said Roger Nabedian, a Gallo vice president and general manager. Gallo produced wine in fourteen foreign wineries stretching across eight countries on four different continents. The company sold its wines in ninety-two countries. Its imported varietals ranged from German Riesling, French Pinot Noir, and Italian Pinot Grigio to Argentinian Malbec, South African Shiraz, and Australian Chardonnay. "Over the last ten years, we have been able to get a good cross-section of the wines from the world's best wine-growing regions," said Nabedian.

In 2002, Gallo added three foreign wineries to its lineup: Don Miguel Gascon in Argentina, Sebeka in South

Africa, and Martin Codax in Spain. Bella Sera, one of Gallo's four Italian wineries, had risen to become the company's best-selling import among lower-priced wines, while Ecco Domani, which Gallo started from scratch in 1997, was its biggest seller in the premium imported-wine category. Wine consumers around the globe were imbibing seventy-five million cases of Gallo products a year under a dizzying array of labels, more than forty in all, most of which did not display the Gallo name anywhere on the bottle. Some of the company's more diverse domestic brands included Louis M. Martini, Mirassou, Rancho Zabaco, Turning Leaf, Gossamer Bay, Indigo Hills, Burlwood, Copperidge, Liberty Creek, Peter Vella, Frei Brothers, MacMurray Ranch (which Gallo acquired from the family of deceased actor Fred MacMurray), Bridlewood Estate, Barefoot Cellars, William Hill, Canyon Road, and dozens of others reflecting various levels of quality.

"We've always been consumer-focused, trying to read the consumer and see what's next," said Chris Gallo, a manager on the import side of the business and Ernest's grandson through David and his wife, Mary. "And we saw consumers branching out, developing an interest in wines they had not had before, including imports. So it was a natural extension for us."

Modesto was more and more a company town, with many residents employed in the winery's transportation, warehousing, and marketing operations just to deal with the increased supply of foreign wine being brought in. The company had grown to more than 4,600 employees, with its products sold across the length and breadth of the globe.

The company achieved a major marketing coup in 2007, when Wal-Mart agreed to sell a line of Gallo wines under its own brand names priced from two to five dollars a bottle, starting in 2008. "There's a large market for cheap wine," said Kathy Micken, professor of marketing at R. Williams University in Bristol, Rhode Island. "The right name is definitely important."

When the media heard of the arrangement, wine wags couldn't resist the temptation of suggesting brand names for Wal-Mart. Among them were Chateau Traileur Parc, White Trashfindel, Domaine Wal-Mart Merde du Pays, NASCARbernet, Chef Boyardeaux, Peanut Noir, Chateau des Moines, and Nasti Spumante. Ernest didn't appreciate the humor, but he was able to laugh all the way to the bank as the Wal-Mart line caught on, soon followed by "two-buck Chuck," an innovation of Ernest's nephew Fred Franzia, sold at Trader Joe's.

Since the labor wars of the 1970s, featuring heavyweight contenders Ernest Gallo versus Cesar Chavez, E. & J. Gallo Winery had established a reputation as a good place to work, as long as you remained loyal to the hand that fed you. Kristen Senseman, who got her start with Gallo after college as a wine saleswoman in Orange County, California, went on to start a small wine business of her own with her former employer's blessing. Kristen founded Hope Wine with seven other partners. The company is a charitable undertaking that donates fifty percent of its profits to people suffering from breast cancer, autism, and AIDS.

"I enjoyed my experience there at Gallo," she said. "I worked for a distributor, and then I was promoted to the wineries in Sonoma and Napa where I met Gina Gallo, who is basically a farm girl with jeans and muddy boots despite her beauty. I even went to yoga class with Matt. They put out a huge training manual for fine wines, and many of their ex-salespeople go into the pharmaceutical industry, where they can earn more money.

"Gallo has come a long way from the old gallon-jug image. They put out excellent wines today for relatively little money because of their vast facilities and land. Many vineyards have to charge more because of the high price for land today."

Gallo's image had undergone a major transition from the days of mob connections, violence, and Prohibition; from

Ernest packing heat as he roamed the nasty streets of Chicago to the modern world of the brilliant and beauteous Gina in her jeans and muddy boots, and her brother Matt Gallo protecting the environment and going to yoga classes. Ernest was still alive and kicking, but he was smart enough to let the new generation do the talking for him.

Chapter Twenty-five

"Unless you've been holed up on a desert island or living without TV," said wine reporter Robert Bradford, "you could have hardly failed to miss a very new, attractive, and articulate young Gallo presence on the scene, who has suddenly emerged in a blitz of international broadcast and print media exposure and coast-to-coast whistle-stop marketing appearances, that are heralding revolutionary new concepts and directions in Gallo wines. Her name is Gina, the granddaughter of Julio. And, as the family's third-generation winemaker, she is taking the family business onto an unprecedented upscale level with an exceptional line of fine, but also notably affordable, handcrafted wines labeled Gallo of Sonoma."

"Wine is pleasure," said Gina. "Wine should make you smile. It has to be beautiful to look at, beautiful to smell, and astonishing to taste. Great wine grapes are fragile things, and each type of grape has a distinct personality that you have to nurture from the vineyard to the glass. The basics of winemaking are pretty simple, but we are not making simple wines. I don't want the obvious. I'm looking for a little mystery and depth, and some 'Wow!' in there somewhere, too."

In 1998, when Gina was barely into her thirties, her 1995 Estate Chardonnay stunned the field by receiving the Best Chardonnay Worldwide award from the International Wine & Spirits Competition in London. The same year, at the Vinitaly Expo Competition in Italy, Gallo Sonoma's entries received the most medals of the 1,482 wines entered from twenty-two countries. Noteworthy among its wines was

Gina's Grand Gold Medal–winning 1996 Russian River Valley Laguna Ranch Vineyard Chardonnay. The prestigious San Francisco International Wine Competition named Gallo of Sonoma its Winery of the Year in 1998 for the second year running, and during a *Wall Street Journal* blind tasting of Cabernet Sauvignon, wine critics Dorothy Gaiter and John Brecher confessed complete surprise at the quality of a wine they had sampled.

"While the wines were, overall, quite good, one stood out," they wrote. "It stood out so much, in fact, that we were sure there had been some sort of mistake. It was everything a fine old 'claret' from Bordeaux should be. We noted: 'Lovely, complex nose; rich yet filled with crisp layers of taste. Alive in your mouth. Dust, soil, oak.' At the end of the tasting, we ripped off the bag fully expecting to see an old Bordeaux. Instead, it turned out to be Gallo! Yep, that Gallo." The wine in question was a 1992 Gallo Sonoma, which cost $9.99 at a neighborhood wine store.

"It's been one step at a time," said Gina, "making sure I'm really balancing my responsibilities. First and foremost, it's the wine and what's in the bottle. This is my first love and top priority. But, when there's time, I also enjoy talking about the wines. Getting out there is really good for me. It helps with my learning and my education instead of just staying at the winery and not exploring. The time I spend tasting and blending will always make a difference, of course. After that, I have to evaluate where I really need to be with all the other stuff to have an impact and do what's important."

In April 2008, Gina showed up for a press conference at the Park Avenue Spring restaurant on East 63rd Street in New York City, during which she presented her family's third annual award to a select group of gourmet food artisans. "It was quite a challenge to pick the Grand Prize winners, given the incredibly high caliber of foods that were submitted this year," said Gina, resplendent in a perfectly tailored dark suit set off by a vivid scarf, her long reddish-brown hair spilling onto her shoulders. "As my family celebrates its seventy-fifth anniversary of winemaking this year, it is especially momentous to honor this hardworking group of people who started out much like my grandfather Julio and great-uncle Ernest, and we are thrilled to welcome them into our extended family today."

Under Gina and Matt, Gallo Sonoma experimented with hundreds of varietal blends, various types of oak, yeasts, fermentation temperatures, and time frames. Matt oversaw eight Sonoma vineyard sites and developed different kinds of grapes to produce new wines. Brother and sister worked well in tandem, complementing each other with their different skills, and both believed that Sonoma Valley offered a better combination of weather and soil than could be found in France, Italy, Australia, or elsewhere in California for that matter. The convergence of microclimates in the Dry Creek Valley, for example, made it possible to make three distinct varieties of Zinfandel at three different vineyards, even though they were only a few miles apart. The soil changed dramatically along Dry Creek Road, which ran west out of Healdsburg over graceful hills and woodland stretching out toward Lake Sonoma. The land ranged from heavy tannins in the soil to a gravelly mix that changed the character of the wine. Some of the wines did better fermenting in French oak, also used for once-fermented Chardonnay, but French oak didn't work well at the Frei Brothers site, where American oak was better at capturing an abundance of spicy elements in the soil.

Farther west, along the cooler and more humid subregion near the coast, Pinot Noir flourished as an amalgam of Pinot from California and the Burgundy region of France. Viticultural problems existed along the coast, however, including bird migrations and powerful winds that made wine production less reliable, but the Gallos experimented constantly with techniques designed to overcome them. The Russian River area was also ideal for Pinot Noir, but it differed in taste and character from the same type of wine produced on the Sonoma Coast.

Marketing remained a challenge for the new generation of Gallos, since the public still identified the name with cheap jug wine for unsophisticated consumers. For the first time in E. & J. Gallo's history, a small tasting room opened on the square in Healdsburg, in an attempt to introduce the wine-drinking public to the higher-quality wines sporting the Gallo label, at prices far below those available at Matanzas Creek, Seghesio, Farrari-Carano, Kendall-Jackson, and other upscale vineyards. Gallo Sonoma hoped that their wine would speak for itself and overcome the public's distrust of the Gallo name.

"What it all comes down to," said Gina, "is getting consumers to really look at themselves and say, 'Do I enjoy this? Is it giving me pleasure?' And so much of the success lies in that second, third, fourth, and fifth purchase. We're finding that once we get people to try it, they're going to come back again. Even with the new line of wines we're making here, we're not going to get crazy on our prices. We're going to keep that value there. It's the reason people will come back and buy another bottle."

Gallo Sonoma wines earned the distinction of being the only American wines that have won the Premio Gran Vinitaly award three times—in 1998, 2001, and 2002. "Many winemakers' best decisions are instinctive, and Gina has great instincts," said Mike Martini, winemaker at Gallo's Louis M. Martini Winery in Napa. "I believe wine is an extension of the winemaker's personality, and as Gina has matured into quite an international personality, the dimensions of her wine have followed."

"The Gallo winemaking empire is putting out better and better wines," said American wine maven Robert Parker. "The gorgeous 2005 Pinot Gris, at thirteen dollars, is a food-friendly crisp and fruity wine. The refreshing 2004 Chardonnay, also thirteen dollars, reveals classic aromas of lemon butter, white peaches, and honeysuckle with little evidence of oak."

Ah yes, butter, peaches, and honeysuckle surely beat the hell out of the acidic plonk sold in gallon jugs two generations earlier.

"It's so unusual that the Gallo family continues to reinvent itself over the years and do well in a totally different market," said Jon Fredrikson, president of wine industry consultants Gomberg, Fredrikson and Associates. "Many companies go through cycles, and some have gone away, but Gallo has survived. To use a grandchild to promote the very same label is a remarkable development and probably not repeated in many other businesses. It's a wonderful legacy to hand down to future generations."

With its acquisition of Louis M. Martini in 2002, the Gallo family made its first foray into the Napa Valley east of Sonoma. Martini was one of the oldest family-owned operations in the state and gave Gallo its first wholly owned winery in the region. The reaction of many of the locals was similar to that expressed by Sonoma activists when Gallo invaded that valley a decade earlier. "Napa hardly has any farmers left," lamented a longtime Napa activist who asked to remain anonymous. "We have to import vegetables and basic foods, in spite of our rich agricultural land. Though wine begins with grapes, it is mainly a value-added product, so most of the money goes to those in the industrial parts of the operation. Who can afford to compete with luxury wines and to farm food here?"

Thirty years earlier, Napa Valley was dotted with numerous small farms where cattle, prunes, and walnuts competed successfully with grapes. In 1965, Napa Valley hosted only about two dozen wineries. But by 1990, that number had exploded to about 200, about the same as in Napa's sister valley to the west. By the turn of the millennium, grapes represented ninety-two percent of Napa County's total agricultural production.

* * *

Seven years into the new millennium, the rest of the old guard finally passed on, leaving the new generations to carry on the Gallo name. Joseph died on February 17, 2007, at eighty-seven years of age. He died at his home in the Central Valley, where he had lived out his life in failing health since the trial against his brothers nearly two decades earlier. The cause of his death was complications from a series of strokes, according to his son Mike. Joe's passing went largely unheralded by the world at large. Just before he died, Ernest had called his sister-in-law Patricia and expressed interest in seeing his brother again.

"I asked Joe if Ernest could come over," she said. "He wants to see how you are. I told Ernest he could come to see Joe. Then Ernest said it would be 'too hard on me'—he was talking about himself," she said with a rueful laugh, "so they had no contact after the trial."

Patricia, Mike, and his sister Linda honored Joe's life quietly with a private memorial service attended by family and some close friends in the community. The business he started in 1979 rolled peacefully across more than 12,000 acres and had grown into one of California's largest cheese-making enterprises. Members of Ernest's and Julio's families issued a statement to the press, stating, "Our family's sympathies go out to Joe's family at this difficult time."

In addition to his children and his wife, Joe left behind his stepson, Sam Gardali, and six grandchildren. Aside from his business interests, his legacy included a love for the outdoors and a devotion to environmental causes. Over the years, Joe had donated several thousand acres of land to the United States Fish and Wildlife Service and to the State of California for wildlife refuges and parks. In 2001, Joseph Gallo Farms received an award from the Environmental Protection Agency for its preservation efforts.

And then it was the old lion's turn to meet his maker. The old man's engine simply wore out. Ernest had not been seriously ill, and he died somewhat unexpectedly at age ninety-seven in his home on Maze Boulevard in Modesto on March 6, 2007, three weeks after the death of his youngest brother. Typically, the family did not give out the exact cause of death, although one can assume that his age was cause enough. In contrast to Joe, Ernest's death made international headlines. Wine insiders estimated that just the year before, E. & J. Gallo Winery had shipped about seventy-five million cases of wine and had produced between one-quarter and one-third of all wine and wine-related products sold in the United States.

At the time of Ernest's death, the Gallo empire encompassed many thousands of acres of vineyards stretching from Modesto to Napa and, from there, over to Sonoma, as well as a network of wineries anchored by the world's largest, headquartered in Modesto.

"No one worked harder to build the base of American wine drinkers that we have today," said Joseph Ciatti, owner of the nation's largest grape and bulk wine broker. "Ernest made quality wine for the masses at a good price."

"Gallo put California on the wine map of the United States and then, through exporting, he put California on the wine map of the world," said Nat DiBuduo, president of Fresno-based Allied Grape Growers, the state's largest wine-grape-growing cooperative. In September 2006, *Forbes* ranked Ernest Gallo and his family number 297 on the magazine's list of the 400 richest Americans, with an estimated net worth of $1.3 billion.

Walter Bregman, vice president of marketing for Gallo from 1974 to 1979, said Ernest was tough because "his name was on the door. While it was true that he suffered fools badly and didn't much care for lackeys, toadies, and lickspittles, he was also a straightforward businessman who didn't play games."

Even at age ninety, Ernest had been putting in full days at the winery plus a couple of hours after dinner, although he shortened his workdays in the years just before his death. "In nothing that my brother and I ever undertook did we have the slightest doubt it would be successful," Ernest said at the time. "We didn't do the impossible. We did the obvious."

"My father was blessed to live a long, healthy life, and he was particularly proud to see his grandchildren and his brother's grandchildren become involved in the family business," said Ernest's son Joseph, the chief executive officer of the family business.

After his father's death, with the son now firmly ensconced at the helm, Gallo announced that it had signed an exclusive distribution deal with Bodegas El Patrocinio, a large wine cooperative in Spain. The partnership was expected to result in higher sales for Gallo wines throughout Europe under their Spanish labels, which included a popular brand named Martin Codex. E. & J. Gallo also ramped up its charitable profile, continuing its support of the "Taste of the NFL Wine Program" to donate between two and three million meals to hungry people. But Ernest's death did nothing to heal the wounds within the Gallo family.

"Once Ernest passed away, we were supposed to be a family again," said Mike Gallo, "but that hasn't happened because, even though Julio's side of the family pretended that this was all about Ernest, in reality it was about both of them. To this day, a lot of people don't like what they did to my father. They tried to pretend afterwards that everything was okay, except it wasn't okay—not as far as my father and I were concerned.

"It continues with Joe and Bob. I see Julio's son Bob and his wife, Marie, maybe a couple of times a year. Bob and I are on the board of trustees of the University of California, Merced. I see them on occasion there at meetings. The other family members I really don't see. Once in a while we'll run into each other. We're friendly and cordial, but that's about it."

In the end, the picture of Ernest and Julio that we are left with is clouded and unfocused. It reflects the variegated portrait of complex human beings and the myriad forces that propelled them. Ernest and Julio were extraordinary people, movers and shakers, empire builders. There is that dark side of them but also the genius of the men, particularly Ernest, who created the most dynamic and far-reaching wine empire in the world. There is a curious balance at play here—light mixed with darkness, good tempered by evil. Ernest and Julio have passed from the scene, but their descendants live on. They are, perhaps, not as driven as the founders of the dynasty in the sense that their challenge, while great, is less daunting. They are charged with being keepers of the family name, with the task of making sure their empire remains intact. Ernest and Julio, on the other hand, had to create an empire from the ruins of Prohibition and its concomitants, including blood, lust, greed, and murder. So far, the transition plan Ernest put in place appears to be working. The latest generation of Gallos has assumed more and more responsibility for the company's operating policies. The youngest members of the clan have begun to fling open the windows, unlock the shutters, and let the sun shed some light into the dark corners of the Gallo empire.

Afterword

"Gallo's big entry into Napa Valley was through Louis Martini, which we had a hand in managing," said Oscar Renteria, son of a Mexican-American vineyard manager who got his start picking grapes in the days of Cesar Chavez. "Gallo is far and away number one by volume. They've got those great vineyards in Sonoma County and are making wonderful wines. They got to be number one through marketing, which a lot of people in this business are not very good at."

The sun beat high overhead, shining down brilliantly on the deck of Oscar's spacious Spanish-style home with its commanding view of the valley from the hills above Napa. His two little girls giggled, scratching on the windows inside the house, beckoning for their father's attention after his long day out in the vineyards.

"My father, Salvador, met Ernest and Julio a few times. My father was one of the first [Mexican-American] growers of fruit in the valley, and he sold grapes to most of the vintners here. He has a long history with the Mondavi family in particular, and he goes back to the days when the Gallos were buying grapes from Napa Valley. We manage about seventeen hundred acres in Napa now and are one of the largest management companies in Northern California. The Gallos are incredibly savvy and sensitive to changes in the market. I think it was last fall that wine overcame beer in consumption in the United States, and the Gallos are extremely well positioned to deal with the changing economy today and into the future. It's amazing that they've managed to keep their company private all these years."

The grape-growing and wine-marketing economy was indeed changing rapidly in 2008. Throughout the Central Valley, where the Gallos still maintained their headquarters, many vineyards had given way to housing subdivisions to accommodate long-distance commuters who could no longer afford houses closer to San Francisco. The farmers were tempted by the allure of cashing out on the skyrocketing prices for land in the Central Valley and were selling to real estate developers for astronomical sums in ever-increasing numbers. Such was the state of economics in California that commuters didn't mind being on the road four to five hours every day— a minimum of two hours each way—in exchange for the luxury of putting an affordable roof over their heads. This development threatened the major vintners in the area, since it was shrinking the amount of land devoted to growing grapes and drying up valuable supplies. The Gallos decided to tackle the problem head-on.

"The Gallos just put contracts out for fruit in the area," said Oscar. "They agreed to pay $450 a ton for Cabernet and $350 a ton for Chardonnay grapes." These prices were almost double what they had been a couple of years earlier. "This is the first time the Gallo family has offered contracts to entice growers not to pull their vineyards out," Oscar continued, "and it's resulted in the highest prices we've seen in maybe ten years. They're very savvy, very smart. They have the foresight, and these big companies have to figure out a way to predict the future. I'm talking about grape supply. I have a feeling that the Gallo family has an incredible data system and vision for predicting what the harvest will be this year and what their estimates are for the next year."

The Gallo initiative led to expanding optimism throughout the industry, a confidence that the future looked bright for selling its goods, given the increasing demand for wine across the country and, indeed, the globe.

"You go to Mexico," said Oscar, "and you'll see Gallo. You'll see the big boys down there, not the small guys.

Gallo serves a very important part of the market since the majority of wine today sells for less than ten dollars a bottle, which is hardly the average price of wine here in Napa Valley. The luxury segment here runs about thirty-five to forty dollars a bottle and up. So Gallo's market is very important. They see the big picture. Their main competition out there is Australian, Chilean, Italian, Argentine, and French wines at those price points. If the Gallos weren't there to command that segment of the market, the foreigners would. Their cost of land, their cost of labor is much lower."

Over seven or eight years through the end of 2007, the cost of farming in general in California rose more than twenty-five percent, largely because of higher labor costs and the soaring price for land. The entrenched wineries that purchased land a couple of decades earlier maintained a major advantage over newcomers to the industry, who had to pay ever-higher prices for a patch of ground on which to grow grapes.

"We can compete very well anywhere in the world," said Ernest's son Joseph. The company that reflected the personalities of Ernest and Julio for decades started to open up after Ernest's death. The newest generation had become adept at spotting trends and taking advantage of opportunities in the marketplace.

The company has continued to maintain a cost structure that can compete with winemakers anywhere in the world, according to Joseph Gallo. He strode purposefully through his massive bottling plant in Modesto, the largest glass factory in the western United States. Joseph planned to expand it further in 2008 and boost its capacity to one billion bottles a year. Nearby, dozens of towering white tanks stored ninety-three million gallons of wine, while Gallo's giant winery thirty miles south in Livingston held 157 million gallons.

"We need to keep the family involved and connected to the business as we get generations away from the founders," said Chris Gallo. "We need to be able to pass down to future generations that this is our land and this is how we make wine."

The Gallos have their vast landholdings, their low-cost distribution network, and the ultramodern, highly technical infrastructure they have built over the decades. In 2008, they were still the most powerful and prevalent wine brand in the world, followed by Hardy's (Australia), Concha y Toro (Chile), Robert Mondavi (United States), Yellow Tail (Australia), Beringer (United States), and Jacob's Creek (Australia). At the moment, the Gallo wine empire appears to be self-sustaining and unlikely to be dethroned from the catbird seat within the industry anytime soon.

Acknowledgments

Researching this book has been an adventure in itself. I began the process during the summer of 2007 by reading everything about the Gallo family that I could get my hands on. I started with *Blood and Wine: The Unauthorized Story of the Gallo Wine Empire* by Ellen Hawkes (Simon & Schuster, 1993). Hawkes's book is a thoroughly researched biography of the Gallo dynasty. The author covers the dark side of Ernest in particular, but what is missing is the genius of the man who created the largest and most powerful wine empire in the world. Nevertheless, her book was a primary source of information, particularly about the early years of the Gallo family before and during Prohibition.

Next I read Ernest and Julio's joint autobiography, *Ernest & Julio: Our Story*, with Bruce B. Henderson (Times Books, 1994), which was written with the intention of presenting the brothers' version of their family and business history as they wanted the public to see it. The book is invaluable for its insights into the wine industry and the Gallos' place in it, but to say that it is a whitewash of the family's beginnings and business style is an exercise in gross understatement. Ernest, more than anyone else, understood the value of perception over reality; Cesar Chavez taught him that lesson in the 1970s, and Ernest was determined to get his and Julio's own record of their history into the marketplace to counter negative press the brothers received in other quarters.

Other books that proved helpful in setting the stage for my original research efforts included Thomas Pinney's *A History of Wine in America Volume 2: From Prohibition to the Present* (University of California Press, 2007), which is a veritable encyclopedia of wine industry facts and figures; Glen Martin's and Jay Stuller's *Through the Grapevine* (HarperCollins, 1994); Julia Flynn Siler's *The House of Mondavi: The Rise and Fall of an American Wine Dynasty* (Gotham, 2007), a well-researched and well-written biography of the Mondavi family and the wine industry in general, with peripheral insights into the Gallo family; John Kobler's *Ardent Spirits: The Rise and Fall of Prohibition* (G. P. Putnam's Sons, 1973); Stephen Birmingham's *California Rich* (Simon & Schuster, 1980); *Winemaking in California* by Ruth Teiser (McGraw-Hill, 1983); and *A Social History of Alcohol: Drinking and Culture in Modern Society,* edited by Susanna Barrows, Robin Room, and Jeffrey Verhey (Alcohol Research Group, 1987).

In addition, I read hundreds of articles about the Gallo wine clan that appeared in the general media, much of it available on the Internet or in the archives of various California newspapers, including the *Fresno Bee* and the *Modesto Bee*. I also sent for and received FBI files on some Gallo family members under the Freedom of Information Act. Other sources, including retired CIA and FBI agents, provided interesting information not otherwise available.

After reading everything available on the subject, I commenced my original research efforts in earnest. I started by sending e-mail messages to more than a dozen members of the Gallo family, letting them know about the book I was writing and asking for their cooperation. In the fall of 2007, I received a message from Donna Bradley, an assistant to Mike Gallo, the son of Joseph Gallo, who was Ernest and Julio's younger brother, saying that Mike would be willing to meet with me on February 14, 2008, during my visit to California. Ernest and Julio's side of the family proved a bit more recalcitrant, but they did ask for a list of sample questions, which I provided via e-mail.

Before leaving for California, I uncovered various sources and interviewed them by telephone. Some of them are former employees of the Gallos who were willing to speak both on and off the record; others occupy prominent positions in the wine industry; others yet were sons of former employees who had worked at the Gallo winery as far back as the 1930s; and one was the son of the man who first discovered the bodies of Joe and Susie Gallo, the parents of Ernest, Julio, and Joe Jr., on their Fresno ranch in 1933. Their names are provided below.

On February 12, 2008, my wife, Marie, and I flew to Oakland, California, rented a car, and headed over to Fresno in the Central Valley. The following morning we drove to the home of Gene and Joyce Brengetto; Gene is the son of Peter Brengetto, who together with Gene's brother (now deceased) found the bodies of Joe and Susie in June 1933. I had interviewed Gene by phone a couple of months earlier, and my wife and I interviewed him again at his home. He and his wife then graciously offered to drive us over to the site of the murders on the former Gallo ranch west of town. We followed them in our own car, driving to the farm about three miles from the ranch, where Gene had lived as a boy and played with Joe Gallo Jr. After snapping a few photographs, we drove over to the site of the murders, got out of our cars, and began to take some pictures.

At this point, a Fresno County police car pulled up alongside our own vehicles. Two officers got out and asked us what we were doing. I introduced myself, explained the nature of the book I was writing, and the reason for my visit to the area. One of the officers, a fellow named Jose, said he used to work at the Gallo winery in Modesto. He took note of our license plate number, and then he and his partner followed us in their squad car for a good ten minutes as we headed toward downtown Fresno to visit the *Fresno Bee* and the local library. We found some old newspaper articles in the library archives covering the deaths on the ranch and printed them for our files. That afternoon, we visited a restaurant owned by Rudy Wagner, the son of a man who had worked for Ernest and Julio during their early years in the wine business following Prohibition. Rudy essentially confirmed accounts appearing elsewhere about his father's involvement with the Gallos before World War II.

The next morning, February 14, 2008, Marie and I drove an hour up Route 99 to the small town of Atwater, the headquarters of Joseph Farms, where we met with Mike Gallo, the son of Joseph Gallo Jr., who died in 2007. Mike spent the next two hours talking to us about Gallo family history, his father's relationship with his older brothers, the startling lawsuit that Ernest and Julio launched against Joe, Joe's lawsuit against his brothers, and Joe's health problems in the aftermath of the trials. Mike supplied us with contact information for his sister Linda, his stepmother, Patricia, and his and his deceased father's lawyer, John Whiting.

The next stop was Modesto, a twenty-minute spin up the road from Atwater. As I describe in this book, Modesto appears to be a company town controlled to a great extent by the Gallo family. Ernest and Julio lived there with their families before their deaths, and, as during their lifetimes, their company continues to supply a significant number of the jobs in town. The Gallos built the art center that is the centerpiece for most of the cultural activities in the area, and the family exerts great influence over the local movers and shakers and the local newspaper, in my opinion. After visiting the Gallo family residence and the Mediterranean-style home built by Ernest and Julio's father eight decades earlier—both of them located on Maze Boulevard west of town—Marie and I drove over to the *Modesto Bee* to see what information the newspaper had in its archives. We were a bit startled when the newspaper's chief librarian greeted us in the lobby and said that it was against the newspaper's policy to sell its photos to the public.

"But I'm an author. I'm doing a book on the Gallos, and I want to buy some photos for inserts."

"We...we don't operate that way."

"I don't understand. I've written books about Donald Trump, Rupert Murdoch, Alan Greenspan, and the Hunts of Texas. I deal with the Associated Press all the time. They show me what they've got, I pick out what I want, and I pay them for the rights."

"We're much more...much more conservative here," she said, visibly nervous.

I had heard stories about how Ernest, when he was alive, had put the fear of God—and the Gallo legal department—into one major publisher to keep it from widely disseminating information he didn't want released to the public. The specter of the old patriarch still loomed high over the town nearly a year after his death.

After Modesto, we drove east of Sacramento to Jackson, an old gold-mining town in the foothills of the Sierra Nevada, to get some information about the area and take pictures of the building that had once been the Central Hotel, a combination rooming house, bar, and brothel owned and operated by the father and mother of Ernest, Julio, and Joe.

The following day, Marie and I drove west to Napa to interview Oscar Renteria. Oscar was a fund of information about the economics of the wine business today, the personalities who dominate the industry, and other pertinent details.

Marie and I finished our research tour in Healdsburg in Sonoma County, west of Napa, where the Gallos maintain a wine-tasting room downtown and operate a well-guarded winery—no visitors permitted without an invitation—along Dry Creek Road west of town on a rolling swath of ranches and wineries stretching out to the mountains in the distance.

Back in Maryland, my home base, I continued with the interviewing process, talking to Mike Gallo's sister, stepmother, and lawyer, as well as other sources who either work currently for the Gallos or did at one time. I interviewed the owners of boutique vineyards and environmentalists in Sonoma, who had criticized the Gallos' land-recontouring practices when they came into the region. Many said that the newest generation of Gallos, particularly the grandchildren of Julio, had changed direction entirely and are currently good stewards of the land that has supplied them with so much of their wealth.

I was still hoping to gain further cooperation from Ernest and Julio's side of the family, and my efforts were rewarded when Gina Gallo referred one of my research assistants to DeVries, Gallo's public relations agency in New York City. The agency also handles PR for Pepperidge Farm, Starbucks, Pepsico, Procter & Gamble, and other major corporations. My contact there, Jessica Miller, was extremely helpful, providing me with detailed information about E. & J. Gallo Winery and the wine industry in general, and she offered to serve as an intermediary with various members of the Gallo family.

I would like to thank the following people, in no particular order, for their cooperation in writing this book: Mike Gallo, Patricia Gallo, Gina Gallo, Susan Hensley, Linda Jelacich, Robert Mondavi, John Whiting, Donna Bradley, Gene Brengetto, Joyce Brengetto, Rudy Wagner Jr., Jon Shastid, Paul Merrigan, Karen Senseman, Oscar Renteria, Jerry Crawford, Caroline Crawford, George Davis, Charlie Barra, Martha Barra, John Parducci, Steve Carmell, Jeffrey Look, Joseph P. Harris, John Giumarra, Amy Trenkle, Jennifer King, Dan Solomon, Jessica Miller, Doug Draeseke, Robert Bradford, Robert Krulwich, Phillip Freese, John Statzer, Michael Presley, Ed Weber, Jaimie Douglas, Laura Goldman, Kathy Micken, Dorothy Gaiter, John Brecher, John Fredrikson, Joseph Ciatti, Nat DiBuduo, Jay DeStefano, Cindy DeStefano, Greg Welsh, Jill Welsh, Tim Fish, Dana Nigro, Larry Cenotto, Loree Stroup, Kimberly Wooten, Scott Baxter, John Poultney, John Nelson, Robert Nelson, Aldo Lavotti, Joanne Sbranti, Kelly Conrad, Dan Michael, Anthony Elia, Lloyd Jassin, Steven Schechter, Mary Burnham, Hal Riney, and countless others who agreed to speak to me off the record.

A special note of thanks goes out to my son, J. D. Tuccille, a freelance writer based in Arizona who provided some valuable research material; to my daughter, Christine Tuccille Merry, a graphic artist based in Maryland who helped with the photographs in this book; and to my wife, Marie Winkler Tuccille, who worked with me as an indefatigable research assistant and photographer.

Finally, but certainly not least, this book would not have seen the light of day had it not been for the enthusiasm and indefatigable efforts of my agent Linda Konner. Linda believed in this project from the beginning and provided insightful suggestions that helped move the book along to fruition. In addition, the look and tone of this biography owes a lot to Michael Viner and his first-rate team at Phoenix Books, including Dan Smetanka, Henrietta Tiefenthaler, Judith Abarbanel, and Ben Prost, who helped with the final design, editorial, and marketing touches.

If I have left anyone out of this list who deserves to be included, I apologize for my oversight.

Chapter Notes

AUTHOR'S NOTE

The statement that Joseph Gallo, Ernest and Julio's father, was connected to the Capone mob in Chicago is well documented in Ellen Hawkes's biography *Blood and Wine* and in newspaper accounts of his activities during Prohibition.

References to Mike Gallo, Ernest and Julio's uncle, as a "West Coast Al Capone" and "notorious East Bay bootlegger" are taken from several sources, including federal investigations of his activities during Prohibition, newspaper reports, and interviews with former Gallo associates.

Rumors that Joseph and Susie Gallo were actually murdered come from Hawkes, various newspaper accounts, and interviews with Gallo family members and associates.

PROLOGUE

Circumstances surrounding Joe and Susie's move to Fresno come from Hawkes, Ernest and Julio's autobiography, and interviews with family members. The differing accounts of Julio's meeting with his father the day before his parents' deaths come from Hawkes and interviews with several Gallo family members. Accounts of Joe Sr. brutalizing his wife and children come from several sources, including the *Los Angeles Times*, Ernest and Julio's autobiography, Hawkes, and the petition for divorce filed by Susie against Joseph.

Details of the discovery of the bodies of Joe and Susie appeared in the *Fresno Bee* and are also taken from Hawkes, testimony given during the investigation of their deaths, and interviews with Gene Brengetto, who corroborated stories of the incident told to him by his father.

The different versions of what happened after the deaths of Joe and Susie come from Ernest and Julio's autobiography, Hawkes, interviews with Gene Brengetto, and various Gallo family members. Also, Ernest admitted in his own book that he had bought a pistol of the same caliber and make as the one found at the crime scene during one of his trips to Chicago during Prohibition.

CHAPTER ONE

Al Capone has been the subject of numerous books and movies dealing with his rise to power in Chicago and his role there as a mob kingpin during Prohibition. The Gallos' connection to Capone comes from many sources: Ernest and Julio admitted in their autobiography that their father was a bootlegger during Prohibition who was charged with violating the Volstead Act, and that they delivered grapes to the Chicago market when they were in high school; Hawkes documents the Gallos' activities in great detail in her own book; numerous newspapers carried stories of the Gallos and their trips to the Chicago and East Coast markets; and Gallo family members and associates corroborated those stories in interviews.

The role of vine-glo—fermenting grapes that were converted into wine within weeks—during Prohibition comes from Hawkes, Thomas Pinney's *A History of Wine in America Volume 2: From Prohibition to the Present*, and interviews with people in the wine industry. Julio discussed the role that Jack Riorda played during his trips to the New Jersey market during Prohibition in his joint autobiography with Ernest. Joe Gallo's brutality toward Ernest and Julio and his leniency toward youngest brother Joe come from several sources, including Hawkes, Ernest and Julio's autobiography, various newspaper accounts, and interviews with members of the Gallo family.

Mike Gallo, Ernest and Julio's uncle, was a notorious con artist and East Bay bootlegger according to many sources, including Hawkes, various newspaper accounts at the time, his own statements during several investigations of his activities, and statements made by Earl Warren, future governor and chief justice of the United States, when he was the district attorney of Alameda County. Mike Gallo served time in jail on several occasions for his activities. The story about the federal agents descending on the family homestead searching for illegal stills and arresting Joe Gallo comes from Hawkes and various family members.

CHAPTER TWO

The early years of Joe and Mike Gallo are based on Ernest and Julio's autobiography, Hawkes, and various newspaper accounts. Descriptions of their appearances and the Biancos come from photographs taken during the period. The history of Jackson, California, and the hotel that Joe and Susie bought is drawn from visits to the area, interviews with local residents, historical monographs of the era, and photographs of the site as it stands today.

Joe's brutality is documented earlier in these notes. His foul language toward his wife comes from Hawkes and from Susie's petition for divorce from Joe. My use of Italian is my own innovation, based on reports that they spoke mostly Italian to each other, and he would have been more likely to use the Italian epithets rather than curse her in English.

Joe's sale of the Central Hotel to Pietro Genolio and Genolio's subsequent attempted suicide were reported in the local newspaper and covered by Hawkes. Ernest and Julio discussed their parents' separation in their autobiography.

Susie's accusations against her husband come from her divorce petition. The reasons for Susie's decision to reconcile with Joe are my own speculation.

CHAPTER THREE

See earlier citations for accounts of Joe's brutality and the details of his separation from Susie. Descriptions of Ernest and Julio are taken from photographs of them at the time. The story about Mike's trial in 1913 comes from Hawkes, accounts in the *San Francisco Chronicle* and *San Francisco Call-Bulletin*, and court records. Details of Battista Bianco's estate come from Hawkes and probate records. The growing fervor for Prohibition has been documented in great detail in various sources, including *The Social History of Alcohol: Drinking and Culture in Modern Society,* edited by Susanna Barrows, Robin Room, and Jeffrey Verhey, and by John Kobler.

Details surrounding the Gallo family's life in Antioch come from Hawkes and interviews with various Gallo family associates. The insinuation that Joe Jr. may have been the product of an illicit affair comes from an interview with a former Gallo executive; its lack of credibility is my own speculation. The existence of the still in Livermore comes from Hawkes, court documents, and the recollections of Gallo family associates. See earlier citation for Mike Gallo's reputation as a "West Coast Al Capone."

Ernest's account of his high school fights appeared in his joint autobiography with Julio. The Gallo family's move to Escalon and their purchase of vineyards are taken from Hawkes and depositions made by Ernest, Julio, and Joe at their trial later. The details about the yields from different types of grapes come from various books, including Ernest and Julio's autobiography and Thomas Pinney's *A History of Wine in America*. The interview with Joe Sciaroni is taken from Hawkes. The description of Joe's Mediterranean-style

villa in Modesto is based on personal observation during a
visit to the site.

CHAPTER FOUR

See earlier citation for Ernest's description of the pistol
he bought in Chicago. Mike Gallo's purchase of the
Woodbridge Winery with Sebastiani is taken from Hawkes
and was reported in the *Lodi News-Sentinel*. Mike's arrest in
1928 was documented in a Department of Justice report and
covered in the *San Francisco Chronicle*. The collapse of the
grape market in 1929 appeared in Pinney's history of wine
and other sources. The construction of underground tanks to
store their wine was mentioned by Ernest in his deposition
during his and Julio's trial against their brother and was
covered by Hawkes. It was confirmed by interviews with
former Gallo employees.

Details surrounding Mike and Celia's divorce
appeared in records of their divorce proceedings and were
covered in the *San Francisco Chronicle*. The confrontation
between Ernest and Julio and their father appeared in Ernest
and Julio's autobiography and Hawkes's book, and it was
confirmed in interviews with Gallo family associates. Ernest's
courtship of Amelia Franzia comes from interviews with
former Gallo executives and other sources. The account of Joe
chasing Ernest and Julio, their flight to El Centro, California,
and subsequent return comes from interviews with former
Gallo executives, Hawkes, *Fortune* magazine, and Stephen
Birmingham's *California Rich*.

See earlier citation for the role of vine-glo during
Prohibition. Capone's threats against winemakers who
attempted to bypass him appeared in the *Chicago Tribune*,
Winemaking in California by Ruth Teiser, and various articles
dealing with Capone's activities during Prohibition. Details of
Mike Gallo's arrest in 1931 come from Hawkes, Department

of Justice files, and newspaper coverage during the time. Joe and Susie's disappearance from Modesto and move to Fresno comes from several sources, including Hawkes, Ernest and Julio's autobiography, newspaper reports, and interviews with Gallo family members.

CHAPTER FIVE

The account of Joe and Susie's move to Fresno is based on interviews with Mike Gallo, Patricia Gallo, and various family associates. Ernest and Julio describe their parents' move in their own book. Hawkes also covers the move and the dispute between Ernest and Julio on one hand and their father on the other. See earlier citation for the differing accounts of Julio's visit the day before his parents' deaths. Julio's courtship of Aileen is covered in his own autobiography with Ernest and in Hawkes's biography.

Ernest's cryptic description of his parents' deaths appears in his book with Julio. The caliber and make of the pistol found at the crime scene comes from Hawkes and the report of the police investigation of the deaths. Hawkes, Ernest, and Julio report different versions of which family members were informed first. Ernest's testimony appears in the report of the investigation. The question of Joe owing money to the "wrong people" comes from an interview with a Gallo family member who asked not to be identified.

The location of fingerprints on the murder weapon appears in Hawkes and in the report of the investigation. The check found in the mailbox is taken from various sources, including Hawkes and newspaper reports from the period. The story about the bodies of the dogs discovered by the neighbor comes from interviews with Gene Brengetto. Gene also said that his father, Peter, was mystified that he was not called to testify at the inquest. Reasons why Joe and Susie were hiding out in Fresno are based on newspaper articles about their deaths and my own speculation, based on interviews with Mike and Patricia Gallo.

CHAPTER SIX

The ditty about Prohibition comes from Thomas Pinney's book, cited earlier. The thoughts about what brought about the end of Prohibition are taken from an article by Don Boudreaux, "The Politics of Prohibition," and represent my own thinking on the subject. The details about Susie's will were revealed in documents unearthed by Joe Gallo's lawyer, John Whiting, many years later and confirmed during an interview with Whiting. The underground lake full of wine is taken from interviews with Gallo family associates and other winemakers. Hawkes bases Ernest's conversation with Leonard Rhodes on a report.

The Gallo family's contributions to politicians from both major parties, and the exact dollar figures, are public information. Ernest discusses the size of the loan he received from the Franzias in his book with Julio. Ernest's meeting with Barbera and Paterno comes from Hawkes and the Gallo autobiography. The proceeds from the liquidation of Joe and Susie's estate are detailed in the court proceedings. Joe's life with his brothers and sisters-in-law in Modesto comes from interviews with Mike Gallo, Patricia Gallo, and other family associates.

The division of labor established by Ernest and Julio is well documented in newspaper reports, in interviews with various family associates, and by Ernest and Julio themselves. Their physical descriptions come from former Gallo executives and members of the family.

CHAPTER SEVEN

The Gallo brothers' wine storage capacity comes from their own account, interviews with former Gallo executives, and various newspaper reports and books on the period. Ernest's contentious relationship with Amelia's family comes from interviews with former Gallo employees. Julio, Pinney, various articles, and interviews cover the logistics of buying grapes, making wine, bringing it to market, and paying off debts with other vintners.

Ernest's disagreements with Julio are covered by themselves and by Hawkes and are also taken from interviews with various sources. Ernest discusses his illness in his own book with Julio. The investigation of the Gallos for using dyes in their wine is covered by Hawkes and is based on public records and interviews with former Gallo employees. Rudy Wagner's comments were confirmed in an interview with his son.

The follow-up investigation of the Gallos' use of wine and caramel in their brandy comes from Hawkes, public records, interviews with former Gallo associates, and Ernest's own recollection of the incident. Figures reflecting U.S. alcohol preferences at the time are taken from various sources, including Pinney, Siler, Ernest and Julio, and newspaper articles. The unintended consequences of Prohibition have been well documented by various scholars of the era. The Gallos' purchase of the New Orleans distributorship is well covered by Ernest and Julio and by Hawkes.

CHAPTER EIGHT

Julio tells the story of his ruptured appendix and his encounter with the doctors in his joint autobiography with Ernest. Julio also relates his version of Joe's reluctance to go into business with them in his book. Julio's interview with the reporter about the winery's origins appeared in the *Modesto*

Bee. The delicate cycle of turning grapes into wine is covered by Julio in his book with Ernest. Ernest discusses his own problems with distribution in their autobiography.

The circumstances surrounding Joe's inheritance of the family estate upon reaching his majority come from interviews with John Whiting, Mike Gallo, and other family members and associates. Julio's illness and his conversation with Wagner are covered by Hawkes and Julio and were confirmed during an interview with Wagner's son. Julio discusses his confinement to the sanitarium in his book. Thoughts about the nature of his ailment and any possible guilt he may have experienced come from interviews with former Gallo executives and from my own speculation.

Ernest's purchase of the tanker cars and the use of tartar by the government are discussed by Ernest and are covered by Hawkes, Pinney, and other sources. Comments by Wagner regarding the sale of molasses to the government come from Hawkes and were confirmed in an interview with Wagner's son. Joe's service during World War II is based on interviews with various family associates.

CHAPTER NINE

The prices of wine grapes and price controls during the war are discussed by various sources, including Pinney, and by Ernest in his book with Julio. Pinney, Ernest, and Julio talk about the main competition during the period and the entry of major distillers into the wine business in their books. The haphazard labeling of various types of red and white wine at the time is covered by the sources mentioned above. Simon's quote is taken from Pinney.

Ernest's conversation with Joe in Denver comes from Ernest and Julio's book; it appears self-serving, considering that the book was written after their court battles in the 1980s. Indeed, Joe later denied that the conversation ever took place. The reasons behind the differing accounts are based on my own speculation. Julio recounts the story of the pig in his book with Ernest.

Joe's courtship of Mary Ann Arata comes from various sources, including Hawkes and interviews with various members of the family. The account of Ernest and Julio pulling Joe in different directions after the war comes from Hawkes, Ernest and Julio in their book, and interviews with family members and former employees. The anecdotes about the advertising campaign are taken from Hawkes, Ernest and Julio, newspaper articles, and interviews with former Gallo employees.

CHAPTER TEN

The figures on wine production in 1946 come from Pinney, Ernest and Julio, and newspaper articles. The lawsuit against Charles Gallo is taken from Hawkes, Ernest and Julio, court records, and newspaper accounts. Wagner's quote comes from Pinney. Cribari's downfall during the period is documented by many sources, including Hawkes, Ernest and Julio, Pinney, Siler, and various newspaper accounts.

Rosenstiel's plan to restrict the supply of wine on the market comes from Ernest and Julio and interviews with former Gallo executives and others in the wine industry. Ernest's defeat of Rosenstiel's plan by a single vote comes from his joint autobiography with Julio and from interviews with wine industry executives. The role played by the cooperatives in the California wine industry comes largely from Pinney. Ernest's and Julio's comments appear in their book.

The details of Ernest's trip to Italy with Amelia are taken from his joint autobiography with Julio and from interviews with members of the family. Hawkes also covers the vacation in her own biography.

CHAPTER ELEVEN

The annual ritual of the *bagna cauda* at Joe Gallo's house comes from interviews with Mike Gallo, Patricia Gallo, Linda Jelacich, and others. Ernest and Julio tried to rewrite history after their lawsuit against Joe by claiming that Julio hosted the gatherings. Hawkes also covers the annual event in her book. Mary Ann's resentment of Ernest holding court in her own home comes from Hawkes and interviews with various members of the family.

Fenderson's arrival at the winery is covered by Hawkes, Ernest, and Julio, and also comes from interviews with former Gallo executives. Armand Hammer's problems with the government because of his pro-Soviet dealings have been well documented in books and newspapers. The tactics employed by Gallo salesmen at the time come from various sources, including Hawkes, newspaper articles, and interviews with former Gallo executives. The evolving relationship between Ernest and Fenderson comes from Ernest and Julio's autobiography and interviews with former Gallo executives.

Julio's comments come from his book with Ernest. His thoughts about experimenting with various types of grapes are based on his own statements and interviews with various Gallo associates. The details of the pruning process come from Pinney, Julio in his book with Ernest, and articles dealing with the subject. The ranking of the various vintners at the time is taken from Ernest and Julio and other authorities in the industry. The anecdotes about the development of a new sweet port cut with lemon juice come from many sources, including Hawkes, Ernest and Julio, Siler, and various newspaper articles.

CHAPTER TWELVE

The anecdote about the naming of the new product "Thunderbird" comes from Hawkes, Ernest and Julio, and various sources in the wine industry. The huge success of Thunderbird is part of wine lore, documented in various books and countless newspaper and magazine articles. The jingle about the product and Ernest's reaction to it appears in Hawkes, Ernest and Julio's joint autobiography, and various newspaper articles.

Julio's discontent about the direction taken by the winery is based on interviews with former Gallo executives and is discussed in some detail by Julio in his book with Ernest. The rift that developed between Ernest and Julio is covered by Hawkes and was confirmed by interviews with Gallo associates. Hawkes describes David Gallo's odd behavior in detail in her biography, and former Gallo executives confirmed much of what she had to say. Comments about both David and Joey are taken from interviews with former Gallo executives.

The description of Julio's offspring is based on interviews with various members of the Gallo family. Speculation about Phillip's possible homosexuality comes from Hawkes. The characterization of Joe's side of the family comes from interviews with Mike Gallo, Patricia Gallo, Linda Jelacich, and other family members. The details about Uncle Mike Gallo's declining years come from interviews with various members of the Gallo family and former Gallo executives.

CHAPTER THIRTEEN

Ernest and Julio discuss their need for a ship in their joint autobiography, and their story was confirmed in interviews with former Gallo executives. Their decision to build a bottling plant comes from various sources, including

Hawkes, Ernest and Julio, former Gallo executives, and members of the Gallo family. Norton Simon's generosity has been well documented and was confirmed by Ernest and Julio in their book. Ernest discusses his insistence on keeping his company private in his book with Julio, and it was confirmed by various sources within the wine industry.

Robert's decision to run the bottling plant comes from Ernest and Julio, Hawkes, and interviews with members of the Gallo family. Phillip Gallo's tragic end is covered in detail by Hawkes and was confirmed by various Gallo associates and members of the family. Julio discussed it briefly in his book with Ernest. Information about the births of the latest generation of the Gallo clan comes from Ernest, Julio, and various members of the family.

The sales figures for the wine industry in 1957 and Gallo's standing in the industry come from Pinney, Ernest and Julio, and various articles on the subject. Ernest's relationships with the Romanos and Fusco in Chicago are taken from Hawkes, Ernest and Julio, and interviews with former Gallo executives. Ernest goes into surprising detail about the arrangement in Chicago in his autobiography with Julio.

CHAPTER FOURTEEN

Ernest's remarks at Stanford Business School come from students who were there at the time. David Gallo's peculiar behavior is taken from Hawkes and interviews with former Gallo executives (see earlier citation). Ernest seemed to be in denial about his older son; indeed, he discusses him in his book as though he had executive ability, an assessment ridiculed by those who worked with him at the time. The comment about how Ernest treated his sons comes from an interview with a former Gallo executive.

Details about the developing problems between Joe and Mary Ann Gallo come from interviews with various members of the family. They are also covered in detail by Hawkes. John Whiting supplied additional information about the divorce proceedings. Ernest discusses his concern that Joe's pending divorce might spill over into their joint business dealings in his book with Julio.

The anecdote about Ernest being arrested for peering into the liquor store window in Texas comes from him in his book with Julio. Ernest and Julio discuss their so-called "Gourmet Trio" in their book, and figures on wine consumption are taken from Pinney, Ernest and Julio, and various newspaper articles. Circumstances surrounding Joe Gallo's meeting with Patricia come from interviews with Shastid and various members of the Gallo family. The details about the ownership of the glass company stock come from interviews with several members of the Gallo family, including Mike Gallo and Linda Jelacich. Julio discusses the firing of his brother Joseph in his book with Ernest, and other details about the incident come from interviews with various family members.

CHAPTER FIFTEEN

The anecdote about Sweeney and his tutelage under the Romanos comes from Hawkes and interviews with former Gallo executives. Information about the contents of the "Big Red Book" comes from interviews with former Gallo salesmen. Details about the new Gallo headquarters in Modesto are taken from Ernest and Julio and various Gallo associates.

The success of the Boone's Farm lineup of beverages is based on several sources, including Ernest and Julio, various newspaper and magazine accounts, and interviews with former Gallo employees. Ernest and Julio discuss their concerns about Gallo's low image in the marketplace in their book, and several former executives were candid about Julio's worries in particular, and Ernest's mixed feelings about the matter. Hawkes insinuates that there was an element of racism in Ernest's attitude about his sons' choices for wives, and it strikes me as more than curious that he barely mentions them in his own book.

Information about Joe's offspring and their mates comes largely from interviews with members of that side of the family. Details about Uncle Mike's final days on earth come from several sources, including Hawkes and interviews with former Gallo executives.

CHAPTER SIXTEEN

Descriptions of the area surrounding Modesto and the site of the Gallo murders in 1933 are based on my own observations. The depiction of Modesto as a company town owned by the Gallos is my own interpretation of the existing power structure. The life and times of Cesar Chavez have been well documented in countless articles and books. Information about Chavez's early relationship with the Gallos comes from many sources, including Hawkes, Ernest and Julio in their book, and various newspaper reports.

Chavez's grape boycott became an international cause célèbre etched in the memories of everyone who lived through the period. Reactions to it from various grape growers are taken from interviews with people in the industry and undercover agents familiar with the boycott, which concerned the government as well. Ernest and Julio discuss their opposition to Chavez, particularly because of his demand for a union hiring hall, and their decision to oppose him in their own book.

Details about the abuses on both sides come from several sources, including Hawkes, Ernest and Julio, and interviews with former Gallo executives. I have tried to draw a balance between the claims made by countervailing forces; the media at the time were virtually united in their lionization of Chavez and demonization of Ernest. Details about the rally at Graceada Park come from Ernest and Julio, Hawkes, my own observations, and interviews with locals. Ernest was forthright about losing the PR battle to Chavez in his own book with Julio. The hard feelings lingered for decades, but the battle essentially ended when Chavez and Fitzsimmons decided that ongoing hostilities were not in the best interests of their respective unions and it was better to bury the hatchet and move on.

CHAPTER SEVENTEEN

The description of the ideal grape-growing climate in Sonoma Valley comes from various articles, interviews with industry professionals, and from Julio in his book with Ernest. The history of the Frei Brothers Winery comes from the Frei Brothers and various articles, and Ernest and Julio discuss their interest in the winery in their book.

FTC charges against the Gallos are public information. Ernest discusses the settlement in his book written with Julio. The Gallo brothers' contributions to politicians from both major political parties are on the public record. Information about how Ernest coordinated and timed his contributions comes from interviews with members of the Gallo family. Details about the dissention within the ranks of the company's senior staff come from Hawkes and interviews with former Gallo executives.

The Gallo brothers' programs of charitable donations have been widely reported in newspaper articles. Comments made by Krulwich and Bradley about the pattern of the Gallos' political contributions are taken from the transcript of a PBS program. Ernest and Julio discuss their ad campaign featuring actor Peter Ustinov, and the failure of their varietal wines to find a market, in their joint autobiography.

CHAPTER EIGHTEEN

The anecdote about Charlie Rossi and the Carlo Rossi marketing blitz comes from Ernest and Julio, various newspaper articles, and interviews with former Gallo executives. Ernest's litigiousness is covered by Hawkes in great detail, particularly the details of the Gallo Salame case. Ernest and Julio also discuss it in their own book. Additional details come from interviews with former Gallo executives. Information about Nathan Cummings comes largely from various newspaper and magazine articles.

The description of the underground storage facility comes from Julio in his book with Ernest. Details about the use of European wood for the casks and the procedure followed to store the wine come from Julio and interviews with former Gallo executives.

Information about the entry of Coca-Cola into the wine market comes from Ernest and Julio and interviews with wine industry professionals. Julio's comments about the vagaries of growing grapes and making wine come from his book with Ernest. Data about wine consumption in the United States during this period, and the competition from foreign wineries, come from Pinney, Ernest and Julio, and interviews with wine industry experts.

CHAPTER NINETEEN

Details about the launching of Joseph Gallo's cheese business in 1983 are taken from Hawkes, Ernest and Julio, and interviews with several members of the Gallo family. Descriptions of the property are based on personal observations. Ernest gives his version of his conversation with Joe in his book with Julio; Joe's recollection of the conversation comes from Hawkes and interviews with members of the Gallo family.

Information about the advertising campaign for
Bartles & Jaymes comes from several sources, including
interviews with Riney and other ad executives, Ernest's
recollection of the event in his joint autobiography with Julio,
and newspaper articles.

Ernest's discovery of the small block of cheese bearing
his brother's label comes from Ernest in his book with Julio
and interviews with former Gallo executives and members of
the Gallo family. Details about the meeting in Modesto come
from Hawkes, Ernest and Julio, and interviews with Whiting
and members of the family. Information about the subsequent
meeting comes from the same sources. The details of Herzig's
letter to Whiting were reported by Hawkes and confirmed by
Whiting. Ernest discusses his counteroffer to Joe in his book
with Julio.

CHAPTER TWENTY

Information about the details of the licensing
agreement comes from Hawkes, Ernest and Julio, Whiting,
and members of the Gallo family. Details about the meeting
in Modesto come from the same sources. Julio's comment
appears in his book with Ernest. Whiting confirmed his
opinion about the charge of unsanitary conditions at the
cheese plant during an interview.

Joe's reaction to his brothers' lawsuit is taken from
interviews with members of the Gallo family. Information
about the discovery of the will by Whiting comes from
interviews with Whiting and members of the Gallo family, and
Hawkes covers the topic in detail in her own book.

Details about the estate left by Joe and Susie and the
continuation of the winery appear in court documents and
were corroborated by Whiting and members of the Gallo
family. The quote from Joe Gallo Jr. comes from Hawkes, and
the quote from Whiting is based on an interview with him.

CHAPTER TWENTY-ONE

The dialogue between Ernest, Julio, and Joe comes from Hawkes, Ernest and Julio in their joint autobiography, and interviews with members of the Gallo family. Shastid's and Whiting's differing interpretations of the meaning of the courthouse documents come from interviews with both lawyers.

Details about the meeting between Ernest and Joe at Joe's ranch are taken from Hawkes, Ernest in his book with Julio, and interviews with members of the Gallo family. Information about the family's reaction to Joe's lawsuit against his brothers comes from interviews with members of the Gallo family, Hawkes, and Ernest and Julio.

Details about the meeting with Julio, Joe, and Bob Gallo in San Francisco come from Hawkes, Julio in his book with Ernest, and interviews with members of the Gallo family. Information about the court proceedings in Fresno is taken from Hawkes, Ernest and Julio, and interviews with members of the Gallo family. The assertion that Ernest had a hand in the appointment of the presiding judge comes from interviews with Gallo family members and others associated with the case.

CHAPTER TWENTY-TWO

Ernest's insistence on protecting the Gallo trademark is discussed by Ernest in his book with Julio and is also based on interviews with Gallo family members. Judge Coyle's relationship with the firm that worked out the Gallo Salame deal comes from Hawkes. Ernest's assertion that Joe Gallo's salesmen tied the cheese to the winery appears in his book with Julio. Ernest's comments at the trademark infringement trial come from Hawkes. Ernest admitted in his book with Julio that Joe's cheese was not responsible for the wedding guests' illness.

Julio's comments appear in his book with Ernest. Hawkes goes into great detail about the trial, which takes up a fair amount of space in her book. Other details are based on interviews with members of the Gallo family and Whiting. Ernest's interpretation of the outcome of the trial appears in his book with Julio. Details about Joe Gallo's subsequent illness are based on interviews with members of the Gallo family.

Information about the automobile accident involving Julio and Aileen comes from interviews with Gallo family members and newspaper accounts. Details about the growing rift between the warring factions of the Gallo clan are taken from interviews with members of the family. Ernest and Julio discuss their succession plans at the winery in their joint autobiography. Julio goes into great detail about the emerging roles played by Bob, Matt, Gina, Jim Coleman, and other family offspring in various facets of the family's operations.

CHAPTER TWENTY-THREE

Ernest's remarks to the Young Presidents' Organization appear in his book with Julio. The list of the politicians who benefited from the Gallos' political largesse is public information. Details about Ernest's role at a fund-raising event for President Clinton in San Francisco come from various newspaper reports. Remarks made by Krulwich and MacIver are taken from the transcript of a PBS show.

The report about Joseph and Ofelia being passengers on the hijacked airliner appeared in various newspapers at the time. Details surrounding Julio's death come from interviews with Gallo family members; a more abbreviated account of the incident appeared in several newspapers and magazines. Ernest's comment about his wife Amelia's death was included in the official public statement released by his PR department.

The details about Gallo's relentless march across Sonoma Valley come from articles by Michael Amsler, Shepherd Bliss, and Rich Cartiere in *Wine Business Monthly*, the *Chicago Tribune*, and other publications, and interviews with former Gallo associates, George Davis, and others in the wine industry. Information about the early days of Sonoma and the practices of big agribusiness is taken from the same sources. Other details come from Glen Martin and Jay Stuller, authors of *Through the Grapevine*. Information about Gallo's arrangement with United Airlines comes from Wendy Melillo writing in *Adweek*.

CHAPTER TWENTY-FOUR

Circumstances surrounding the death of David Gallo are based on interviews with members of the Gallo family. The idea that he might have committed suicide is my own speculation. Information about the role played by Jess Jackson in Sonoma comes from Rich Cortiere, Michael Amsler, and George Davis. Gina Gallo's comments come from interviews with her by Madelyn Miller in *TravelLady Magazine* and Robert Bradford in *Beverage Business*.

The story of Gallo's lawsuit against Jennifer King is based on an article by Mark Stuertz in the *Dallas Observer* and an interview with her attorney, Jeffrey Look. Information about Gallo's trademark infringement suit against Gallo in the Philippines comes from court documents. Nabedian's and Chris Gallo's remarks come from interviews appearing in the *Modesto Bee*. The lineup of Gallo wines under different labels is taken from various sources, including the Gallo Web site and various newspaper articles.

Information about Gallo's link to Wal-Mart and the suggested names for the retail outlet's brand of wines comes from my own memory about jokes making the rounds at the time, which were also posted on the Internet. The link to "two-buck Chuck" was mentioned in the *Sacramento Bee*. Kristen Senseman's comments come from an interview with the former Gallo employee.

CHAPTER TWENTY-FIVE

Gina Gallo's remarks are taken from an interview with her by Robert Bradford, from comments she made at a press conference in the Park Avenue Spring restaurant in New York City, and from information supplied by the Gallo family. Gallo's awards and comments made by wine critics Dorothy Gaiter and John Brecher appeared in various newspaper accounts. Information about the ingredients in the soil that make Sonoma Valley unique comes from Bradford. The description of the terrain is based on my own observations.

Robert Parker's comments about Gallo come from his Web site. Remarks made by Jon Fredrikson appeared in various newspaper accounts. Information about the conditions for growing wine in Napa Valley comes from interviews with various people in the region's wine industry.

Details surrounding Joseph Gallo's death, including Ernest's expressed desire to see his brother before he died, are based on interviews with various members of the Gallo family. The description of the land surrounding the dairy farm comes from my own observations. Ernest's death was covered in great detail in newspapers throughout the world. The size of the empire he left behind comes from various newspaper accounts and interviews with wine industry professionals. Bregman's comment appeared in the *Los Angeles Times*. The quote attributed to Ernest's son Joseph is taken from the *Sacramento Bee*. Mike Gallo's quote comes from an interview with him.

AFTERWORD

Information about the Renterias is based on literature supplied by the Renteria family, an article by Tim Fish and Dana Nigro in *Wine Spectator*, various newspaper accounts, and an interview with Oscar Renteria.

Details about the changing conditions in the Central Valley come from my own observations. Information about the Gallos and the economics of the wine industry today comes from an interview with Oscar and from statements made by the Gallo family. Oscar Renteria provided the details about the Gallo presence in Mexico and competition from foreign wineries.